ASTROLOGY

ASTROLOGY

*

Your Place in the Sun

By

EVANGELINE ADAMS

Author of

THE BOWL OF HEAVEN

New York

DODD, MEAD & COMPANY

1930

FOREWORD

This book does not undertake to teach Astrology—that vast and complicated subject which would require many volumes—but it does present authentic astrological information gathered by the author during her more than thirty years of devotion to the furtherance of the science of Astrology and its application to the needs of humanity.

Part I of the book is largely based on Solar Biology, which concerns itself only with the influence of the Sun, and does not take into consideration the attributes contributed by the planets. Those who will consult the table in Part III to ascertain the sign that was rising when they were born (provided they know their hour of birth) can make use of Part I for the purpose of understanding better their general characteristics. If they will synthesize the description of their rising sign and the sign in which their Sun is located at birth (which is determined by the part of the month in which they were born) they can have a very good idea both of their true nature and of the nature that appears on the surface.

Commencing with Part II, more scientific material is given. When one has fully familiarized himself with this knowledge, all that is necessary is to balance the influence of a planet and the sign in which it may be placed, as well as the aspects operating with it, in order to get a very good understanding of what the effects must be. For example, if you find the cold, conservative Saturn in the practical, noncommittal sign Scorpio, the effect will be very different from the effect of this same restricting planet in the unselfish benevolent sign Sagittarius. You might consider placing a very vicious character in the home of a humanitarian, God-fearing man, and it would be merely a matter of time for the less desirable individual necessarily to take on some of the nobler characteristics of his host.

If this suggestion is followed in considering the Sun and Moon, the seven planets and the twelve signs, as well as all the aspects, a very workable *modus operandi* of the science will be obtained.

The Ancients discovered that the planets were more sympathetic and exerted a more powerful influence in certain signs than in others. This was because the fixed stars which constituted the signs harmonized with certain planets. As an example, they determined that Mars, which stands for physical energy, aggressive force and ambition, was at its height of power when in the signs Aries and Scorpio; Mars is, therefore, the Star of Destiny, or ruling planet, when either of these signs is on the eastern horizon. If the reader will refer to the Table of Ascendants (Part III), he will find that on January 1 of any year, between 2 and about 4.20 A. M., and between about 11.30 A. M. to 12.30 noon, the signs Scorpio and Aries, respectively, will be on the Ascendant, and therefore Mars will be the ruling planet.

If the hour of birth is not known, it is not possible to say definitely just what the ruling planet or Star of Destiny will be, although the sign in which the Sun is placed will determine what planet will strongly influence the native. For instance, if one is born from March 22 to April 21, the Sun will be in the sign Aries, which partakes of the vibrations of Mars. Therefore, with no knowledge of the hour of birth, Mars can be considered as the dominating force in the horoscope.

It will be noted that Mars, Venus and Mercury are found to be powerful in two different signs, whereas the other planets are apportioned to one sign each; for instance, Aries is the diurnal house of Mars and Scorpio is the nocturnal.

The chapter on Horary Astrology describes particularly the author's special contribution to the science —a theory evolved during her years of practical experience, whereby she considers not only the mundane position of the heavens at the time the query is made, as was done by the Ancients, but combines with this the natal horoscope of the querent.

As the aim of this book is primarily to point out a way to the practical use of the science of Astrology, a long discourse on its history will not be attempted—that can be found in the Encyclopedia Britannica or in special volumes—but a brief outline may be of interest as an introduction to the following descriptions and directions.

Astrology is the science that describes the influence of the heavenly bodies upon mundane affairs and upon human character and life. It is the oldest science in existence; it is not only prehistoric, but pretraditional; it is the science of the effects of the Solar Currents on the living things of our earth, especially on human life.

Astronomy is an outgrowth of Astrology, just as chemistry is an outgrowth of alchemy. Astrology was the mother; astronomy, the daughter—it is only within historic times that astronomy has become the study of man. The Astrologers of Babylon were interested in astronomy only so far as it was necessary in computing the positions of the stars. They wanted to know what was in store for the nation even more than for the individual. They consulted the history of former kings, together with their horoscopes. Looking backward, they saw where good fortune was promised the kingdom by the ruler born under a lucky star, and they also saw where misfortune, also promised by the stars, had been realized.

So far as we know, they had no knowledge of the theory of vibration, but they did know that certain impulses dominated persons born under a certain arrangement of the stars and the planets and that other impulses were given those born under other configurations. In the light of modern science, we know that all matter vibrates, and it therefore follows that planetary vibrations quicken or retard the action of the brain and body with far-reaching consequences. Radium is only one element about which man has learned something within the past generation; he is using radium emanations for the good of the race. He also knows that the colors of the spectrum have a curative effect on disease.

The stars and the planets vibrated in the days of ancient Babylon; just as they had vibrated for ages and ages before; just as they are vibrating to-day; and just as they will vibrate in ages to come. Those vibrations register with greater or less intensity upon every living atom. The stars and the planets have been performing their creative work since they were hung in the heavens. Their influence on the human mind has been studied in accordance with established laws from time immemorial, just as the influence of present-day phenomena is studied by the modern scientist. Instead of records of only a decade or two, however, such as the scientists have, the Astrologers have the compiled records of ages.

The wisdom of the Chaldean Astrologers spread to Greece and to the Western World, and also to the Orient before the Christian era. With this spreading of knowledge came also the spreading of its application. At first, only the horoscopes of the royal families were read, for as rulers they were looked to by their people for the preservation and growth in power of the nation—but to-day, as is the case with all knowledge, Astrology is open to the man in the streets, as well as to the rulers of the earth.

Astrology is divided into four distinct branches; i. e., Natural, Mundane, Natal, and Horary.

Natural, or Physical Astrology, pertains to the action of the Sun, Moon and planets upon the tides of the ocean and other terrestrial phenomena, the atmosphere, climate, seasons, weather, earthquakes, and volcanic eruptions.

Mundane Astrology considers the heavenly bodies as they relate to prosperity and adversity of nations and communities. Consequently, it treats of matters respecting governments, rulers, peace, war, revolutions, famines, plagues, and everything that has reference to people generally.

Natal, or Genethliacal Astrology, is that department of the science which considers the individual and everything that pertains to him from the moment of his birth to the end of his existence. While this branch of the science can be of inestimable value in assisting the individual to know himself and to be forewarned, it is important that it shall be clearly understood that the horoscope indicates tendencies only and shows what will happen if knowledge and will power are not used to avert the evil or to take advantage of the opportunity provided by Fate at the moment.

We quote from Claudius Ptolemy, who lived in the first half of the second century A. D., and to whom Astrology is indebted for some of the earliest expositions of the science. He writes as follows: "Judgment must be regulated by thyself, as well as by the stars; for it is not possible that particular forms of events should be declared by any person, however scientific, since the understanding conceives the idea of some sensible event and not its particular form. It is, therefore, necessary for him who practices therein to adopt inference. They only who are inspired by the Deity can predict particulars."

Horary Astrology, as the name might imply, has reference to a figure of the heavens erected at the moment when a person is seriously agitated concerning the result of any undertaking or impending event. A figure is then erected for the minute in which the question was asked, and if the Astrologer is competent and the querent sincere and really desirous of obtaining reliable information, there is no reason why the question should not be completely solved by making use of the author's new method of Horary Astrology.

Although all branches of Astrology are equally fascinating and instructive, the problems and perplexities with which we are confronted during the present century make Natal and Horary Astrology seem most important to the ordinary individual. Natural and Mundane Astrology are more necessary in the study of national and international affairs, especially concerning industry, tariff, weather conditions, and all matters relating to peace and harmony of the world. In order to obtain the necessary statistics to arrive at accurate conclusions on these two branches of the science, tremendous research work is required, which cannot be done by one individual. This is a field of research that offers great possibilities to an endowed organization.

Among modern writers on the subject, Dr. Richard Garnet, who was a famous English writer, translator and editor, and who for many years before his death was the Librarian of the British Museum, has done much valuable work for Astrology. Among his works, which were multifarious, he published in the *University Magazine,* under the pseudonym of "A. C. Trent," a well-recognized treatise on Astrology with the title of "The Soul and the Stars." His death prevented the publication of a second volume on the same subject.

On page 8 of "The Soul and the Stars," Dr. Garnet writes: "It is the more necessary to insist on the strictly

empirical character of Astrology, inasmuch as it is
generally regarded as an occult science. The Astrologer
is considered as a kind of wizard. . . . The fact, nevertheless, remains that Astrology, with the single exception
of Astronomy, is, as regards the certainty of its data, the
most exact of all the exact sciences. The imperfection of
the geological record may mislead the Geologist; an error in analysis may baffle the Chemist; the Astrologer
takes his data from observations which the interests of
Astronomy and navigation require to be absolutely fault-
less. He works, as it were, under the surveillance of his
brother, the Astronomer, and cannot falsify his data without instant detection. The principles of his art have come
down to him in essentials from the most remote antiquity;
they have been published in a thousand books and are
open to the examination of all the world. His calculations
are performed by no more cabalistical process than arith-
metic."

Again, on page 25, we find: "It will be conceded that
there is nothing occult or mystical in the line of argument we have been pursuing. We have appealed throughout to the testimony of facts, partly the notorious and
indisputable facts of history and biography, partly astronomical observations derived from no more recondite
source than the ordinary ephemeris. Anyone can verify
or disprove these observations in a moment by the same
process; anyone who will be at the trouble to search for
examples can investigate the subject for himself."

He goes on to show that nine sovereign princes who
were notoriously insane or deficient in intellect had Mercury and the Moon afflicted by Saturn, Mars and Uranus;
and that eight religious enthusiasts and visionaries had
the Moon and Mercury in aspect with Uranus. Fourteen
instances of eccentricity accompanied by great mental
power had Mercury in aspect with Mars and Uranus, and

two noted French socialists had practically the same aspects in their horoscopes. He further shows that Mr. Gladstone and Cardinal Newman, who had intellects of so similar a character, both had Mercury in conjunction with the Sun and quartile with the Moon and Mars in aspect to Mercury. He also shows that Bacon and Bishop Thirwell had Mercury and the Moon aspected very similarly.

Many other instances could be quoted from his valuable work, which goes to prove that he made a very thorough and scientific study of his investigations; and he is only one of the many students of Astrology who have done similar work.

Dr. Joseph Butler, the author of "Analogy of Religion" —"Butler's Analogy," as it is known in our theological schools—decided to attack and confute Astrology, and that he might do so most effectively, began to study its principles and teachings. Through this study, he became so convinced of its truth and wisdom that he wrote an able defense of astral doctrines. This was published in 1680 and is one of the rare books on Astrology.

Part of the dedicatory epistle of Bishop Butler's Defense of Astrology, to Sir Thomas Doleman, one of the clerks of the Privy Council, reads as follows:

You have here, Sir, three propositions, or a sacred stool on three feet, each of them carrying their several weight, and you may sit safely thereon. The first leg bears this position, that there is an astrology certainly written in the heavens. And this leg stands fast. The second bears up what skill in some measure may be attained, in the understanding of the same. And the third upholds the legitimacy of the means; shows how by true art, and without infernal help, it may be lawfully compassed.

If, Sir, I may add light to a lawful and honest Science, I hope I have done my God, and my country, good service, espe-

cially in an age where true treasure is a scarce commodity; and
as God shall bless mine endeavors, my hearty prayers and good
wishes are, that mine Honorable Patron, may have an honor
worthy of his name and fame; and, that, worthy Sir, the good
blessing of God may crown with honor and felicity, the whole
work of your virtuous life, is the continual prayer, and wish of,
Sir,

Your most humbly devoted,

JOHN BUTLER.

Archbishop Whately, of Dublin, also changed his
opinion through study of the science. He says: "When
young and inexperienced, I preached a sermon against
Astrology, denouncing it as anti-Christian and infidel in
teaching and tendency. I had never read a standard work
on the subject and had no knowledge of it save that
gained at the addresses of itinerant lecturers quite in-
competent to deal with it. . . . The study of this science
has removed my ignorant prejudice and I now find pleasure and profit in the perusal of its literature. . . . It has
opened up fields of thought before unexplored and it
has furnished arguments and illustrations for the unfold-
ing of truth, before unknown."

Henry Ward Beecher, when asked his opinion of Astrology, said: "I have never made it a study, but if its
principles are sound, and I think they are, then the practical application of Astrology should interest every human being who cares to rise above the common level of
humanity. Its value is in that it does for the human race
what no other science pretends to do, and that is to show
man his proper place in life."

THE RISING SIGNS

Preliminary Remarks

The sign that is rising and the sign in which the ruler is placed at a person's birth seem to determine his physical appearance, more than any other factor, in the majority of cases. There are instances, however, where the position of the Sun or of the Moon, in male or female nativities respectively, seems more important, but this could only be where the ruler of the rising sign is weak or afflicted.

There may also be modifications of practically all characteristics of any rising sign when there happens to be a planet in close proximity to the Ascendant. For example, the ordinary idea of the Leo face is of a ruddy complexion and frank expression. Saturn or Uranus rising will darken the complexion; Uranus will not alter the general shape of the face, but it will make all its lines sterner and more resolute, with a hint of subtlety; Saturn, again, might lengthen the face and give an expression of great gravity and melancholy.

It may be asserted that, in general, the planets being far more positive in their influence than the signs of the zodiac, it is hardly possible to get an absolutely pure example of the unmodified action of any sign, since its ruler is always somewhere in the heavens, modified in diverse ways by his position. The zodiacal sign is of the nature of an atmosphere rather than a unit of force. This may seem a somewhat intangible quality, but to the trained observer the signs of the Zodiac are more recognizable at a glance than any planetary combination.

The general characteristics of a rising sign will naturally be most modified when a powerful planet of an opposite nature occupies the sign. Taking, for example, the sign Cancer, we have two main types, the passive, watery, Luna type, and the cardinal, aggressive, Jupiter type. Imagine Mars and Uranus rising in conjunction in this sign and it will be evident that they will almost wipe out the former, while emphasizing the latter. Such elements of confusion must, of course, be taken into account, but it must not be supposed that any combination of planets, however powerful, can wholly destroy the general effect of the rising sign. No possible modification of Aries can give the effect of Taurus. The general characteristics or temperament of the individual will remain as a background. One may slow up the action of Aries in all kinds of ways, but the result is to produce hesitation in the execution of rash action, not to prevent the original hasty resolution. Never forgetting the cardinal point of our doctrine, that we are describing a negative and not a positive condition, we may say that the signs of the Zodiac divide humanity into twelve major classes.

No one, it is to be hoped, will be so simple as to suppose that the infinite variety of face and figure which humanity presents is to be classified in so rough and ready a fashion. It is probable that every degree has its own peculiar magical image, but the difficulties connected with the measurement of time are enormous, and there is usually an inaccuracy of minutes at least in the casual observation taken of a nativity. However, patient experience is leading us to distinguish finer and finer vibrations.

But the infinite variety in the details of feature, complexion, size, and proportion which all go to make up the appearance of an individual depends to a considerable extent upon other factors than the Zodiac, the modifications caused by rising planets or by the ruler of the Ascendant sign. Every planet contributes its work. Mars rules the muscular system, so that even where we have a general type inclined to femininity, softness, or fatness, the muscularity will depend upon Mars and be modified by his strength or weakness by position or aspect. Take, for example, Venus rising in Pisces. That will determine the general appearance, but if Mars should be in Capricornus, the muscular system, particularly in the lower parts of the body, will be lean and strong, as if of steel and whipcord. It is further to be remarked that every planet possesses multiple functions. Mercury rules the conscious mind, but his position and aspects will also determine the appearance of the mouth as well as all those parts of the body that are ruled by him and the part of the system itself which he governs.

In describing the personal characteristics from a nativity, every detail must be considered separately, and a judgment formed as to its probable effect in modifying the main type. The general welfare of a being depends on the harmony of all the elements of his make-up, and a single bad fault is likely to ruin the rest of the structure. A body like that of Hercules is not much good if the head happens to be hydrocephalic. A man may have all the qualities of a great statesman, but if he should be a hopeless drunkard, these qualities will have no chance to operate.

Another complexity is introduced into the problem of

the rising sign by the fact that there are usually certain quite characteristic elements in the physical appearance which are manifestly due to heredity, and would seem, on superficial view, to have nothing to do with astrology. But when we separate the indications of heredity from those of the native's own chart, we find large confirmation of astrological laws. For example, there will be great unlikeness due to the different horoscopes between a child born with Cancer rising, whose father has Capricornus rising, but there may be a great likeness due to the heredity. The astrologer should be able to determine which influences are responsible for which effect.

Enlarging this subject, we may suppose two children born in the same house at the same moment, one a Spaniard and the other a Chinese. Where is the resemblance to come in? Unless there is a resemblance, astrology is utterly false. The explanation of the dissimilarity is really very simple. The same causes are in operation, but each set takes place within a separate sphere. The Chinese race is ruled by Libra, the Spanish race by Sagittarius; consequently, in all specimens of either race will be certain great basic sets of conditions, corresponding to those signs. Now take a Chinese and a Spaniard, each with Scorpio rising, and you will perceive a certain similarity in the midst of the dissimilarity.

Most of our shallowness of thinking on this subject has arisen from our failure to make proper observation. Every sheep in a flock of sheep seems to look like every other, but only to the man who does not know sheep intimately. The shepherd knows each one by sight and is familiar with every little trick of every little lamb. In the same way, one is overwhelmed by the insistence of the main type whenever one comes into contact with an unfamiliar race, and one may take some days to learn to recognize new servants in a foreign country; but live among the foreign race for any length of time and experience will make them just as individual as one's own people. Indeed, the converse phenomenon often takes place in the case of explorers who return to civilization after months or years of sojourn among alien peoples; they may think they recognize an old friend in each stranger they meet—the very general likeness has become emphasized by the acquired unfamiliarity. It would be well for the astrologer to select people of some alien race and compare them very carefully with reference to their horoscopes. Practice in this will enable him to recognize with certainty the effect of a nativity considered as a microcosm within the sphere of the great ruling race signs.

It should thus be possible in every case to work out with minute accuracy a complete physical description of the native, and this accuracy will evidently be increased as we progress to a fuller understanding of the attribution of each degree of the Zodiac, the power of each planet in each degree and a better knowledge of the limits within which aspects become operative.

From the foregoing it should be clear that an astrological diagnosis of the physical characteristics of any given person is an exact science; still suffering, it is true, from the lack of completely organized data based on accurate observation. It should also be evident that this branch of astrology, lending itself as it does to unquestionable demonstration, should serve to the science much as the discovery of the laws of constant and of multiple proportions did to chemistry. Nevertheless, whatever may be the planetary influences in the horoscope, they never wholly outweigh the general type given by the Zodiacal sign rising. Bearing this in mind, and remembering all the factors of differentiation, we may now proceed to consider the main classification of humanity in the twelve-fold zodiacal division.

It should be remembered, throughout the following descriptions of the influence of the rising sign upon the moral characteristics, that many of the qualities considered will be much more dependent upon the position and aspects of a specific planet than upon the nature of the ascendant. The influence of Jupiter will be paramount in financial affairs, just as that of Venus and, to some extent, Neptune, will govern the love nature. These influences will be fully discussed in the consideration of the planets. There are certain general tendencies in the character which depend upon the rising sign and it is to these that we shall direct the reader's attention in the following pages, reminding him that even these general tendencies are subject to modifications by the pertinent planets.

ZODIACAL SIGNS, PLANETS, AND THEIR SYMBOLS

	SIGN	SYMBOL OF SIGN	RULING PLANET	SYMBOL OF PLANET
1	Aries	♈	Mars	♂
2	Taurus	♉	Venus	♀
3	Gemini	♊	Mercury	☿
4	Cancer	♋	Moon	☽
5	Leo	♌	Sun	☉
6	Virgo	♍	Mercury	☿
7	Libra	♎	Venus	♀
8	Scorpio	♏	Mars	♂
9	Sagittarius	♐	Jupiter	♃
10	Capricorn	♑	Saturn	♄
11	Aquarius	♒	Uranus	♅
12	Pisces	♓	Neptune	♆

Aries	♈	opposite	♎	Libra
Taurus	♉	"	♏	Scorpio
Gemini	♊	"	♐	Sagittarius
Cancer	♋	"	♑	Capricorn
Leo	♌	"	♒	Aquarius
Virgo	♍	"	♓	Pisces

CONTENTS

Foreword v

PAGE

Part I. The Signs of the Zodiac 3

Part II. The Planets 197

Part III. Table of Ascendants 263

Part IV. How to Cast a Horoscope 303

Part V. Horary Astrology 317

Part VI. Description of the Twelve Houses . 325

Part VII. Free Will versus Destiny 337

PART I

THE SIGNS OF THE ZODIAC

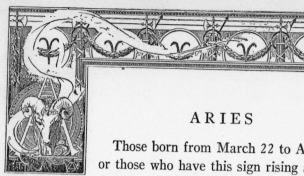

ARIES

Those born from March 22 to April 21, or those who have this sign rising at birth (which can be ascertained only through a knowledge of the hour of birth), will come under the dominion of the fiery, cardinal sign Aries, symbolized by the Ram, which rules the head.

The sign of Aries, or the Ram, is the first in the zodiac. Mars, the "God of War," is its ruler, and the Sun is exalted therein. In the Tarot, it refers to the card called "The Emperor," and by putting together these four facts we get a fairly complete hieroglyphic of the meaning of the sign.

Each of the signs is divided into two main types, the active and the passive. As a general rule, the active type may be called the masculine; the passive, the feminine. In Aries, on the one hand, we have the restless and butting ram; on the other, the helpless and unoriginal sheep.

It should be remembered that Aries is a sign of short ascension, so that the Ascendant is always complicated by Taurus. The pure Aries type is rare, which is fortunate, perhaps, as the active type especially needs the steadying modification of a more stable sign and the passive type can be strengthened by forceful characteristics due to such modifying relations.

PHYSICAL CHARACTERISTICS

The personal appearance of those with Aries rising is very often characteristic of its symbol and, in the great majority of cases, the expert Astrologer can distinguish at a glance what sign was rising at the nativity of any Aries person. The indications are not infallible, however, because it sometimes occurs that planets of a nature contrary to the sign are rising in it, or the lord of the sign may be so weak and afflicted that the characteristics are blurred. Sometimes this blurring is not sufficient to upset the judgment. It is of the utmost importance that the Astrologer practice constantly his judgment in this respect, verifying it wherever possible. In this way he will be able to make sure of obtaining the correct time of birth in cases where people do not know their hour.

The active type of Aries is tall, slim, muscular. The physical energy is very great, but somewhat spasmodic; there is no great power of endurance. The energy increases as long as things are going smoothly, and momentary opposition is easily broken down, but there is little capacity to fight an uphill battle. The head is usually marked by a cranium long in proportion to its breadth. The hair is often light brown or reddish; the eyes are somewhat blue and cold, with a keen and haughty expression. The Aries man is intensely proud, often insufferably so. This characteristic is seen in the general expression of the face. The most characteristic of all the Aries signs is the shape of the nose. This need not be actually very big or long, but even when small it has a trick of standing out from the face: it is an uncompromising nose. Its line is sometimes aquiline, but more usually straight. In the latter case, it sometimes possesses a slight waviness. It seems to radiate independence and strength of character, but this is only too frequently somewhat delusive. The mouth is usually thin and the chin sharp and prominent. There is a severity and reticence in the type. The body is usually well formed, with a tendency to length of limb. This type very rarely accumulates fat.

The constitution is powerful, but rather delicate. Sudden effort is more natural to it than endurance. Aries governs the head and face, and people born with this sign rising are particularly liable to fevers, apoplexy, stomach trouble, headaches and violent diseases in general. The nervous system is high-strung, and people with this sign rising often have trouble in this respect, particularly if subjected to any long-continued strain. They sometimes die suddenly, and in any case are not likely to suffer from long or chronic illness. Either they die or they recover in a short space of time, because their constitution is not adapted for a long fight. These people are peculiarly liable to wounds and accidents, possibly because of the physical fearlessness they possess.

The passive type of person with Aries rising is rather like a caricature of his more fortunate brother. The skull is more rounded, the eyes are also pale and blue, but they have a timid and furtive expression. The nose is fleshier, the mouth fuller, the chin less pronounced, and the profile exceedingly like that of a sheep, or suggestive of it. The body is short and given to quick, restless movements, timid and purposeless, as if perpetual irritation were present. There is no general physical activity; the ambitious and dominating attitude of the noble type of Aries is replaced by a cringing greed. The eyes often bulge like those of Pisces people. The man seems always to be apologizing for his existence.

With women, the active type is so unfeminine that those who are built on this model are apt to be sympathetic to the average man. They lack seductiveness and repose. The lower type is, in a way, more tolerable, because more tractable. To those, however, who see deeper than the surface, the active type of Aries woman will appear one of the best that exists. To such minds there is something extraordinarily attractive in the clean, proud appearance of such women with their highly developed personality.

MORAL CHARACTERISTICS

Aries is the pioneer among the signs. He may not discover a new continent but he is the man with the ax who makes the clearing for the settlement. He is capable of initiative, but lacks persistency in execution. The right orders being given, though they may be accepted with some impatience, are carried out with immense energy. There is something of the cavalryman about the Aries man. If his charge is successful, well and good, but if it is broken he can do little to repel a counter-attack.

The characteristics of the ram are singularly strong in these people. They are extraordinarily aggressive and self-willed. Their ambition is boundless, and opposition merely excites them to greater effort. At the same time, they occasionally lose interest in a matter as suddenly as they take it up. They are headstrong, excitable and impulsive.

People born with Aries rising are often narrow in outlook. To begin with, their horizon is apt to be limited by the material plane. The English, who bitterly opposed the introduction of the steam engine, were totally unable to conceive that their beloved commerce would ultimately be made easier and more profitable by this "crack-brained invention." Not only is the horizon limited in this way; it is narrow in that the ambitions and desires of the Aries man are in a small groove, even with regard to things which more sensible people look upon as parallels; thus, a lawyer with Aries rising will have little comprehension of the work of a doctor or an architect. Indeed, in his own profession he is likely to have little sympathy with other branches than his own specialty. In religion, Aries people are naturally extremely intolerant. It is difficult to say whether the characteristic pride of the type is cause, effect or a concomitant of this mental narrowness.

The Aries man is intensely practical, once he is set to a business he happens to understand, but even in this case, he lacks the power to carry on against opposition, especially if it be of the type of reasoning that goes over his head. He is bewildered by men who are in advance of him, either mentally or morally. He feels that it is horribly unfair when people will not fight him with weapons of his own choice. He is, as a rule, incapable of visioning new ideas, but he always believes himself an original thinker, and he is extremely stubborn and bigoted with regard to everything that he believes.

His enthusiasm is infectious. People seek his company because he has the air of being so original, yet says nothing to shock. The Aries man is, in a sense, always young. He is optimistic because he has no means of gauging the forces opposed to him. He goes ahead magnificently, without in the least appreciating the size of his job, and so confident is he of his own strength that he often fails through sheer lack of proper preparation. The attitude of the English in the present war is extremely typical of Aries—they had no idea of the power of Germany. They expected to finish the business without any trouble. It took months to arouse them to a sense of the seriousness of the situation. Similarly, at the outbreak of the Boer war, everyone was quite sure that the British Army would eat its Christmas dinner in Pretoria. It is fortunate that Taurus, the succeeding sign, has also an influence on the English, for it is to this sign, not to Aries, that they owe their bulldog power—the ability to reorganize in the midst of disaster and to hang on in spite of whatever blows may be inflicted upon them. The result of all his optimism is that the Aries man is constantly getting into trouble. When he can take any reputable step without too much bother, he does so. He marries without reflection or starts a business without calculation.

But although original thought is not a mental characteristic of this type, the brain is extraordinarily fertile in the devising of expedients. The Aries man is a master of diplomacy—that is, the diplomacy of the moment, the diplomacy of emergency. In the Napoleonic wars, England continued from combination to combination in a masterly fashion, until the quarry was pulled down. It will be noted, however, that such combinations are based entirely upon the expediency of the moment; consequently one finds what seems the most extraordinary reversal of policy. The man with Aries rising can think of only one thing at a time, and when Paul has to be paid, he has no hesitation in robbing Peter for the purpose. The subsequent explanation with Peter must take care of itself. He has no idea that he is being insincere or tricky, and he is furiously indignant if anyone calls attention to his policy as a whole. He cannot grasp the significance of an operation that extends over a lengthy period, and derides, as theorists or doctrinaires, those who do habitually so conceive of things.

In regard to money, people with Aries rising are extremely honest. They are generous and ready to spend freely, but they are extremely meticulous in their conceptions of what is right to spend money upon.

Aries people make very bad correspondents; their style is usually curt and dogmatic, so that the recipient is likely to feel that he is being dictated to.

Aries people are not fond of home ties; they resent parental authority, and they like to break new ground. This frequently leads them to leave home early in life. As a rule, however, the conventionality of their ideas makes them slow to recognize that they are unfilial or impatient.

In matters of love, the Aries man is very rigid and conventional. He is passionate and selfish, taking somewhat the attitude of the Oriental. If he is immoral, it is in a very conventional way. He has a contempt for any advanced ideas on this subject, and is irritated at the idea of anybody presuming to think for him on this matter. The Aries woman is often quite contrary to her male parallel in matters of love. She is exceedingly independent, active and unhampered by any considerations beyond her own desires. Such women may be described as "free lances."

In dealing with children and inferiors, Aries people are kind and generous but not sympathetic or considerate.

There is much of the martinet in the character. In the base Aries type, this amounts to studied brutality; systematic bullying. The domestic relations are consequently rarely fortunate; revolt is bound to be excited by such an attitude.

Aries people are impatient of sickness. The Aries man is naturally irritable, and sickness not only offends him, as if it were the inexplicable revolt of a previously well-mannered animal (for the Aries constitution is usually sanguine and strong), but there is mingled with it a sense of extreme alarm, for Aries people are very much afraid of death. They lack consciousness of immortality and like to have somebody in authority promise it to them.

In dealing with public affairs of a routine character, the Aries man is more capable than almost any other type. Similarly, in a matter like marriage, he knows his own mind so well that he wins out against men greatly superior to him, who are hampered by some lurking doubt of the wisdom of the proceeding. Routine business where the habit of quick decision, of authority, of unbending firmness is more valuable than many higher qualities, is the very atmosphere for Aries people. They fall down only when confronted by something outside of the routine. The unexpected leaves them without resources, except those of mere adroitness; once get them off the beaten track, confront them with a genuinely new problem, and they are completely at sea.

In general mental work, we find the same traits of character. A man of science, for example, will do a great deal to advance his particular branch on conventional lines. He will be unable to get new light from analogy or to take advantage of development in other lines of life, unless the parallelism be extraordinarily close. His con-servatism will often allow other people to get ahead of him. He is not sufficiently adaptable to make himself the equal of constantly changing conditions. In commerce, what was good enough for his grandfather is good enough for him, but always with the latest improvements. He can progress on given lines, but he cannot change radically.

There is some danger that the Aries man, especially of the more thoughtful type, may be a jack-of-all-trades. He is usually very quick at picking up elements of any-thing, but when he comes to the hard work, where his energy has to be supplemented by a great many other qualities, he is only too likely to throw up the whole busi-ness in disgust.

Similarly, his friendships do not easily stand the stress of disagreement. In all friendships there comes a time when the fundamental differences come to the surface. Then it is that friendship is really tested. Aries people are apt to fly off in a rage, and though the anger may be short-lived, it often ruptures relations.

Aries people are often very eloquent and make the most popular orators because of their power to arouse enthu-siasm in their hearers. They are quick, sharp, and precise in speech and go straight to the point, and while in pri-vate friendships these qualities often lead to disagreement, in appeals to the masses they are invaluable assets.

Aries people find it difficult to distinguish between the creations of their imagination and facts, and often seem to be untruthful or irresponsible. For this reason, Aries children should be encouraged to transmit their vague imaginings to paper, as this will release their pent-up energies, and may lead to something creative later in life. If their imagination is suppressed, it is likely to have a very disorganizing effect on their nervous system.

Parents would do well to train their Aries children not to live too much in their imagination, and to realize the realities of life. Their mental faculties are very alert, and their whole mentality keen and passionately organized; so there will be a constant tendency for them to embroider facts and present reality under an imaginative guise. The Aries nature is naturally very proud, as well as sensitive, and in youth it is inclined to resent control. Instead of protecting these children from a hot stove, let them find out by experience that it burns, bearing in mind that each succeeding stove that Fate provides may be hotter than the last.

Lack of concentration and application, as well as exaggeration, are the paramount faults of the Aries child. These children should be taught the value of rest as apart from sleep, for as a rule the nervous system is overactive. If they lose their ability to sleep, it is a sign of danger, and if insomnia is neglected it can result in their suffering from a hypersensitive, overcritical, and most unhappy disposition. Even when given great care, they are naturally restless in mind and body, even in repose. They should practice the art of taking moments of relaxation frequently during the day.

People born from the 24th of July to the 24th of August, when the Sun is in the fiery, magnetic sign Leo, and from the 23rd of November to the 23rd of December (Sagittarius) are naturally sympathetic and helpful to those born under Aries. Because their characteristics are complementary, they are good partners for the Aries born, matrimonially or otherwise. If too intimately associated with those born from the 22nd of June to the 24th of July (Cancer), 24th of September to the 24th of October (Libra), and 23rd of December to the 21st of January (Capricorn), the Aries people will find it necessary to be very adaptable; such an intimacy might result in the native of Aries becoming too dictatorial and overbearing.

Even if associated with congenial souls, there is still a tendency for the Aries people to take an attitude indicating that they give too much thought to their own importance, or that they are disregardful of the rights or feelings of others. They must hold themselves in check and be most considerate or they will court misfortune and misunderstandings. They should cultivate the attitude of not showing authority, and strive to live in harmony with their associates.

A period of about seven days—April 19 to April 27—when the vibrations of Aries are merging into those of Taurus, and Taurus still retaining some of Aries, is known as the cusp. People born between these dates will partake of the idealistic side of Aries as well as the practical side of Taurus, or a combination of the two. As Mercury, ruling the mentality, and Venus, the love nature, are so close to the Sun, they, too, may partake of some of the qualities of the adjoining signs of Aries. This will account for some of the complex personalities so difficult of comprehension.

As these deductions are drawn from the position of the Sun or Ascendant, it is probable that, among one's best friends or uncongenial associates, some will be found who were not born at the times mentioned above. In such cases the individual horoscopes must be consulted to ascertain how the stars combine with those of the Aries-born, and thus determine what effect the combinations of influences have upon each other.

These indications are only general and will not cover all the characteristics of an individual as he knows himself, since those born under the sign Aries are subject to modification by the planets. All the planets vibrate true to their own laws at any given moment of time, and it is evident, therefore, that a detailed statement or horoscope must be made to discover the whole truth.

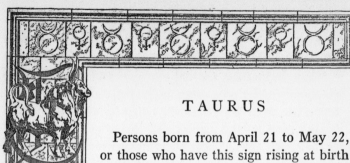

TAURUS

Persons born from April 21 to May 22, or those who have this sign rising at birth (which can be ascertained only through a knowledge of the hour of birth), will come under the dominion of the earthy, fixed sign Taurus, symbolized by the Bull and governed by the "lesser Fortune," Venus.

In the case of Taurus, the difference between the active and passive types is by no means so remarkable as in Aries, and with this sign the passive type is, in some ways, the more harmonious and well balanced. It is the difference between the angry bull in the ring and the hard-working ox and the placid cow.

PHYSICAL CHARACTERISTICS

Taurus almost always gives extreme sturdiness of body, with great breadth of shoulder; there is at least a stockiness, a thick-set figure, probably with rather short limbs in comparison to the general size of the body. The muscular development is usually great, but with some danger of fat if proper exercise is not taken. However, Taurus being full of natural energy, this tendency is usually held in check.

The cranium is distinctly short in proportion to its breadth, and the general shape of the face is square, with flat planes and an expression of stubbornness and endurance, indicating great force of character capable of with-

15

standing whatever strain may be put upon it. The hair is usually dark. When it is not so, the type is very often so blond as to be almost albino. In the dark type, the hair is generally crinkly and very often shows a thick tuftlike growth above the center of the forehead, curiously similar to the growth between the bull's horns. The eyes are usually dark, and their expression, though determined and courageous, is exceedingly soft and affectionate when not in anger. The tendency of the nose is to be short and fleshy, the mouth large but shapely, and the lips often full and voluptuous. The chin is strong and the jaw square, but not necessarily prominent; the neck is short and powerful. The general expression is very characteristic of the symbol of this sign; combining great mildness with great strength.

In the active type, the aggressive qualities are accentuated. There is a great deal of self-indulgence and laziness in the lower form of Taurus, and where this is combined with an exceptionally strong will, there is apt to be a certain harshness in the features. The native is usually patient, calm and long-suffering, but a very small cause of irritation may throw him into a fury which is at times positively dangerous, being totally ungoverned by reason. People of this type seem to have no higher conception of victory than the imposition of the will by means of brute force. The lower type is a sort of degeneration of the active; coarseness marks the expression, greed and sensuality are very clearly indicated. This is sometimes combined with that curious type of cunning which one associates with people like the Norman peasants of Guy de Maupassant.

It is fortunate that these types are rarely seen in their

integrity. It may be noted that every Ascendant has a tendency to take something from its succeeding sign. We have just noticed the modifications of Aries by Taurus, and here again we see in Taurus something borrowed from the diplomatic and suave qualities of the impinging Gemini. The average Taurian is an exceedingly pleasant person. The influence of the ruler, Venus, softens any brutality, and that of the Moon, that is exalted therein, confers a purity which raises the sign from its natural tendency toward the sensual. Ireland is governed by Taurus, and one gets a very good idea of its main characteristics from the people of the Island of the Saints. There is a plump, physical beauty and graciousness which is rendered yet more charming by the exquisite delicacy and chastity of thought. Just as we have seen that Taurus contributes its stubbornness to the English race governed by Aries, so in the Irish race, we see some of the Gemini qualities just mentioned.

People with Taurus rising are naturally somewhat slow and heavy in their movements. They are very much creatures of physical habit. It takes them a long while to acquire an aptitude, but having done so they never lose it. As a general rule, however, it may be asserted that people born with this sign rising are best suited for heavy work, although the sign gives great equilibrium, and it is remarkable that many acrobats and trapeze performers are born under Taurus. A study of these people at their work will convince the observer of this fact, not alone from their physical appearance, but also because one will see that their mind is in their muscles.

The strength of Taurus people is very much beyond the average, and their endurance almost superhuman. The nervous system seems not to be so finely ramified as with many people and they are therefore more fitted to endure a severe strain. They do not complain, because they are not sensitive to pain, and this of course makes it sometimes difficult for them to understand the comparative frailty of others.

Taurus governs the throat, and its natives are extremely liable to trouble with this part of the body. The general constitution is usually robust, its power of endurance and resistance making it possible for them to stand privations which would wreck others. They are not nearly so liable to acute sickness as the natives of Aries, but they are slow to throw off any disease that may afflict them. It usually requires a very long and severe illness to pull them down. Their recuperative power is exceedingly strong, but slow to operate. A Taurus native will be reluctant to admit that he is ill and his convalescence may be equally protracted.

Sympathetically, Taurus also governs the heart and organs of generation and circulation. The diseases to which people born under Taurus are susceptible when depleted nervously, or if they are not eliminating properly, are those connected with the throat, such as mumps or quinsy, with the heart, or those peculiar to their sex. They should not neglect any symptoms of scrofula, glandular swellings of the neck or throat, tonsilitis or diphtheria.

Taurus people should avoid too many fats and heating foods. Stimulants in moderation may be taken safely, but malt liquors should be avoided. Moderation should be made the rule of life in eating and drinking, as well as in all things for these people with the bull-like tendencies, as they are by nature addicted to a fondness for excess in every direction.

MORAL CHARACTERISTICS

All cherubic signs hold the greatest force, because they represent at its maximum the power of the elements to which they belong. It is not the fresh burst of youth or the fading fire of age, but the power of manhood at its zenith. There is energy to begin and there is energy to carry on and to finish. All cherubic signs have this great quality of endurance.

Though Taurus represents the least active of the elements, and though its planetary influences are the passive Venus and the Moon, the cherubic nature of the sign is sufficiently strong to make its action upon the character thoroughly positive. For example, the influence of earth in Taurus is to make the native intensely conservative; but this is not the conservatism of idleness or the laziness of contentment, it is the positive conviction that things are right as they are and must not be changed. The Taurus native is therefore always on his guard against influences which make for so-called reform. His mental attitude is like that of the landed gentry or the farmers in an old established civilization, who, feeling that things have gone pretty well on the whole for centuries, are determined to resist radical interference with them, fearing even a desirable reform, lest it should be the thin end of some disastrous wedge. For this reason, the Taurus native is often called stupid, especially by people like the natives of Gemini, who can see nothing but the pure logic of the situation.

The moral character corresponds very closely with its physical indications. The degraded Taurus type is extraordinarily lazy, sensual, and self-indulgent. Even its affection may be a form of debauch, and the mother who spoils her child by overindulgence is showing the worst qualities of Taurus. The tendency in Taurus to overindulgence in the appetites is correlated with the Taurian influence over the throat, which contains the palate. Even the sensual excesses that sometimes are characteristic of the lower type in this sign are likely to be the results of too free dining and wining. In all forms of unrestrained appetite, there is more regard for quantity than for quality.

In the aggressive type, these qualities are largely reversed. The Taurian native loves work for its own sake. He rejoices in conquering and his other pleasures are subsidiary. People of this type are admirable workers, when once interested; nothing frightens them, nothing turns them from their appointed tasks. Obstacles only impel them to greater activity. Taurus men and Taurus women therefore make excellent servants or employees, and they are admirably fitted to act subordinately as superintendents or "bosses" of labor.

The great difficulty of the Taurian native is the difficulty of starting. Neither the planets nor the elements nor the character of the sign itself shows much initiative. Taurus people always need to be trained; they have to be shown exactly what to do, but once they grasp that, they go on forever. Where a new task is imposed upon them, there may be difficulty in consequence of the stubbornness of the type. There is an obstinacy, which often makes persuasion difficult. Loyalty and fidelity are particularly characteristic of Taurus people. Their affection is indeed almost a doglike devotion without any marked self-assertion.

It is not too much to say that this quiet, steadfast, unimaginative mind is one of the greatest assets of humanity. People with Taurus rising are soundly constructive, but exceedingly cautious. They are always very careful to see that a superstructure, however elegant, should not spoil a building on which it is placed. Their main interest is in the stability of the foundation. Their sense of beauty is great, but they care little for mere decoration, without a foundation of usefulness. Their aspirations are strong, but they insist on proceeding step by step and never make a jump. They never draw a bow at a venture, they never gamble; they are content to work and reap the results in due season and they are not at all cast down by misfortune.

It is perhaps a fault that they are so patient under oppression, but their method is a good one. When their life's work is ruined, they go on steadily, almost as if nothing had happened, and very often this course of conduct is crowned with ultimate success. By means of this, Taurus people acquire the respect even of those who are naturally inclined to despise their stolidity. In any case, they attract affection; even the most frivolous are compelled to recognize the value of their solid virtues.

In dealings with money, the native of Taurus is extremely trustworthy and honest. He is not a spendthrift and at the same time anything but mean. He is what we call a sound, conservative financier.

In the management of business affairs, his integrity and gentleness combine with his steady, purposeful power to produce excellent results, particularly if of a constructive character. He is quite useless in the management of the vulgar and immoral intrigues which so often pass for diplomacy, whether in business or politics. He has no great gift of speech or of writing. He expresses himself with difficulty, though he feels so strongly.

He is extremely fond of home, the place where he was born; another evidence of his general conservatism. His domestic life should be placid, and generally speaking, happy; indeed, he makes an ideal marriage partner, being much more suited for conventional sex life than for any irregularities of conduct, and he is very fond of children, another safeguard for the home.

The Taurian native is very faithful and warm-hearted in his friendships. He is patient and self-controlled, but goad him to a certain point and he will break out in the most violent and dangerous manner. So gentle and kindly is he that it may seem impossible to make him angry. Rash persons presuming on this sometimes go too far with him and find themselves swept away by what appears to them a totally irrational fury.

Parents would do well to realize that their Taurus children are easily hurt and that they become indifferent, unless constantly loved and encouraged. Because of their self-control, they may appear self-sufficient and over-confident, when in reality they are subject to an excess of modesty which amounts almost to an "inferiority complex." They find it difficult to believe that they are loved or appreciated and naturally underrate their own abilities; for this reason they need to be praised whenever possible rather than criticized. These children have an excess of physical force at their disposal, but unless they have a real interest they may become too stolid or indifferent, which later could develop into laziness. Life should not be made too easy for them; an indulgent parent is likely to be their worst enemy, as the pressure of necessity is helpful to those born under Taurus.

It is necessary that these children should have the advantages of a specialized education, as they are more dependent on mental training than the average child. It is also essential that wisdom be shown in the selection of their early companions and pleasures, as they naturally gravitate toward self-indulgence.

People born from the 24th of August to the 24th of September, when the Sun is in the earthy, intellectual sign Virgo, and from the 23rd of December to the 21st of January, when the Sun is in the earthy, conscientious sign Capricorn, are naturally sympathetic and helpful to those born under Taurus. Because their characteristics are complementary, they are good partners for the Taurus born, matrimonially or otherwise. If too intimately associated with those born from the 21st of January to the 20th of February (Aquarius), 24th of July to 24th of August (Leo), and 24th of October to 23rd of November (Scorpio), Taurus people will need to be very adaptable in order to get on harmoniously; such an intimacy might result in the natives of Taurus becoming too stubborn and too resentful.

A period of about seven days—May 20 to May 27—when the vibrations of Taurus are merging into those of Gemini, and Gemini still retaining some of Taurus, is known as the cusp. People born between these dates will partake of the mercurial side of Gemini as well as of the practical side of Taurus, or a combination of the two. As

Mercury, ruling the mentality, and Venus, the love nature, are so close to the Sun, they, too, may partake of some of the adjoining signs of Taurus. This will account for some of the complex personalities so difficult of comprehension.

With this sign, as with Aries, these deductions are drawn from the position of the Sun or Ascendant, therefore it is probable that among the best friends of a Taurus native, or those with whom he is uncongenial, some will be found who were not born at the times mentioned. The individual horoscopes must be consulted to ascertain how the stars combine with those of the Taurus-born, and thus determine what effect the combinations of influences have upon each other.

These indications are general only, and will not cover all the characteristics of an individual as he knows himself, since those born under the sign Taurus are subject to modifications by the planets. A detailed statement or horoscope must be made to discover the whole truth.

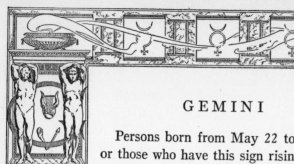

GEMINI

Persons born from May 22 to June 22, or those who have this sign rising at birth (which can be ascertained only through a knowledge of the hour of birth), will come under the dominion of the sign Gemini, symbolized by the Twins.

Gemini is an airy, mutable sign, so lacking in stability that it, or its equally impressionable ruler, Mercury, will nearly always be influenced by some other planet in such a way that the type is constantly and radically varied. Gemini is the all-wandering air, the ever-varying and fluctuant mind of man which changes its color with every new impression.

Consequently it is very difficult to find the pure type; and Gemini may often be indicated as the rising sign when a face is so intensely planetary in character that the zodiac seems to have little influence upon it. The extraordinary profile of Dante, for example, is thus characteristic of Saturn.

PHYSICAL CHARACTERISTICS

As a general rule, people with Gemini rising are rather small, rather slim, generally blond, with gray or brown eyes and a pale complexion, but a very slight planetary influence may change any of these indications, or all of them.

One characteristic, however, is sufficiently pronounced

to be practically always present. This is the alertness and the activity pronounced both in the eyes and in the movements of the whole body. Where planetary influence accentuates this, it becomes greatly exaggerated and the restlessness amounts at times almost to St. Vitus Dance. Where it is modified favorably by such steadying planets as Saturn or Jupiter, the effect is admirable, since their dignity corrects the boyishness of Mercury, and the agility of Mercury lightens the gloom and heaviness of Saturn, or gives more joy to Jupiter.

Another marked characteristic of Gemini is seen in the mouth, which is almost always small with rather thin lips, frequently somewhat contracted. The nose is nearly always a recognizable feature, being long and generally aquiline. Altogether, these significant points combine to give the alert, birdlike face, which is a marked characteristic of the influence of Mercury, the ruler of the sign. Another almost invariable indication of Gemini rising is found in the unusual length of arms and fingers.

The health of the Gemini native is usually very good. He is rarely robust, and may sometimes be of the frequently ailing type, but disease commonly sits lightly upon him; it does not seem to take strong hold. He is almost entirely dependent on his nervous system, which is extraordinarily sensitive. It is often hastily supposed that this means exceptional liability to derangement, but this does not seem necessarily to be the case. The real danger of this sign is lung trouble, since Gemini rules the breathing apparatus of man. There must, however, be a quite definite affliction of a serious character, if this danger is to materialize. The sign also rules the hands, arms, shoulders, the brain and nerve centers, and sympathetically, the thighs, feet and intestines.

MORAL CHARACTERISTICS

An Ascendant Gemini typifies the mind of man, considered as a mechanism. It is capable of doing any kind of work, and of itself does not care in the least what that kind of work is, for the mind of man is entirely unmoral; the same ingenuity of invention may be used to combat a disease or to plot a murder. This being so, the activity of Gemini needs the right kind of direction, for unless the mind is kept busy with useful and uplifting work, it will occupy itself with the useless and deleterious. Moral education is therefore all-important to people with this sign rising. The mind is not wicked in itself, but under temptation it makes all the difference whether there is any principle in the man to prevent his mind from working in improper ways. The unmodified native of Gemini has little or no inborn sense of discrimination.

The childishness of Gemini is very characteristic of the nature of his mind, and this is further indicated by the dual nature of the sign. We have to deal not merely with one child, but with twins. This readiness of the Gemini native to work on any material, without much consideration of whether it is inherently good or bad, is practically always to be found in these people. It is not only a moral question; such matters as æsthetics are equally to be included. Whatever be the subject presented to it, the mind works logically and accurately on that subject, produces the conclusion and presents it with the perfect confidence

that it has done a very fine piece of work. The logical mind
being an extremely rare object, other minds are very apt to
be shocked by the coldness and rigidity and formality of
its productions. People born under warmer signs instinctively resent the method of presentation, even where they
agree with the conclusion. They feel the absence of heart
and account it devilish. St. Paul's method of argument is
very typical of Gemini. There are many earnest Christians
who resent St. Paul's teachings as incompatible with those
of Jesus, but this is really more because of his style than
because of his conclusions. The real difference is that
Christ invariably appealed to the emotions; St. Paul only
to the intellect.

The mind of the native of Gemini being thus exceedingly quick to seize upon any material and work it out to
a logical conclusion will reach the very highest results
in existing channels. It has also the power to combine, to
perceive the relations between all sorts of things, and thus
to produce results which appear entirely original; but the
Gemini mind of itself does not do more than combine,
clarify and develop—it never creates. We may take Dante
as a superb example of this sign. In his "Divine Comedy,"
he has used practically the whole of the knowledge of his
time. He presented it with matchless lucidity and, thanks
to his rising Venus, in a most attractive form; but it
is impossible to find in the whole poem a really new
idea.

The Ascendant of Immanuel Kant is nearly all Gemini,
and Mercury is particularly strong, in exact conjunction
with the Sun, just above the horizon, and in his philosophy we find an incomparable power of analysis and resolution. Dissatisfied with this, he attempted to create, but

his later work is little more than an example of cleverness in concealing fallacies.

It is, of course, rare to find the native of Gemini with such high power of concentration; indeed, in the cases quoted, this is due to the strength given by planetary aid. The natural tendency is to spread the intellectual energy over a great diversity of subjects. Most Gemini natives try to walk in two directions at once. There is no beginning or end to any occupation of the average Gemini mind. Unless the education has been so thorough that a real liking for intellectual pursuit has been created, the mind scatters itself and what, in properly trained people, is a thirst for knowledge, becomes a mere craving for novelty and excitement of different kinds. There is apt to be a great lack of heart, and to natives of such signs as Leo and Pisces, Gemini people seem to be ungrateful, disloyal, lacking in affection and incapable of true comprehension of serious matters. The native of Gemini is quick to retort and finds no difficulty in winning the argument—as if argument settled everything, or indeed anything.

The United States of America is ruled by Gemini, and one sees its influence in the quick-change method of its inhabitants in the matter of occupation. One never sees such perfectly common and characteristic types as one finds in England; for instance, the old butler, who was born in the house; the lawyer's clerk, who has outlived half a dozen partners in the firm; the agricultural laborer, whose forefathers have tilled just that one bit of soil since England was. The average American has engaged in a dozen different kinds of business before he is fifty. The acuteness of his intellect, its rapid comprehension of anything new, is assisted rather than hampered by the complete lack of solid mental training. An Englishman is frightened when he is asked to make even a slight change in some business method.

This adaptability, of course, is the most valuable of all qualities in an undeveloped country, since specialization of labor is a late development in building up a civilization. It is natural, therefore, that such qualities should persist, even after the need of them has passed.

In America we find an extraordinary diversity of occupation which works without appreciable friction simply because of the pace. If the expansion of the country should be stopped for any reason, the situation would immediately become critical. A *modus vivendi* would have to be found; a settlement of the million questions demanding adjustment would become urgent. It would be impossible to carry on a government where the laws of every state, even on so important a matter as marriage, conflict with those of every other state, and many of these again with Federal laws, if anybody would spare the time to consider the matter.

An extreme freedom of thought and speech is characteristic of this sign. It may be said paradoxically that the native of Gemini is so busy thinking that he never stops to think. Fortunately, as we have seen in our consideration of England and Ireland, modifications of national character come from the impinging influence of the succeeding sign. The domesticity of Cancer makes the love of and pride in the home a strong factor in our national life, and gives immense power to our operations in war when once started, although, crablike, we are slow in getting into motion, the sign steadying to a large extent the almost scatterbrained, tumultuous Gemini activity. In the survival of the Puritan instincts, even beyond their spiritual reality, may be seen another Cancerian trait. The average community is often accused of a hypocritical regard for conventions that it does not actually observe.

The nervous sensitiveness of the native of Gemini does not particularly imply ill health; for example, he is not nearly so irritable as the native of Aries, and his magnificent Sensorium, acting like a perfect network of sentinels, warns him of danger of which the Taurus man is quite unaware. Such a man would be inclined to assert that the perpetual alertness and activity of the native of Gemini was bound to tire him out and break him down, but Gemini is a very enduring type. His power to resist pressure or to push obstacles aside is not great, but he is warned so early of any difficulty that he can sidestep it. The Gemini native, therefore, represents rather closely Herbert Spencer's idea of the fittest. If his surroundings do not suit him, he changes them or adapts himself to them. The result is that, as a rule, he has a pretty good time during life.

Coincident with the disinclination to resist is the lack of any wish to attack. It is true that the Gemini native is up in arms very easily in a fussy kind of way, but to him this is only an argument. The senses of the Gemini native are, as a rule, exceedingly acute. It would take a serious affliction of the Moon to upset this natural tendency. There is, therefore, not merely the faculty of picking up things easily in a rough-and-ready sort of way, but there is the possibility of extreme advance in any subject which depends primarily on delicate and accurate senses. One may, therefore, expect such people to make good musical critics, workers in anything that requires extreme fineness of perception, observers of minute differences, and so on.

In money matters, the native of Gemini is not always reliable. In well developed types, the mercurial influences will be shown in a tendency to acquire money by schemes, and the nature of the sign will often incline him toward handling a number of different schemes at the same time. In undeveloped types, this scheming may degenerate into actual trickery.

In speech and correspondence, the Gemini native is exceedingly eloquent, logical and clear. He has some tendency toward diffusiveness and repetition, and he is not always very good at keeping to the point, nor is he very honest in his method of argument. St. Paul's Epistle to the Romans was a masterpiece of this kind of writing. He was obliged to tell the Gentile that circumcision was unnecessary to salvation, and in writing to the Jews, bound by his previous utterances to that effect, he had to answer the question, "Then of what use is circumcision, since salvation is the only important good in life?" His efforts to solve this contradiction are classical. It is the legal type of mind entirely unscrupulous in its method and rejoicing in its own cleverness, only the more because it has fooled the opponent.

This type of mind being limited by the formalities which it has devised as safeguards of truth is sometimes rather blind to the truth behind the fact, the truth of the deeper planes. It is possible for accurate statement to convey profound falsehood. Gemini is often shallow and superficial. It is too little understood that the mind contains more powers than those of pure reason, and that those other powers are based upon fundamental principles quite opposed to those of reason. Purely intellectual analysis ends in an irreconcilable duality, whereas the higher principles of the mind are founded on an irrational, or rather, super-rational unity.

True family life does not appeal very strongly to the Gemini native, but it is not distasteful to him. He acquiesces in the domestic circle without being moved either to intensity of affection or to revolt. This is pretty true of all his relations with humanity. To him, human beings are only factors in his problems. He has no strong inclination to travel, but it is likely that he will do so as soon as opportunity arises. He accepts all the facts of life so easily that he does not mind very much where he may be. Once he is away from home, he will not hanker after it.

The Gemini native is apt to be as shallow in love as in all his relations. In fact, he may fail altogether to understand it. St. Paul, for example, remarking "it is better to marry than to burn," can hardly be considered as having shown a complete comprehension of the subject. He sees nothing in it but an animal passion, as gross as a gorilla's. Bernard Shaw's treatment of the sex problem is almost equally untrue and unsatisfactory, and he has four degrees of Gemini rising. To him the passion of love is rather contemptible, rather ridiculous, a great nuisance, and so far as it is explicable at all, is a manifestation of a mystical abstraction of his own invention called the life force.

Compare this with the profound understanding of the subject shown by Alexandre Dumas, *père*, who has Leo rising. While not a profound writer, his understanding of love is perfectly normal with that of the average human being, and he never falls into a mistake or commits a solecism. Compare this again with the feeling shown by Robert Burns, who has Taurus rising, or Byron with four degrees of Cancer on the Ascendant.

The study of the signs is enormously facilitated by observing the expression of their characteristics through those few children of humanity who are capable of self-expression. We might just glance at the case of Rossetti, who has the reputation of being an extraordinarily passionate poet, whereas a closer examination reveals the Gemini point of view very clearly. It is somewhat derivative; he gets his passion from Petrarch. It is reflected and idealized. Tennyson is another Gemini poet. We get the same idealization of the passion, the vision of it from afar through a beautiful literary telescope. To Tennyson, love is a branch of good manners. None of these Gemini people have the idea of it as a consuming fire. They try to separate it from those powerful and primitive elements that sway the soul; that shake it to its depths, and make it an instrument by which man is identified both with the Most High God and with the lowest of the brutes.

In their treatment of inferiors, the natives of Gemini are often unsuccessful, because they are unsympathetic. They are apt to regard the relation as of a purely business character, and neither give nor acquire the affections of those whom they employ. In the management of public affairs, the native of Gemini is an ideal administrator as long as things go well, but he is quite incapable of understanding the depth and strength of a really unpopular movement. He will try compromise and arguments; failing altogether to touch the source of the trouble. Even so, his intellectual ability will often enable him to succeed in pacification of a temporary character, though sometimes his confidence in the efficacy of argument may lead him into great error.

With regard to marriage, it may be said that the native makes an amiable and useful partner. No great trouble is to be expected, unless produced by adverse planetary conditions; petty irritations arise from time to time, but it is not likely that any serious cause of disagreement will come into the household. Those who are married to the native of this sign may, however, suffer a good deal of unhappiness, if they happen to be of such types as Taurus, Cancer or Leo, which demand a great deal from the marriage partner, for the native of Gemini is incapable of giving himself; one might say that he had little self to give, and the attitude of the other will appear to him absurd, objectionable, and perhaps rather disgusting. Moreover, so far as Gemini ever loves, he loves diversity; he is a flirt, and if he is taken too seriously, great unhappiness will follow. It is a great mistake to be angry with a person of this type.

Parents would do well to realize that their Gemini offspring are highly organized nervously, that they require a calm atmosphere, and should not be told exciting or terrifying stories or anything that would work on their imagination, as this would upset their nerves. They require more sleep and fresh air than the average child; it is essential that they should not only be put to bed early, but that they have frequent periods of sleep or relaxation during the day, for their great excitability and over-wrought imagination often cause them to suffer from sleeplessness or restlessness. If they do not get the proper care during childhood, they will suffer from "nerves" all their lives, and their natural tendency to be dissatisfied will be intensified.

While everything should be done to encourage composure, their imagination or love of physical activity should not be suppressed. Parents should allow Gemini children to express their "different" side, either through masquerade, their love of "pretending," dancing, or outdoor activities. On the other hand, they should be made to realize that becoming bored so quickly with their toys or playmates is due to their own changeable or dissatisfied disposition, and contentment with their environment and appreciation of what they have should be encouraged. The parents should, however, be careful as to the associates of these children, as they are so mercurial that they will take on the coloring of those about them.

In determining the education of Gemini children, it would be well to study their natural leanings or desires, for their great adaptability may cause them to acquiesce in the wishes of their parents or guardians, and keep them from entering the field they prefer; consequently, they are likely to be "square pegs in round holes."

People born from the 21st of January to the 20th of February, when the Sun is in the airy, humanitarian sign Aquarius, and from the 24th of September to the 24th of October, when the Sun is in the airy, balanced sign Libra, are naturally sympathetic and helpful to those born under Gemini. Because their characteristics are complementary, they are good partners for the Gemini-born, matrimonially or otherwise. If too intimately associated with those born from the 20th of February to the 22nd of March (Pisces), 24th of August to the 24th of September (Virgo), or the 23rd of November to the 23rd of December (Sagittarius), Gemini people will find it necessary to be diplomatic but firm in order to get on harmoniously together; such an intimacy might result in the native of Gemini becoming too vacillating and adaptable to the extent of being insincere. For this reason, people born under Pisces, Virgo and Sagittarius would not make the most sympathetic or helpful partners, either matrimonially or in a business way.

A period of about seven days—June 21 to June 28—when the vibrations of Gemini are merging into those of Cancer, and Cancer still retaining some of Gemini, is known as the cusp. People born between these dates will partake of the mercurial side of Gemini, as well as of the maternal and conservative side of Cancer, or a combination of the two. As Mercury, ruling the mentality, and Venus, the love-nature, are so close to the Sun, they, too, may partake of some of the qualities of the adjoining signs of Gemini. This will account for some of the complex personalities so difficult of comprehension.

With this sign also, the deductions have been drawn from the position of the Sun or Ascendant, therefore it is probable that some friends or uncongenial associates will be found under other signs than those mentioned. In such cases, the individual horoscopes must be consulted to ascertain how the stars combine with those of the Gemini-born, and to determine the effect of the combinations of influences upon both persons.

These indications can be only general, and will not cover all the characteristics of an individual as he knows himself, since the influence of the planets modifies the signs. A detailed statement, or horoscope, must be made to discover the whole truth.

CANCER

Persons born from June 22 to July 24, or those who have this sign rising at birth (which can be ascertained only through a knowledge of the hour of birth), will come under the dominion of the watery, cardinal and maternal sign Cancer, symbolized by the Crab, which is ruled by the Moon, the "Time Measure" and the ruler of the senses.

The active and passive types characteristic of Cancer are more clearly differentiated than those of any other sign.

PHYSICAL CHARACTERISTICS

In the active type the skull is long and the face aquiline. The complexion is rubicund, the eyes piercing, the mouth usually thin and firm, the chin pointed, the jaws sometimes suggesting the mandibles of the crab. The body is somewhat large and not very well proportioned. There is something a little clumsy in its appearance. The bodily strength is generally great, but there is a decided liability to disease, especially the kinds that come from self-indulgence.

In striking contrast to this picture is that presented by the passive type. Here we find at its fullest the influence of the element of water, accentuated by that very similar force, the Moon, the ruler of this sign. Here there is nothing whatever masculine to balance. The head is unusually large and broad-skulled, so much so that sometimes it is even broader than it is long. The face is round and flat, the complexion is very pale and has a look as of unhealthy fatness. The mouth is usually large, greedy and sensual; the nose is wide and snub, often extremely turned-up. The eyes are large and often pale, and the arching eyebrows give an expression of placid curiosity. The hair is usually blond or of an indefinite color. When black, it is unusually black, very straight, and dull rather than glossy. The body is squat, with short, rounded limbs, and in the case of women has abnormally large development above the waist. This appearance is that of a pure Cancer type, but in its passive aspect the sign readily takes impression from any planet that happens to be strong in the horoscope.

In both types there is a tendency to become very fleshy in later life, even when this does not manifest itself in youth. People with this sign rising are very liable to illness, especially chronic illness. There seems little resistance or recuperative power in the tissues. Everything in its vicinity tends to mix with water, and Cancer is more prone to contract disease than almost any other sign. The weakest point is in the digestion. The arrangements for nutrition are sluggish, and almost any organ is likely to degenerate. Physical laziness is a marked characteristic of this type; bursts of energy may be frequent, but only when under the influence of some strong motive. The general characteristics of water and the Moon are thus adequately represented in the physical habit of the Cancer native.

The appetite is unusually large and is indulged indiscriminately. It is very frequently of a morbid type, the

Cancer native preferring the foods that are worst for him, such as sweets or condiments. This doubtless conduces to the general ill health which one so often finds with the sign. In fact, the typical Cancer native is never really healthy, for in a proper definition of health we must include energy and activity, and in pure examples of people with Cancer rising these rarely exist. The active type is much less liable than the passive to any of these discomforts.

The type of disease will probably be determined by the position of the Moon or by the ruler of the sixth house and his aspects. For example, the ruler of Madame Blavatsky's sixth house is Jupiter, which is in Aquarius, retrograde in the eighth house in opposition to the Sun. A dropsical condition is easy to predict from such a configuration. There is a great liability to death in early childhood, but if these dangers are avoided, and they may be by careful training on the part of the parents, who should be particularly careful to correct signs of morbid or excessive appetite, there is not likely to be much trouble until the age when diseases consequent on self-indulgence become threatening. If these are avoided, the type is rather long-lived, unless there is something to disturb it; it does not disturb itself. There is, however, always a fear of degeneration of cell or alteration in tissue. Diseases such as Addison's or diabetes are very common; so also are all kinds of malignant growths.

Cancer rules the stomach and solar plexus, and sympathetically the head and kidneys. It is most necessary that those born under this sign be very careful in all matters pertaining to their digestive organs, as they are susceptible to inflammatory diseases, infections and tumors. If they are not wise in the selection of their diet, or if their constitution becomes depleted, they are likely to suffer from asthma, bronchitis, loose coughs, gastric disturbances, weak digestion and kidney complications. Under suppression or excessive use of alcohol, they may develop ulceration of the stomach. Women born strongly under Cancer frequently have ovarian trouble.

All people born under influence of Cancer find it difficult to withstand bodily suffering. They are inclined to exaggerate their symptoms to such an extent as to bring on the very disease they fear. They abhor pain and are very trying patients. Unless they are exposed to contagion, or they abuse nature's laws, these people should enjoy excellent health after they reach adolescence. As children they are just like sensitive plants and are likely to be very delicate, particularly during the first four years of life.

MORAL CHARACTERISTICS

In the moral, as in the physical world, there is an extreme contrast between the active and passive types presented by Cancer. It will be simplest to describe them separately, leaving the question of modified or mixed types to be adjusted to each particular case by the Astrologer. Cancer being a cardinal sign of water, represents the most active or fiery part of water, that quality of water which makes it the most universal of solvents, eating up solids in a way similar to that of fire itself. It must not be considered paradoxical to speak of the fiery part of water; in nearly all cases the solution of a solid body in water generates energy which manifests itself in heat.

When sulphuric acid is mixed with water, the temperature of the liquid is raised almost to boiling point, while the solution of caustic soda in water generates so much heat that an engine has been devised to use this for its source of energy. There was, therefore, nothing unphilosophical in the theory of the alchemists and early chemists when they described every substance as composed of the four elements in varying proportions.

With regard to the active type of Cancer, we shall not forget that it is water, but we must not think of water as passive, easily molded, incapable of offering resistance, quiet and reflective. That is rather the type of water represented by Pisces, or by the passive type in which Cancer's natural acerbity is modified by the influence of the Moon. We must think of it as the corrosive element, as the sea which eats away great cliffs, eternally breaking back upon itself, and eternally coming on again, wave upon wave, until it has eaten up the defiance of the cliffs. This image is very accurate in describing the method of attack of the native. He does not expect to gain his ends immediately. Rebuffs do not perturb him in the least. It is all part of the business. He is broken to pieces apparently, but he goes on exactly as if nothing had happened.

One sees excellent examples of this method in the lives of William Blake and Madame Blavatsky. These were both persons of what may be called the prophetic type. The corrosive action is shown in the subtlety and persistence of their criticism, which has produced such immense results on the trend of the thought of the world. Not in either was there vehemence of swordstroke. The method employed was insidious. Constant rebuffs had no effect upon the work of Blake. He went on with a serene confidence that he was dissolving the conventional ideas of right and wrong. The same is true of Blavatsky. In face of the most damaging attacks, she persisted quietly and on the rare occasions when extreme provocation caused her to lose her temper, she was the first to recognize her error, and continue her submarine operations, so to speak. It is impossible for a thoroughly educated person nowadays to hold the view that salvation, whatever that may be, is the prerogative of some particular creed. Blavatsky may be fairly given great credit for this fact and she helped to bring about this revolution without destroying religion, merely by showing the essential harmonies in apparent diversity. Her share in this work is really much larger than that of science, which used a purely destructive formula. Blavatsky did not destroy the barriers and the warring faiths with them. She merely dissolved the artificial dams.

People with Cancer rising do not attack effects; they seek causes and undermine them. For this reason, such people constitute a serious menace to established order. Their work is accomplished while people are still pointing them out as examples of fatuity and failure. Swinburne is another example of this principle. The world is extremely lucky to have had three such persons within a century. Swinburne had been tabooed, reformed, and nullified. Victorianism was convinced that he was a negligible quantity, but the younger generation knew him by heart and was already acting on his revolutionary conceptions. Victorianism died without knowing that it was sick.

A fourth member of this revolutionary Cancer body was Huxley, who sapped dogmatic Christianity in the same insidious way that the other three had used on somewhat different planes. A perusal of his essays on the subject will be found extraordinarily illuminating on the method of attack characteristic of natives of this sign. He says such innocent things. He leads his opponent on from one apparent victory to another, until the latter is suddenly overwhelmed by the realization that Huxley has been causing him, without his knowing it, to admit the very propositions which he set out most strenuously to deny. The educated world was leavened with Huxley's agnosticism, even while it was proclaiming that the school of Darwin had been superseded.

The vision of these people is usually comprehensive and idealistic. They always think in large units of time and space. There is a strong tendency to the poetic or romantic view of the Universe. Life is to them a species of knight-errantry. They understand themselves as pilgrims or as guardians of some grail. Even a comparatively fleshly type like Byron pictures himself as his own "Manfred." In fact, there is a tendency for the individual, even when he is not a prophet, to regard himself as one. It may be that the Cancer native is a little apt to overlook the practical details of life. His imagination may bewilder him, so that he takes windmills for giants. Furthermore, this quality often causes extreme conceit and egotism. The habitual exaltation of one's self or one's functions frequently leads to contempt and lack of consideration for others. This is a fault against which the native should be constantly on his guard, for it is in reality the most terrible threat, even against the vision itself, which he so dearly cherishes.

Although Cancer represents the fiery part of water,

even its most active form retains the quality of reflection, but moving water distorts and exaggerates these images. We may say here that in the passive type of Cancer this reflection becomes enormously important. Cancer is pre-eminently the sign of memory and its natives dwell intensely upon the past, having a profound affection for everything that represents rest and serenity, but in the active type this quality is transmuted; the images of the past are magnified and idealized. In the Tarot, "The Chariot" is the card attributed to Cancer and the Charioteer is, in one sense, the herald of the divine, of the god-man or Messiah, who comes into the world to create a new era. The herald, therefore, has no conception in consciousness of the message which is to come, and he gets his ideas by reference to antiquity. Thus we see Blake going back to the Old Testament for his inspiration; Blavatsky founding her philosophy on the Vedas; Swinburne exalting Paganism; and Huxley arguing about the Eohippus. The adoration of the past has a tendency to falsify the picture and there is little sense of true proportion.

Consequently we find the native of Cancer drawing the absurd caricatures of the periods which he happens to affect. Consider for a moment the eighteenth century. There is the Watteau shepherd-and-nymph Versailles idea of it. There is the oppression of the poor, spiritual-deadness idea of it. The philosopher will not take one without the other, but people with Cancer rising do not see this. They ignore everything but that which suits their purpose. Thus, though devoted to history, they make the most untrustworthy historians. The effect of this romantic temperament is to make the Cancer native rather inspiring as a teacher or guide. People like to have things painted *couleur de rose*. They dislike people who point out that the Knights of the Round Table are but an astrological legend and that whatever knights there were at that period slept on dirty straw. They are even more offended if the same thing is said about Jesus or Buddha, each with his twelve disciples, with some allusion to the fact that Easterners do not use forks in eating.

The Cancer native is rarely of a strong intellectual type. He lives far too much in sensation and emotion. He may be spiritually developed to a high extent, but rarely gets rid of ethical implication. He is bound by conventions, not those which he finds close at hand but those of the period of history that excites his admiration. He is, therefore, often extremely superstitious, in the true sense of the word. He is scrupulous in fulfilling conventions whose very object may have been forgotten.

The type is extremely sensitive in its emotion. You cannot destroy its activity by ridicule, but it will feel the wound personally. There is a distinct tendency to go hunting martyrdom. The Cancer native takes pleasure in his misfortune. In one of St. Paul's Epistles, Christians are advised to console themselves for any sufferings that they may endure by recalling the fact that these things always happened to the prophets and martyrs of times past. One cannot help saying that this is very unwholesome advice. It kills at the root self-criticism, the most useful faculty that the average self-sufficient human being has as a corrective. It prevents him from inquiring whether his misfortune may not be due to his own stupidity. The more misfortunes he has, the more he is convinced that he is a fine fellow; and this may develop ultimately into a persecution mania. One often finds a touch of the charlatan in perfectly sincere Cancer natives.

The Cancer native has the idea of appeal to authority and antiquity, and he finds it necessary to defend himself by exalting his own personality. Besides this, he will go for proof to analogy and to history, but he will not use modern scientific methods. If one quotes Huxley as an example of a person whose thought was the exact contrary, one need only go into the horoscope in detail to see how the planets governing his intellectual side were able to overcome the original tendency. In everything except science, Huxley held the conservative, authoritative position. It is not unusual to find special training causing a development in one particular line, which is apparently altogether out of keeping with the general character. Such artificial aid as the imagination can confer is, of course, somewhat in the nature of morphia. There are periods when the dose has worn off. Despondency is the natural antithesis of vanity; and the Cancer native is therefore prone to times of extreme depression. This alternation of moods must be carefully distinguished from what is called a mercurial temperament, which is elastic, and depends for its modulations much more upon facts. Its resisting power is much greater. The mercurial mind never reaches such heights or depths as that which we are discussing.

The passive type of Cancer is altogether governed by the Moon. It has hardly anything in common with the active type. It lives almost entirely upon reflection, like Selene herself. The conservatism is quite complete, yet there is practically no resistance to change when the impression arrives. It reflects any image with equal docility and is itself not really impressed. There is something philosophically false in saying that water takes the shape of the vessel into which it is poured. Water has no shape. The only thing that it insists upon is a level surface. Just as the active type wins by subtle and persistent attack, so the passive type remains itself by virtue of resistance of the Tolstoian kind. It resists by the simple process of not resisting. Water can no more be compressed than steel. Its apparent docility is a delusion.

This type is not imaginative or prone to the same romantic illusions as the active type. It replaces these qualities by sentimentality. There is little real depth of feeling; the most affectionate wife, and affectionate is the right word to use, is hardly disturbed by the death of her husband. She accepts the new situation with perfect equanimity and probably slides into another marriage a year later without enthusiasm or regret. Things are taken as they come, not as in the case of Gemini, because of conscious adaptability to new circumstances, but from pure laziness. The easiest way is the only way.

There is very little moral stamina in these people; a great many women of the street are of this type, but one never finds the real courtesan with this sign rising in its passive form. They are never really wicked, any more than they are really good. They simply accept without forethought or design. They never originate; there is no activity in them. Although these people appear the most domesticated and reliable, they are not at all to be trusted. They come under a new influence and respond to it as completely as to the old. It is as absurd to be angry with them as it would be to blame a looking-glass for reflecting opposite images in succession.

In speech and writing, the general characteristics of both types are the same. There is a strong tendency to employ the appeal to antiquity. Byron was always writing of past times and filling his work with allusions to the classics, even in his most modern efforts. A much stronger case is Swinburne, who was literally saturated with antiquity. He wrote almost entirely of classical mythology or legend; he imitated the actual meters used by Greek poets or French, using such forgotten forms as the ballade and the *chant royal*. He even wrote poems in Greek, Latin and French, so admirably framed on ancient models that scholars admitted that they might have been written three thousand years before. He then spent twenty years with Mary, Queen of Scots, and the Elizabethans. He wrote numerous ballads in the style of different authors of almost forgotten periods. Even his most modern work was suffused with the ancient spirit.

In less brilliant cases we find failure instead of success. The average writings of natives of this sign are repetitions of worn-out platitudes. Many are too lazy to write; even in speech, they are deliberate and placid and seldom say anything worth hearing. They say the easiest thing and are particularly careful to avoid giving offense. The last remark is not at all true of the active type, which is very sharp and often offensive in its utterances, outspokenness of criticism being characteristic of it.

The native of the active type is quite likely to contract a marriage of convenience, but he is not particularly keen on doing anything of the sort, having a feeling that it may interfere with his activity. The passive type welcomes marriage as a settlement and remains in it with the same feeling. This type is not especially faithful by nature, but would be so rather than have a domestic up-set.

In love, the active type is tenacious, enduring and even self-sacrificing when its affections have once been fixed, although because of their normal good nature and desire to please, these people may be accused of fickleness. The passive type is purely receptive; it is sensual rather than passionate. It is often mercenary because ease is its chief consideration. These people adore children, but have little patience with their naughtiness. This is an exceedingly bad type of mother. The child is petted and spoiled in every way, yet at the first fault which happens to irritate the mother, unreasonable punishment is inflicted. When the active type of Cancer becomes a mother, there may be a tendency to err by undue severity, but the comprehension is better and the whole attitude more reasonable.

In their dealings with inferiors, people of the active type are apt to be just, but severe; those of the passive, careless and overindulgent. In public affairs the active type is exceedingly dangerous, owing to the qualities of his method of attack as already described. The passive type is useless, even for routine. He can hardly bring himself to attend to business and he has no perception of the necessity for dealing with individual cases, as such. He wants a single formula to cover everything. He may not exactly create, but he performs the miracle of resurrection. The passive type is a complete nullity in science and religion. He has not that discontent which is the basis of all inquiry. The disposition to travel, especially mentally, is strong in the active type.

From what has already been said about the general character of both types, it will be seen how they react to attempted control. The active breaks, but continues the attack; the passive yields in appearance, but receives no real impression.

The Cancer-born are thin-skinned, hypersensitive and suffer acutely from fancied slights. It is necessary for them to have congenial surroundings and associates who hold similar views on the essential aspects of life, otherwise they will not make the best use of their opportunities. They are dependent on sympathy and approval, both in private relations and in public matters. Discord or opposition tend to divert their best endeavors. They are inclined to be changeable and restless, but at the same time possess great perseverance and tenacity of purpose. They are very easily influenced by those they love, but if coerced, even though they may appear to be adaptable, they will display a very determined and even stubborn spirit. Those who are intimately associated with people born under this sign should encourage them to cultivate independence of thought and action. This may be difficult to do, for in one breath they express the desire to be "let alone," and in the next, feel entirely at sea without a directing force.

People born under this sign are often attracted to spiritualism and psychic phenomena. There is great danger, however, that they may delve so deeply into the supernatural realm as to interfere with their health and worldly success.

Children born under the influence of this sign are inclined to have a weak constitution during childhood, but they grow more robust in after years, particularly after the age of forty. It is most essential that the parents choose nurses and governesses who are robust physically and normal mentally, and who have good dispositions, as Cancer children are so impressionable and sensitive that they become easily depleted when associated with uncongenial, weak or elderly persons. Vice versa, these children draw on the life forces of those stronger than themselves or from those who love them.

They have a tendency to be contrary and sullen, and to brood over slights, imaginary or otherwise. They have very delicate digestions; they do not require as much food as the average child, and are very "faddy" in their likes and dislikes. They must be taught to like simple and nourishing food, and not be allowed to select their own diet, which, in many cases, is just what they should avoid. They should not be exposed to infectious or contagious diseases, for, because of their receptiveness, they are likely to catch the germs from others.

These children are not only affectionate, but crave love, although it is difficult for them to be demonstrative because of their modesty. Because of their lack of self-preservation and unselfishness they are often taken advantage of by their playmates, and later in life may be foolishly indulgent rather than wisely kind.

Because of their lack of initiative and their tendency to go along the line of least resistance, their possibilities and limitations should be studied, and wise direction given to their education. Unless they have some very strong bent, which, of course, will be due to aspects in their horoscope, or they express a desire for a college education, it would be unwise for parents to insist, or make too many sacrifices in order to send them to college. The Cancer-born have great manual dexterity and are very thorough workers. If they show any desire for a manual training, it would be well to encourage it. They do not derive knowledge as easily through books, but rather absorb it through association, travel and experience.

People born from the 20th of February to the 22nd of March, when the Sun is in the watery, unselfish sign Pisces, and from the 24th of October to the 23rd of November, when the Sun is in the watery, mechanical sign Scorpio, are naturally sympathetic and helpful to those born under Cancer. Because their characteristics are complementary, they are good partners for the Cancer-born, matrimonially or otherwise. If too intimately associated with those born from the 22nd of March to the 21st of April (Aries), 24th of September to 24th of October (Libra), or the 23rd of December to 21st of January (Capricorn), Cancer natives will need to guard well their own interests and fight to preserve their own individuality. Such an intimacy might result in the native of Cancer becoming too introspective, too fretful, and too lacking in self-confidence. For this reason, people born under Aries, Libra and Capricorn would not make the most sympathetic or helpful partners, either matrimonially or in a business way.

A period of about seven days—July 21 to July 28— when the vibrations of Cancer are merging into those of Leo, and Leo still retaining some of Cancer, is known as the cusp. People born between these dates will partake of the supersensitive, conservative Cancer, as well as of the overconfident, masterful side of Leo, or a combination of the two. As Mercury, ruling the mentality, and Venus the love nature, are so close to the Sun, they, too, may partake of some of the qualities of the adjoining signs of Cancer. This will account for some of the complex personalities so difficult of comprehension.

The position of the Sun or Ascendant only has been considered in drawing these deductions, therefore it is probable that persons born under other signs than those mentioned will be congenial or uncongenial to the Cancer-born. The combinations of influences indicated by the individual horoscopes will make clear the reason for such variations.

These indications can be general only, and will not cover all the characteristics of an individual as he knows himself. A detailed statement or horoscope must be made to discover the modifications made by the planets.

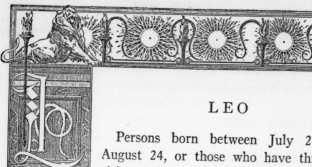

LEO

Persons born between July 24 and August 24, or those who have this sign rising at birth (which can be ascertained only through a knowledge of the hour of birth), will come under the dominion of the fiery, fixed, executive and magnetic sign Leo, symbolized by the Lion, which is ruled by the Sun, the "Giver of All Life."

As the Sun is the center and archetype of his entire system, the native of Leo is the most complete and balanced representative of humanity. All his faculties and proportions are in just equilibrium and harmony, and this is particularly the case in his physical appearance. The Greeks instinctively recognized this, making Apollo and Hercules the adolescent and adult types of Sun Gods, the models of manly beauty.

PHYSICAL CHARACTERISTICS

The typical cranium is neither too long nor too broad; the brow is brave and clear, with the frontal lobes well developed. The hair is usually blond, sometimes reddish. The eyes are fearless and commanding in expression, with sometimes a trace of haughtiness. Leo natives are keenly observant when in action, but often seem to sink into themselves as if they were preoccupied with their own thoughts. They are frank and challenging, seeming to regard every new person upon whom they fall as a possible enemy, but for all that, they are immensely good-humored. The natural color is florid. The forehead is high and broad. Premature baldness, especially frontal, is very common. The nose is well formed, neither too large nor too small; as a rule it is straight, though there is sometimes a slight tendency to aquilinity. The mouth is small and well shaped, firmly held, but not pursed. The chin is more square than pointed, and the planes of the face have the characteristic flatness of the cherubic signs. The only deviation from the Greek ideal is the general shape of the face, which is square rather than oval. The body, which in youth is rather elegant, settles down towards the end of its period of growth into a robust type; activity hardens into strength. The limbs are well proportioned.

There is usually what is very generally recognized as a leonine expression in the physiognomy, and also a similar suggestion in the breadth of shoulder and slenderness in hips and flank. The passive aspect of Leo is not distinguished from the active in any such way as we have noticed with Cancer. It is merely a degeneration of the noble type. Indeed, this extreme diversity of type, which characterizes certain signs, appears to be due to some conflict in the nature of the planetary influences that affect them. Leo is a perfectly straightforward sign, with a harmonious ruler. There is no incompatibility between the Sun and the elements of fire, and there is no planet exalted in the sign to create a second type. The exaltation of Jupiter in Cancer may logically be considered as the cause of the markedly superior characteristics of the active type in that sign, since the ruler of the sign is herself passive.

A degenerated Leo is very easy to recognize. The expression is more of the bulldog than the lion. The complexion, which in the noble type is clear and rosy, is usually dark and flushed, with a heavy grain; the whole face is pinched and pursed and wizened; all the salient strength of it seems to have been removed. The body is much smaller and weaker, but may sometimes tend to grossness and heaviness. The fighting spirit of Leo is present, even in these bad types, but it degenerates into quarrelsomeness.

The constitution of Leo is exceedingly robust in all respects; not only nerves and muscle, but the vital organs of the body are highly developed and exceedingly well balanced in function. The recuperative power is immense. The native is perhaps susceptible to malady, but no sooner is he sick than his whole vitality seems to come to his aid and he throws illness off with great rapidity. Many apparently serious disorders will prove to be merely functional derangement. The Leo native is sometimes rather easy to alarm with regard to the condition of his health, but he rapidly regains his courage and fights even the most serious disease with confidence.

Leo rules the heart and back, and sympathetically the circulation, the throat, and organs of generation. Disorders affecting these parts will be easily aggravated when the system becomes depleted.

He should try to rise above any sorrow he may have, for if he nurses it, it will have a very disorganizing effect on his health. His heart is both his strong spot and his weak spot, for his vitality is so enormous that he sometimes exaggerates it, and puts too great a strain upon his powers. His heart is particularly liable to dilation and hypertrophy. The latter condition is indeed rather characteristic of the Leo native and may be considered normal unless extraordinarily marked. Diagnosis of it should not alarm the physician unduly.

MORAL CHARACTERISTICS

The moral character of the native of Leo can best be understood by those who have made an intimate study of the rites of the Sun God. He is the royal and tragic figure, intensely conscious alike of his glory and of his fate, and possessing infinite confidence in his resurrection. He thus represents humanity in its royal and sacramental sense. He bears constantly within himself this subconscious knowledge. The typical organ of Leo is the heart. The Leo native has not perhaps the analytical understanding of the Universe which we shall find associated with Aquarius. His understanding is subconscious, but in one respect he excels even the native of Aquarius, for not only does he regard all life as one, from century to century, but he perceives it as a sacred ceremony of a wholly divine character. Of course, in the ordinary type, this amounts to little more than the exercise of the three cardinal virtues, Faith, Hope and Love, but in the greatest types there is a perception of the entire Universe as an eternal feast, an endless pageant of joy, in which suffering is but an incident necessary to emphasize the reality of happiness. Adversity is needed to bring out true sweetness of character, and it is only in the climate which has a touch of frost that the fullest flavor is found in fruit.

The character of the Leo native is bold and confident, his carriage assured and his mien lordly. Most other types spontaneously respect or fear him, and he makes a great many enemies through their instinctive envy. Here we come back once more to the symbolic figure of the Sun God, who is slain through the envy of his brethren. Leo produces fighters rather than workers. As a general rule, they have not nearly so much capacity for continued effort as natives of Taurus. They do not fight the uphill battle so well. They are more easily wounded. This applies also to the fighting qualities—the buffalo once roused to battle is a much more terrible opponent than the lion. The pride of Leo rather hampers him, even in fighting; he wants to fight with knightly weapons. He dislikes details. He has not the capacity of thorough preparation for war, such as has been shown by the Germans. He cannot prepare industrially, or develop an elaborate system of spies. He likes to go into battle with his flags flying and his bands playing. His nature is extraordinarily noble; he detests the mean, the base, the underhand, and in a conflict where these qualities are the essentials of success, he is sometimes rather a failure. For another thing, he values glory more than material benefits. He does not wage commercial war; he desires universal empire. France, which is ruled by Leo, illustrates this spirit. It is interesting to note that the first Napoleon had the Sun in this sign.

The appeal of Leo is always to the ideal. He is singularly slow to comprehend baseness, and imagines that if he founds his arguments upon great principles, justice and humanity and righteousness, he must necessarily succeed. He does not at all realize that most people decide questions by considerations of material advantage. For another thing, he expects the question to be considered from all angles, with reference to the past and the future, and to general propriety, whereas people in reality calculate the petty expedients of the moment. Leo also errs through his generosity and faith in others. It is partly the pride of the Leo native that makes him think deception impossible. He himself not only tells the truth but acts directly and frankly without subterfuge or concealment. He is the easiest of all men to deceive, and even when he discovers his betrayal, he is too noble to take revenge. "Father forgive them, for they know not what they do," is a typical attitude of this type.

Leo himself suffers acutely and is, perhaps in consequence, extremely sympathetic with the sufferings of others. The idea of revenge or even of punishment is entirely foreign to his nature. He understands so well the heroic and tragic destiny of humanity, with its inherent quota of misfortune, that the idea of inflicting additional pain is revolting to him. He loves mercy rather than justice. He understands clearly that error, in whatever sphere, must certainly produce a corresponding result, but he would regret the fact, and he would certainly refuse to aggravate the situation by the deliberate infliction of a penalty.

One might draw an illustration from the character and quality of Bismarck, who had Leo rising. It was his aim to consolidate the German-speaking people, and he did so in a comprehensive and royal manner, brooking no opposition; but he would probably have let France alone had it not been for the recrudescence of the Napoleonic position in its worst form. Napoleon III had nothing of the Napoleonic qualities. He was weak, fussy, petty, ambitious without the real stuff of ambition, and he aroused

the just alarm of Europe by his apish emulation of the
exploits of the great Corsican. But when France lay in
ruins, entirely at the mercy of her conqueror, Bismarck
opposed the policy of annexation. Having beaten France
fairly, he had no wish to humiliate her. He would have
preferred to leave her territory intact, and by the exercise of generosity, lay the foundation of a permanent
friendship. That he was overruled has been Germany's
misfortune and danger from that day to this.

It will indeed be a bright moment for humanity when
it comes to understand that two blacks do not make white,
or two wrongs a right; that "forgive and forget" is a better
rule than "an eye for an eye and a tooth for a tooth."
Europe lies in ruins to-day because Bismarck's generosity
in 1871 was above the level of thought of his contemporaries. Material consideration and sympathy both belong
to all time.

Leo is somewhat prone to anger and to excess of pride.
He is excitable and, however good his qualities may be,
when they are in the slightest degree overdeveloped or
let loose, they become fatal. Restraint is always necessary for Leo. His tendency to expansion is his greatest
danger. He should learn above all things "to walk humbly
and with his God." In extreme cases, megalomania is not
at all infrequent. An unrestrained Leo means arrogance,
but, despite the superb self-confidence, when opposed effectively, he is apt to find himself suddenly without re-
source. At this moment, he will remember his tragic destiny and turn at bay, determined to die fighting. These
qualities are less useful than the patience and perseverance of Taurus. On the other hand, they are much

better than the similar qualities displayed by the two other fiery signs.

Leo is the airy part of fire; the fire in its full strength and well balanced; and further, Leo is a cherubic sign. There is, therefore, a robust and persevering quality, but it lacks the solidity which some earthy force might have conferred upon it.

Leo, feeling his royalty as he does, is much too inclined to expect everything from others as his natural right. He takes the attitude that everybody should pay him tribute and that he is a very fine fellow to return a fraction of it in the shape of gifts. The commercial idea is entirely absent from his mind. He constantly bemoans the ingratitude or disloyalty of others, who happen not to do immediately whatever he may require of them. Has he not conferred upon them the inestimable benefits of his smile? He is easily accessible to flattery, and is offended if warned that it is insincere. It is so obvious to him that the statements are true that he cannot believe that the person making them is otherwise than sincere. He will admit that that person may be praising with the idea of getting something out of him, but that is excusable; it is quite natural—is not he the dispenser of all favor? It is right that inferiors should expect his bounty. The lion is very easily managed by the jackal, as Æsop is at pains to point out. The lion despises that mean beast, and is often very angry with him, but in order to restore himself to favor, the cunning animal has only to remind the lion, in the height of his rage, that he is the king of beasts and must not expect too much from a poor little jackal.

In matters of money, Leo is generous and expects

generosity in return; he cannot understand any kind of pettiness. When he thinks of money, he thinks in large, round sums. He never thinks of money for its own sake and the thought of sordidly hoarding it disgusts him. He likes to possess it, recognizing that it is useful as a force, especially for the higher purposes of life.

The native of Leo is often eloquent, both in speech and writing. His appeal is invariably frank and direct, and it is addressed to the heart rather than to the brain. He rather despises dialectical skill. He tells the truth, but is inclined to exaggerate, to boast, and shows a tendency to dangerous optimism.

The Leo native gets on well with his family as a rule, owing to his goodness of heart. In a sense, he may be said to be domesticated, but he insists upon being the center of any circle. His family must revolve around him; however humble may be his station in life, he makes himself the king of a little court. Sometimes the effect is unpleasant; beggars on horseback rarely manage their steeds well. The desire for adulation is exaggerated when the outside world refuses it, and some of these people consequently become tyrants in the home circle. They expect everything to be done for them, not from laziness but from a desire to exercise their rights as they see them. They feel constantly obliged to prove their position. This only occurs when life goes rather hardly for them; when it goes well, they can hardly conceive that anyone might ever challenge them. It does not matter much to them whether they are at home or abroad, so long as they have a sphere in which to shine.

In the matter of love, Leo is noble and rather conventional, but he is usually somewhat unfortunate, on accepted ideas. His one thought is to give himself to the uttermost, and his sense of his own value is so great that he cannot conceive of any person favored by the offer declining to accept it. When accepted, he is at the same time too lax and too exacting. He is likely to spoil the other party, and he feels ridiculously wounded when he finds neglect or ingratitude. These may not even exist, but he expects so much that he attaches quite absurd importance to the veriest trifles. He is not fickle, but he is at heart polygamous, feeling himself such a big personality that he could easily keep a dozen planets revolving around him and shining by his light.

The quality of the love of the Leo native is what literary people call normal; that is, it is the romantic, chivalrous idea that appeals to him. It is very likely to degenerate into sentimentality. The ideal has been expressed by Mallory in his "Morte d'Arthur."

It is impossible for the Leo native to harbor a grudge. The clouds which hide the Sun are but temporary, and besides, they do not belong to him, but to the earth whence they are born. It is significant to observe that such clouds are generated by his own excess of heat.

The Leo native likes danger and adventure because they seem to him to ennoble the passion. He has a certain power of maintaining illusions, even after discovering them. His faith in his ideal leads him to overlook the faults of his inamorata. This also is vanity.

Leo rules not only the physical heart, but also the love nature. It is most necessary that one born strongly under the influence of this sign should have a normal outlet for his emotions, as he is very dependent on affection. In fact, his desire for praise and approval may tend to become an exaggerated ego, or "exhibition complex." It would be well for this type to remember the old adage that "He who has the greatest authority seldom shows it." The Leo native should avoid giving way to "fits" of temper and to over-exertion, because of the ill effects they may have on the heart.

People with Leo rising have no sense of moderation in their labors, and are rather in danger of killing themselves with overwork. When filled with enthusiasm, they allow themselves no rest. "It is better to wear out than to rust out" is their motto. They understand the joy of life to the full. "A short life and a merry one" is much nearer their ideal than a long and sad one; they are miserable only when they feel that time is being wasted.

In dealing with servants, the tendency is to be generous and somewhat lax; but they are very severe if they fail to receive what they consider proper respect. They have the power of kindling loyalty and enthusiasm, and they are exceedingly sympathetic and considerate, but their good-heartedness puts them at the mercy of deliberate malice. They find it difficult to believe evil of anybody, and even on discovering disloyalty, though they may be swift to punish, they bear no malice. They are open-handed in giving presents, not only to servants, but to everyone with whom they come in contact. However, they bitterly resent any demands on them, any assumption that the other party has a right to favor. They are, in fact, very anxious to put everyone in his place and keep him there.

What has been said about love applies very much, paradoxical as it may seem, to marriage. The Leo native is inclined to take the sacramental view of marriage. He is extraordinarily loyal to his own idea of an oath. His word, his honor, these are the most sacred of all things to him. If he swears to "love, cherish and protect" a woman until death part them, he holds himself to his vow. However worthless the woman may prove, it often makes her seem the fitter subject for his protection. Where divorce becomes absolutely necessary for some reason or other, he will allow his character and his material interests to be sacrificed in order that he may feel that he kept his oath rigidly to the last.

Self-satisfaction is a very characteristic trait of Leo, and the pleasure which he takes in contemplating his own generosity lasts him throughout life. The Leo native is often misunderstood, for there is hardly any action that cannot be set down to two wholly opposite motives, and selfish people will often accuse this native of selfishness when, to himself, he appears to have been the very soul of magnanimity.

The capacity for business of the Leo native is apt to be weak owing to lack of interest. Only when his imagination has been strongly excited can he expect to make marked success in this department of life. In the conduct of public affairs, the same characteristics have play. This native never departs from the kingly attitude. His self-confidence enables him to make up his mind very quickly, and no argument really shakes him, though with a lordly graciousness he may allow himself to appear to be convinced. It is necessary for him to smile on every one, to seem acquiescent even when most resolved upon resistance. Arguments fail to reach him, because he is sure of his own righteousness and truth and there is no more to be said on the subject. Arthur James Balfour,

who has the Sun in Leo, is an excellent example of this
manner. When Chief Secretary for Ireland, night after
night confronted by eighty angry men in the House of
Commons—"Irish wolves howling against the Moon"—
he would sit as if half asleep, rise when necessary and
proffer exquisite nothings in reply to the most detailed
charges. He never changed his policy in the slightest degree.

In matters of state, generally speaking, this native is
bold and sagacious, always obviously ready to fight for
his principle and thereby often avoiding the necessity of
fighting. Bismarck, with Leo rising, and Napoleon with
the Sun in Leo, are great examples of this temperament.
In science, philosophy, and religion, the Leo native is, as a
rule, sound and practical, but his comprehension is passionate rather than intellectual. The greatest men of
science are not found with this constellation rising. Every
progress implies a disturbance of balance, and Leo is
always harmonious with the totality of things.

The sign is capable, however, of two methods of advance, both of the highest importance. The first is that
it possesses the power to generalize, to bring up to date
in perfect arrangement and beauty the sum of all knowledge, extracting the heart of it and making it manifest.
Such a step is real progress in no mean sense of the word,
for it is the constant tendency of the pioneer to advance
in specialized direction but to lose touch with the general
situation. Every business needs occasional auditing; to
attempt to judge of its prosperity by details is to go
hopelessly astray. A giant example of the faculty of summing up is found in Balzac, who had Leo rising. Leo revolts instinctively from the accumulation of petty detail,

realizing that it is often impossible "to see the wood for the trees." The other point in which Leo excels is that of sheer creation. Such creation, however, is not that *genus de nova* kind which pertains more to Neptune and Uranus than to any other sign; it is rather a resurrection in glory of a dead body. The Renaissance was a characteristically Leo creation. It was Paganism come to life, renewed in beauty and immortality, and it is significant that it had its birth in Italy and France, both ruled by Leo. This quality is in strict keeping with the traditional mystical significance of the sign.

Those shallow Athenians who are always clamoring for something "original" often look with contempt upon the creations of Leo, as if it were something wonderful that truth would continue to be truth. "There is nothing new under the Sun"; there are only unfamiliar combinations. It is the kaleidoscopic beauty of these that produces the effect of new creations by creating new impressions. There is nothing eccentric in the operations of Leo; the sense of beauty is intensely keen and the love for it overwhelming, but balance is always kept by the innate instincts for harmony. It is part of the general normality of the sign.

But as the Sun at high noon is on the edge of his decadence, so the native of Leo always finds danger in the moment of his glory. His reputation is likely to suffer sudden reverse.

Leo children are warm-hearted, overgenerous and sympathetic. They are inclined to be rather boastful, concerning not only their family, their friends and their belongings, but also their achievements. The fact that anything belongs to them makes it, in their eyes, the best in the world. They are very unhappy if they cannot be first in a game, a contest, or in the esteem of their playmates. Unless this is tempered by good judgment, instead of helping the Leo child to happiness and success it often proves to be a stumbling block, as their associates resent their air of superiority and tendency to "show off." Teach them to realize that if they have done anything worthy of praise or merit, others will recognize it and it is not necessary for them to "blow their own horn."

One of the greatest weaknesses of the Leo-born children is their desire to dominate others; so they should be made to realize, even as children, that others also desire freedom. They will be happiest when they feel responsibility, or are in a position of authority. A free expression of their emotional nature will be absolutely necessary in order that they may be at their best, either physically or mentally. Their natures will be very rhythmic, and if they show any particular talent it will be well to have it cultivated, as they would have executive ability, more especially along musical or artistic lines. Praise and appreciation are necessary for the younger Leo-born. If they are found fault with, they become very irritable and indifferent.

They are quick to detect inconsistencies, and these not only confuse them but are unpardonable in their eyes. Because of their powers of observation, it is necessary to be very precise or literal in making promises or in stating facts. While this is more or less necessary with all children, it is especially marked in the case of the Leo-born, for children are often wiser than the average adult realizes.

Again, because of their keen observation, they are inclined to imitate more quickly than do most children the examples of those around them, which makes it imperative that their parents or guardians set them a wise example by being polite, kindly and attentive. Because of their love of adventure and their tendency to idealize everything about them, it is necessary to give strict attention to their early training, to the books they read and the companions with whom they associate.

Children born under the influence of Leo are naturally robust and have great endurance. They are likely to suffer if held down or not given an opportunity to work off all their physical vitality.

People born from the 22nd of March to the 21st of April, when the Sun is in the fiery, magnetic sign Aries, and from the 23rd of November to the 23rd of December, when the Sun is in the fiery, intuitive sign Sagittarius, are naturally sympathetic and helpful to those born under Leo. Because their characteristics are complementary, they are good partners to the Leo-born, matrimonially or otherwise. If too intimately associated with those born from the 21st of January to the 20th of February (Aquarius), 21st of April to 22nd of May (Taurus), or 24th of October to 23rd of November (Scorpio), Leo people will find it necessary to avoid being too dictatorial, stubborn or conceited. Such an intimacy might result in the native of Leo becoming too irritable, impatient and dissatisfied. For this reason, people born under Aquarius, Taurus and Scorpio, would not make the most sympathetic or helpful partners, either matrimonially or in a business way.

A period of about seven days—August 21 to August 28—when the vibrations of Leo are merging into those of Virgo, and Virgo still retaining some of Leo, is known as the cusp. People born between these dates will partake of the dominant, splendid qualities of Leo, as well as the analytical and intellectual side of Virgo, or a combination of the two. As Mercury, ruling the mentality, and Venus, the love nature, are so close to the Sun, they, too, may partake of some of the qualities of the adjoining signs of Leo. This will account for some of the complex personalities so difficult of comprehension.

As with all the other signs, these deductions are drawn from the position of the Sun or Ascendant, and it is probable that some of the best friends of a Leo native may have been born under an apparently uncongenial sign. In such cases, the individual horoscopes must be consulted to discover what influences combine to produce the unexpected effect.

These indications cannot cover all the characteristics of an individual as he knows himself, as the influence of the planets must also be taken into consideration. A detailed statement or horoscope must be made to discover the whole truth.

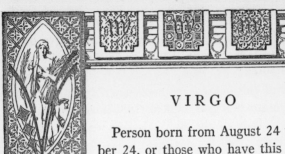

VIRGO

Person born from August 24 to September 24, or those who have this sign rising at birth (which can be ascertained only through a knowledge of the hour of birth), will come under the dominion of the earthly, mutable, discriminating and critical sign Virgo, symbolized by a Virgin holding some ears of corn, and ruled by Mercury, the "Messenger of the Gods." The intellect of people born under Virgo is as intelligent as that of the other sign which is ruled by Mercury (Gemini), but, fortunately, it is not so vacillating or restless.

Virgo is a somewhat contradictory sign, being the most earthy and passive of the three earthy signs, and at the same time doubly influenced by Mercury, which is exalted therein. It is to be observed that this sign is the only one in the zodiac that claims as ruler the planet thus exalted, and that astrological tradition describes Virgo's ruler as "the negative side of Mercury."

These facts give peculiar significance to the claims of certain esoteric astrologers that the true ruler of the sign is Vulcan, an undiscovered planet whose existence has been suspected by some astronomers, and whose invisibility could easily be accounted for by its nearness to the Sun and the effacement of its small light by that body. Further plausibility is given to this speculation by the discovery of Neptune in 1846, and astrological observations of its domain lead us to accept it as the true ruler of Pisces, a sign in which similar incongruities have been found in the attempts to justify any of the previously known planets as its lord. A complete and fascinating analysis of this occult claim, reasoned from the symbolism of the ancient god, Vulcan, will be found in Isabelle Pagan's study of the zodiacal signs, entitled "From Pioneer to Poet"; but, as our purpose has been throughout to hold strictly to scientific interpretations, we shall discuss the sign from its mercurial significances, which are not contradictory when we bear in mind the ancient statement that it is the negative side of this planet that operates through this sign.

PHYSICAL CHARACTERISTICS

Mercury is in all respects the very opposite of earth, for he is mutable, mobile, airy, restless, ever-changing; and this antinomy is hard to resolve. Therefore, also, as we have seen to be the case in Gemini, it is extremely difficult to find natives of Virgo whose appearance has not been modified by planetary factors. The earthy type of Virgo native is big, the mercurial type small; but there are no great contrasts between an active and passive type such as we have seen with other signs.

In the earthy type, generally speaking, the head is broad-skulled, sometimes large for the body. The face is generally homely, with a tendency to wide nostrils, and is rather aggressive, sometimes even overbearing in appearance. The eyes are clear but small, frequently with an expression of cunning; they are hardly ever sympathetic. The mouth is small and thin, the very gross lips, occasionally seen, can probably be attributed to planetary interference. The body is often ungainly and with the limbs ill set; there may often be some actual deformities. Nature seems to delight in playing tricks with these people; giants and dwarfs are usually found to have this sign in the Ascendant. The hair is rather indeterminate in color, but though it may be either light or dark, there is a peculiarity of shade which strikes the expert eye. It is often crisp or wavy, and it stands up and away from the forehead in an extremely characteristic manner.

The mercurial type of Virgo native is a very different object. It should be said at once that this type is much more common when the latter degrees of Virgo are rising, and it is a somewhat doubtful point as to whether this type is not really caused by the influence of the entering of Libra into the Ascendant. However this may be, the fact remains that the type is dissimilar in almost all respects, the chief similarity being the tendency to a slight deformity or lameness.

The stature of the Virgo native is unusually small; he is exceedingly well knit, well proportioned and active. The skull is very long, the features small and regular, tending to a slightly feminine delicacy. The color of the hair is usually light brown, and that of the eyes hazel or gray; in rare instances, blue. The nose is straight, small and sensitive, though still with rather wide nostrils; and the same adjectives describe the mouth well enough. The expression of the eyes is rather frank and simple; they are inquisitive and active and express a keen intelligence.

Virgo rules the bowels, the solar plexus and sympathetically the lungs and nervous system; disorders of these organs should be guarded against. We must differentiate

between the diseases of the intestines that are secondary to stomach troubles and those that arise directly. The
region especially under Virgo is the alimentary canal
itself.

There is also a connection between Virgo and the roots
of the nervous system, Gemini's influence upon this part
of the body being more peripheral. Many nervous disorders of the seat of the primary lesion, such as locomotor
ataxia, may be traced to afflictions of Virgo. Here again
will belong the chlorosis of adolescence. The Astrologer
will soon learn by experience to determine in what way
planetary influence will cause one disease rather than
another; thus, a Saturnian affliction of Virgo might cause
tuberculosis of the bowels. Mars might produce typhus,
enteric fever, cholera or inflammatory troubles such as
colitis. Uranus or Neptune, on the other hand, would be
more likely to give rise to *tabes dorsalis* and probably such
maladies as Graves' disease, Addison's disease, and perhaps diabetes.

People with Virgo rising are usually very sensible in
matters of health and avoid most of the troubles commonly brought about by mismanagement or self-indulgence; they are temperate, with no strong temptation to
abuse pleasure. They like quiet, regular and active lives
and, as a rule, do not require violent exercise to keep
them in health. They are inclined naturally to thinness
rather than to fatness, though as a rule the balance is held
very even, and any error in diet will usually be on the side
of abstemiousness. The lure of the senses has no strong attraction for these people. The simple life agrees with them.
It will have been noticed that most of their characteristic

maladies are somewhat obscure in origin. A physician, therefore, when consulted by people born under Virgo, will do well to search very deeply into the primary cause of the affliction.

Virgo is one of the signs that confer great length of life, if the perils of early infancy are avoided. Convulsions and infantile diarrhea are the principal dangers at the beginning of life. After that, it is likely that Virgo people will never know a day's illness until the time comes when obscure degenerative diseases begin to menace the constitution. If the Virgo native be under good direction and transits during this period of life, say from thirty-five to fifty, he will probably escape altogether, and may then expect to live to a green old age; in which case, life is likely to be terminated by paralysis.

Baudelaire offers a striking illustration of the way in which these influences operate, for he has Mercury the ruler within three degrees of the conjunction of Mars, which is in exact square to an exact conjunction of Uranus and Neptune; accordingly, he was struck down by complete paralysis, which left him entirely incapable of speech or movement while apparently permitting him the full use of his intelligence and consciousness. In this state he continued for about a year. Contrast with this the case of Oscar Wilde, whose Mercury is in Scorpio, squared by the Moon, and in opposition to Uranus. Such aspects overpower the natural abstemiousness of Virgo. It was indulgence in absinthe, aggravating specific disease, which caused his early death; and the influence of Virgo is indicated strongly by the spectacular manner of that death, so graphically recorded by a biographer.

MORAL CHARACTERISTICS

Mercury being so strong in this sign, there is a great similarity between it and Gemini in the matter of mentality, but the earthiness of Virgo diminishes the pure rationality of this native and his reasoning powers are not valued for their own sake, as we found to be the case with the more positive Mercurial sign.

The Virgo native is extremely practical and his aims are usually influenced by some so-called material advantage. His outlook is apt to be petty and his reason itself hampered by the perpetual intrusion of the pragmatical viewpoint. He is, therefore, practically incapable of producing anything with the fire of true genius, and however talented he may be, it is difficult to conceal the fact that he has "an ax to grind." Thus Charles Dickens sacrificed his art in his attempt to use it for moralizing propaganda; instead of being engaged with beauty, as was Balzac, he deliberately wrote his novels to help abolish imprisonment for debt and to reform all kinds of abuse. His Sun in Aquarius gave him a humanitarian objective instead of a sordid money gain. It is to be observed in passing that his characters are all moral caricatures, suggesting the tendency to deformity which we have already learned to associate with Virgo, and it is also desirable to call attention at once to the extreme care in matters of detail shown by the master and his weakness in the construction of his plots.

Before leaving the subject, let us glance at a very different individual, an infinitely greater artist, a child of the spirit, whose sense of beauty is so profound that there was nothing feminine upon which his glance fell that he did not transform into a radiant goddess glowing with all the splendors of the spring. But on what material did his poetic imagination work this miracle? A giantess, a dwarf, a negress, an absinthe drinker, or an *affreuse Juive*—in short, deformity of some sort. Such was the effect of Virgo rising at the nativity of Charles Baudelaire. The meticulous precision and attention to detail which characterize this sign manifested itself in his choice of words; minute perfection in form was as necessary to him as the intensity of the thought behind it. It is for this reason that, though he left only one book of poems, that book is one of the greatest volumes in all French poetry. Baudelaire's horoscope has so many powerful planetary influences that the ruling sign is little more than a background. A far more characteristic example of the mental influence of the sign is Cornelius Agrippa, whose books showed an astounding capacity for collecting and arranging facts without any ability to harmonize and comprehend them.

The practicality of Virgo and its love of order and arrangement, its patience and foresight, give it a regard for the conventions of life which may easily be mistaken for an ethical morality that the sign itself does not possess. The tendency with Virgo is to talk about ethics instead of feeling in itself what is right and what is wrong. Every fact of nature is a basis for its investigation, but the fact is always observed from outside, and so never really understood. The Virgo type of reformer is a hopeless doctrinaire; he works out by mathematics what is best for everybody and is simply annoyed at the stupidity of people who passionately attack his proposals as callous and immoral.

The Czar Nicholas II and Louis XVI of France both had Virgo rising, and the destinies of the two monarchs are very similar. Both monarchs finding themselves threatened by popular discontent, proceeded to grant Parliamentary Government and then made that government farcical. They were both under the delusion that people who were suffering from real grievances would be satisfied by paper remedies.

It is the prime source of error in Virgo that the native of this sign cannot understand irrational human passion. The lack of humanity and sympathy too often characteristic of Virgo is even more striking than that which we found in Gemini; for that sign, after all, justifies itself by the completeness of its intellectuality, while Virgo habitually applies the intellect to the more material side of every problem. People born under both of these signs should attempt to form a link between heart and mind. Thus the airy quality of Aquarius becomes noble by reason of its humanitarian direction; that of Libra by its close relation with beauty; but Virgo drags down air to earth. There is something repugnant in the idea of compressing and confining air. The very spirit of liberty is in it, and when, instead of wandering unconfined, it is debased to wheeze through old bellows, our conception of its divinity is affronted.

The qualities described are characteristic only of the more or less intellectual types, of course. The average man born under this sign has for his type the husbandman; he is the steady and patient worker, but his work is always routine work.

Virgo, however, is the critic *par excellence*. He never of himself creates, but he discriminates and distinguishes,

often indeed with quite unnecessary accuracy. He is the
purist, the statistician, the man who works by rule and
who generally interprets rule in the narrowest possible
way. He instinctively prefers the letter to the spirit. Especially in the earthy type, he has a certain sense of his
own failings which is quite subconscious but which operates to make him contented with hard work and little pay.
One of his troubles is that he cannot grasp the idea of the
dollar because it is such an awful lot of cents, and he
really does understand the cent. He lacks the imagination
requisite to greatness, even in such a matter as a salary.
Success comes to him very slowly and it is usually well
earned. In this respect the sign resembles Taurus; but
Virgo, being more adaptable, gets around obstacles rather
than through or over them, and so achieves the same result as Taurus without anything like the same expenditure
of energy.

The Virgo native is often too humble, though he is
sometimes very sensitive about the little dignity he may
happen to possess. He is an object of strong dislike to
those of warmer and nobler signs, but he is very fascinating to such people as would fear Aries, Leo, or Scorpio. He
gets along easily because he is not aggressive. His insignifi-
cance excites no envy and his manner no resentment. His
plodding patience assists his capacity and cleverness, and
though he will never beat another man to anything, he will
sometimes get a first-rate job without asking for it; while
the lion and the bear are fighting, the fox slips off with the
booty. These people are often what are called compromise
candidates in political circles. Whenever a man is wanted
to fill a place harmlessly, one should look around for somebody with Virgo rising. There are many situations when

the struggle between the really powerful forces is so intense that the triumph of either cannot be attained without the ruin of both; and, in such a case, a person who is neither acceptable nor unacceptable, positive on neither side but actually negative to both, offers the only solution.

Virgo is thrifty and very constructive in financial affairs. The Virgo native is accurate in his accounts and inclined to pay much attention to petty details, believing concretely that if he "takes care of the pennies, the dollars will take care of themselves." He is thus open to the accusation of stinginess and, in undeveloped types, may be very mean.

Mercury being the god of commerce (as well as of thieves), the native of Virgo is extraordinarily well adapted to routine business and is exceedingly clever at driving a bargain. He will expend infinite trouble on saving a penny, and finds great pleasure in getting the best of a bargain. It exasperates him to find himself outwitted by one of the moral types, whom he looks down upon but whose imagination has a far wider range of vision than is possessed by the man who is limited by Virgo. The narrowness of his horizon is frequently the cause of his being overreached. He painfully adds up columns of figures while the other man, having made a rough estimate, is occupied with the dynamic qualities of his scheme. In other words, Virgo makes an excellent bank clerk or cashier, but rarely produces a financier.

In his speech and correspondence, Virgo is usually tedious to a degree, filling his page or his discourse with every kind of unnecessary detail, and laboring in argument over what the other man is perfectly willing to accept without discussion; thus he may wear his subject threadbare without ever touching the heart of it.

In his domestic life, the native is usually happy enough; he does not provoke trouble and he does not respond easily to it. Anger with him is apt to be as shallow as his other passions. He dislikes change and does not care to leave his home. He prefers the life of the village or small town to that of the city, and in the city he will choose a commercial career in preference to one of the professions. He makes a good lawyer, though not so good a one as a native of Gemini, so far as the controversial part of law is concerned, but he is certainly wholly admirable in those departments of law which are really specializations of business; for example, conveyancing. He is a reliable guide for the investment of funds and his advice with regard to any matter is shrewd and politic, provided it does not call, as many matters do, for considerations that lie deeper than the visible facts. In a dispute with another in business, one may often have a very good case and lose a lot of money by winning it. Virgo may sometimes see as far as that, but seldom farther. He is always very much alive to present advantage.

In love, Virgo is an impossible mate for temperamental people. He is not passionate and he is not especially affectionate. Narcissus, who is attributed to this sign, is an excellent symbol. He is cold because he is self-centered; he has no conception whatever of the inmost secret of love, the mutual abandonment of the self for the beloved resulting in a true spiritual fusion into divine oneness. Indeed, the dividuality of the ego and the non-ego is the quintessence of pain, but Virgo is entirely unconsious of this. He detests the idea of self-surrender. He does not even care much for the idea of conquest, and thus he fails to arouse true enthusiasm, either in himself or in others. Thus we may say quite flatly that he is incapable of loving. Paradoxically enough, this very quality makes him popular with the very large class of the community that likes to play at love. Men with this sign rising often are successful at lovemaking in the lighter sense of the word, where nobler types would fail for the simple reason that they will not *play* at the game. The woman has also a feeling of safety in having a so-called love affair with such a person, because of the instinctive recognition of the fact that the whole affair is taken so lightly by Virgo that there cannot possibly be any serious trouble.

With regard to children, one could hardly find a better parent; the Virgo native is extraordinarily careful to attend to every detail of the child's welfare. A child with a personality worth preserving will easily learn to exercise a proper influence over its parents in all important matters, while at the same time the placid routine of the Virgo life is perhaps the best soil in which its genius can develop.

In their treatment of inferiors, natives of this sign are usually successful; though lacking in sympathy, they attend carefully to detail and see to it that they are well served. The person employed knows that no carelessness will be permitted, and though he may acquire little affection for his master, he will not be offended by arrogance or overbearing disposition on the part of the latter.

Virgo people make excellent partners in marriage or business; small comforts and conveniences are diligently attended to. The partner is businesslike, whether in housekeeping or in office work. Even flirtations will usually be of a mild order; nothing will occur to threaten the home. In business, he will not seek to dominate, and a man of great initiative should look for such a partner for this reason.

In public affairs, the Virgo native makes a useful secretary. He is likely to be able to suggest useful improvements in any organization, and his activity and alertness may prove a valuable safeguard to those whose minds, intent upon great projects, are likely to lose sight of all the little things that count. The native is trustworthy and diligent in all affairs, those of state as well as his own personal concerns. There is, however, a certain exception to be noted which extends over the whole gamut of his activity. Virgo being like Gemini, a mercurial sign, is in itself neither good nor bad; it lies somewhat apart from those passions which create great happiness or great misery. Mercury is cold-blooded and indifferent, but there is this factor which renders Virgo less dangerous than Gemini, that the sign is earthy, more stable and practical than its airy brother. There is, therefore, a certain conservatism in Virgo. The mental activity is less obsessing—in a word, Virgo has an anchor. It is easier for the native of this sign to observe conventions and routine. He is not carried away by ideas as is the native of Gemini, but the possibility of such violent impression remains, and the very practicality of Virgo sometimes implies greed.

When there is no definite moral bias, such as we find in Taurus and Leo, a powerful planetary interference with the natural tendency of the sign will operate easily. There is no subconscious revulsion against crime. Suicide is somewhat common with natives of Virgo. We may notice the horoscope of Guy de Maupassant, whose Sun is squared by a retrograde Uranus, and the ruler of whose ninth house is in conjunction with Mars in the Ascendant.

With such aspects, one can hardly be surprised at his suicide. It might also be remarked that in his stories he sometimes shows an exceedingly detached point of view. He has several tales of cold-blooded cruelty, which are agonizing even to read. Though this great realist doubtless observed them from life, he indicates at least the possibility that such ideas were not beyond the range of his temperament.

In science and philosophy, the Virgo native may be preeminent, for he has the power to perceive minute differences, to make careful measurement and to analyze appearances until the ultimate secret is laid bare. He can distinguish the false from the true; the real from the seeming. These qualities above all are necessary to the successful prosecution of research in either of the departments mentioned. In religion, the Virgo native is not likely to achieve great things. He lacks enthusiasm; he lacks emotionalism. His perception of truth will lead him to reject all spiritual revelation as superstition, and while he may remain perfectly content with the faith in which he is educated, he will take it very superficially.

It will be instructive here to glance at the nativity of Brigham Young. It was not he who founded Mormonism; he was the clever, calculating administrator; the Sun, Venus and Mercury all in the tenth house and Mars nearly conjoined with Jupiter and exactly sextile to Uranus, conferred upon him a tremendous power of making his will paramount. Contrast this with the founder of that interesting faith, the visionary Joseph Smith, with the prophetic sign of Cancer on his Ascendant, and the Moon and Mercury in conjunction on the cusp of the seventh house in exact square to a conjunction of Saturn and Uranus. Brigham Young could have administered a federation of the world; Joseph Smith had no such executive ability. Just as Christianity owes its tremendous spread and power to the organizing and administrative genius of St. Paul, so with Mormonism we find the spread of its teachings dependent on the power and energy of its leading apostle.

The friendships of the Virgo native are frequently intimate and durable, but they exist by virtue of community of interests, usually upon the intellectual plane. Such friendships are easily broken by divergence of view, for the native of this sign is exceedingly jealous of interference and suspects its existence even where the danger is quite imaginary.

The Virgo native is not especially impatient of constraint; he feels it but little. Hamlet says, "I could be bounded in a nutshell, and count myself king of infinite space, were it not that I have bad dreams." Virgo has no bad dreams. It seems natural to him that all things should be arranged in a somewhat petty order, and he sees no reason to complain.

Virgo children should not be discouraged in their tendency to ask questions. They are living interrogation points and should not be suppressed, as this is their way of acquiring knowledge. Any tendency toward being too critical or faultfinding should, however, be held in check. They are naturally orderly and particular, but are inclined to let little things overshadow the more important things of life, much like their elders. Teach them to take lightly small disappointments; otherwise they will not be able to surmount greater trials or difficulties which are bound to overtake them later in life. It is very easy for them to become depleted nervously by worrying or fretting over petty annoyances; from a larger standpoint, however, they have a very hopeful and buoyant side, which should be developed. These children should have frequent rest periods, as they use up much nervous force with their great mental activity, and it is more necessary for such children to retire early (as with Gemini) than for the average child. It is also essential that they should live in an atmosphere of calm and harmony and not be attended by excitable, exacting, or nervous persons. Virgo children should be given every opportunity to acquire not only a sound education but the advantages of good environment and of much travel, if at all possible, as they would be unhappy if they felt they were mentally inferior to their associates. They are not spontaneous "mixers," however, and because of their indifference to others, they should be given an opportunity to cultivate their latent talents, in order that they may be less dependent on friends or family. It would be well to teach them to modulate their voices, if there is any tendency towards shrillness or too high pitch.

People born from the 21st of April to 22nd of May, when the Sun is in the earthy, practical sign Taurus, and from the 23rd of December to the 21st of January, when the Sun is in the earthy, conscientious sign Capricorn, are naturally sympathetic and helpful to those born under Virgo. Because their characteristics are complementary, they are good partners to the Virgo-born, matrimonially or otherwise. If too intimately associated with those born from the 20th of February to 22nd of March (Pisces), 22nd of May to 22nd of June (Gemini), or 23rd of November to 23rd of December (Sagittarius), Virgo natives will find it necessary to be less critical and more sympathetic in order to get on harmoniously together. Such an intimacy might result in the native of Virgo becoming too petty and stressing small things to such a point as to upset his nervous system. For this reason, people born under Pisces, Gemini and Sagittarius would not make the most sympathetic or helpful partners either matrimonially or in a business way.

A period of about seven days—September 21 to 28— when the vibrations of Virgo are merging into those of Libra and Libra still retaining some of Virgo, is known as the cusp. People born between these dates will partake of the discriminating and intellectual qualities of Virgo, as well as the just and balancing side of Libra, or a combination of the two. As Mercury, ruling the mentality, and Venus, the love nature, are so close to the Sun, they, too, may partake of some of the qualities of the adjoining signs of Virgo. This will account for some of the complex personalities so difficult of comprehension.

Again we must say that, as these deductions are drawn from the position of the Sun or Ascendant, it is probable that among the best friends of the Virgo-born, or those with whom he is uncongenial, there will be some who were not born at the times mentioned. The individual horoscopes must be consulted to ascertain how the stars combine with those of the Virgo native, and to determine the effect of the combinations of influences upon each other.

These indications will not cover all the characteristics of an individual as he knows himself, since they do not take into consideration the influence of the planets. A detailed statement or horoscope must be made to discover the whole truth.

LIBRA

Persons born from September 24 to October 24, or those who have this sign rising at birth (which can be ascertained only through a knowledge of the hour of birth), will come under the dominion of the airy, cardinal, just and balanced sign Libra, symbolized by the Scales and ruled over by Venus, the "Goddess of Love and Beauty."

It is very easy to recognize people who have Libra in the Ascendant, in spite of the fact that there are two distinct types; one swayed by Venus, the other by Saturn and Scorpio.

PHYSICAL CHARACTERISTICS

The general build is small, slim, delicate, excellent in proportion; and the movements are lithe and graceful. There is an unruffled activity which is not at all like the nervous restlessness of Gemini.

The head is long-skulled; the features are small, regular and pleasing. Ancient statues of Hermes, Antinous and Aphrodite give a fair idea of the type, though sometimes there is a tendency to floridity or buxomness, which is anything but characteristic of Libra. The natural complexion is olive; the hair very dark brown or black, though possessing a luster and a warmth which is exceedingly pleasing. It is straight and very soft in texture, with a tendency to grow low upon the forehead. The nose is

89

small and Grecian, being straight with practically no identation in its bridge; the lips deep-hued, seductive and exquisitely shaped. All the lines of the face are soft, elegant, delicate, and gracious. Most people feel instinctively drawn to this plastic beauty. The limbs are small and admirably proportioned, the hands and feet being particularly well molded. Even in the strongest types there is something of feminine delicacy.

But all this applies to Libra as the sign in which Venus bears most active sway. There is an entirely different type which 'is due to the exaltation of Saturn in Libra; his power modifies the Venusian influence to a very marked extent, accentuating the fact that the sign is cardinal and counteracting its airy nature.

When the Saturnian influence predominates in the sign, it makes the native much more thick-set, muscular, robust, and square than the regular Venusian type; approaching, indeed, the personal appearance of Scorpio. In fact, this type is usually found when the latter degrees of Libra are rising, since a good deal of Scorpio is then actually in the Ascendant.

There is one trait which is easily recognizable and excessively characteristic and this is what may be called the intriguing expression; the eyes of Libra are naturally subtle and fascinating, but they are exceedingly soft, gentle and affectionate.

In the Saturnian type the Libra eyes have the two first characteristics, but their expression is somewhat sinister. There is an intense love of power in them. One can see that they are scheming and unscrupulous. One would go too far in saying that they were necessarily untruthful, yet the effect is an effect of untruthfulness. Peo-

ple of this type are apt to say things intended to deceive
and to deceive very successfully, but their method of deception is often to tell the truth in such a way that the
hearer will obtain a false impression. The whole face bears
out the eyes. It is sly and secret. One always feels
that such people constitute in some special way a power
behind the throne. They are very economical in their
methods of attack and defense. They never put all their
goods in the shop window. There are always aces up the
sleeve.

The most mysterious people in the world are the Chinese, who are ruled by Libra. When Sir Robert Hart, after
fifty years spent among them, was going home to England, he told a young friend, who had just completed a
walking tour through the country, and who sought assistance in psychological interpretation from the man whose
very life had depended for half a century on his just estimate of the character of these people, that he now knew
pretty well what a Chinaman would do in any given set of
circumstances, but had not the least idea why he would
do it. This type understands the all-important, psychological truth, that no one can defeat your purpose, except
by some accident, if he does not know what that purpose is. Many women instinctively follow out this method
in their dealings with men. It is quite generally recognized
that no woman is so dangerous as the woman of mystery,
but the type of intelligence implied is by no means a feminine intelligence, any more than it is a male intelligence.

The influence of Saturn often gives a coarseness of texture to the complexion, and there is often a touch of brutality in the countenance, but with these qualities goes
eternally a suavity which to most people makes the type

seem yet more formidable. Simple-minded people have an instinctive distrust of such a type. Those who are conscious of their own essential force, though it be entirely different in character, tend rather to admire and to like it. It seems to hold such profundity of knowledge that those who are afraid of knowledge fear it beyond anything else.

The shoulders of this type are more square than those of the purely Venusian type. There is a greater appearance of physical strength, and much less gracefulness. The limbs are shorter, the hands and feet stronger and more practical in appearance. All these modifications, however, are more characteristic of the impinging influence of Scorpio than of Saturn.

The general constitution of Libra is very good, but it lacks robustness. Slight causes produce rather serious disturbances in health. In no other sign does well-being depend on such fine poise. On the other hand, disease yields quickly to treatment.

Libra governs the loins, kidneys (the ovaries in the case of a woman), the spinal cord and lumbar region, and sympathetically, the head, stomach and knees. The affections of these parts, involving many obscure conditions which may result from structural changes in the nerve centers, and sympathetically digestive disorders, are the troubles to which those born under this sign may be subject, provided the system becomes depleted or they abuse natural laws. The most serious troubles the native should guard against are those involving the kidneys and the spine.

The Libra native delights in harmonious movement; dancing, for example, is a characteristically favorite amusement. The sense of rhythm is as strong as the sense of form, and these things, being as it were the blossom of the Libra nature, are the first to suffer in the event of frost. With the exception mentioned, there is no special liability to disease, but this will generally depend on planetary positions or aspects. The vitality of the Libra native is very great within a certain limit but he should never permit himself to suffer undue strain. He can go on forever taking things in moderation; but excess, which throws him out of poise, is most dangerous for him. He is usually conscious of this fact; he will never run when he can walk and will often pull through cheerfully where a much stronger man collapses. He understands how to conserve his energy and seldom wastes an ounce of strength.

The natural temperance of the sign serves him in good stead in all matters of health. He has a strong revulsion when tempted to eat or drink too much. A feeling of disgust dominates him before he makes any error of this kind. Nature herself, too, is very kindly in this respect; intemperance in eating or drinking usually producing nausea. The Libra native; therefore, though not nearly so strong in appearance as many others, often outlives those born under more powerful constellations.

MORAL CHARACTERISTICS

Libra, being the cardinal sign attributed to air, represents that element in its most active form. Air has no shape; it cannot be seen; it hardly resists the movement of material objects, and it is, therefore, difficult for some people to understand how this innocent-seeming substance can be a destructive force; but when air becomes aggressive, it is the most terrible and irresistible of all agents. The tornado and the hurricane, the cyclone and the typhoon tolerate resistance as little as the volcano. Air is the chief nourisher of the life of man, yet in one way or another air kills more men every year than all the other elements combined.

We must never, therefore, think of Libra as in any way passive. The passive type of air is given by Gemini, which is a thing unstable, easily swayed, opposing no resistance. The balanced type is given by Aquarius, representing the settled and consecrated thought of humanity. The latter is the soaring man-eagle of the zodiac and is closely connected with the idea of the Holy Spirit of man, but Libra is rude, primitive and untamed. It works on the intellectual plane like the other airy signs, but its function is intensely dynamic. There is something paradoxical in the idea that the invisible steam which issues so quietly from the spout of a kettle can be turned into a force which can ultimately be used to tear up the surface of the earth. This paradox can be carried yet deeper. The principal constituent of air is nitrogen, one of the most inert of the gases, yet for this very reason nitrogen is the principal constituent of practically all high explosives.

These facts of physics and chemistry have their precise counterpart in the moral make-up of the native of Libra, particularly in the Saturnian type. The gentleness and amiability are apparent, but they are always, one should not say a mask upon a passionate face, but the smoothness which enables a sharp spear to penetrate with the minimum of resistance. Libra recognizes that rude frankness is the worst possible detriment to the carrying out of one's secret purpose.

So far we have spoken of Libra in its most intensely active form, with the influence of Venus glossing its sharpness and serving to conceal its intense energy under a cloak of graciousness, but Libra has a static as well as a dynamic force. Libra is the sign of the balance, and its card in the Tarot is "Justice." The power of Libra is accentuated by the possession of this greatest of all qualities, the power of weighing everything accurately and never attempting to employ force without consideration of equilibrium. Libra never acts at all unless the conditions are exactly favorable. The tornado itself is controlled by the forces which set it in motion, and the true explanation of its actions is that it restores a disturbed equilibrium; fills a void. The aim of Libra is always to compose a disturbance, and its apparent activity is a misnomer. Things may be very wrong without people perceiving it. Libra is the one who discovers the trouble and proceeds to adjust it. The habit of acting in equilibrium is absolutely necessary to the efficiency of any machine; the arrow will not fly straight unless it be balanced by feathers. The Egyptians, noticing this fact, made the feather a symbol of their goddess of justice and truth, and their gods and kings wore the feather in their headdresses to symbolize that they stood for righteousness and for a force irresistible because its application was in accordance with the general law.

Libra is the most effective of all the forces of the zodiac, because it works invariably according to the laws of nature. It never attempts to intrude where it has no business, although to others it may seem to be doing so. It has calculated all the probabilities and as its action progresses it will be seen that its object has been peace. If Napoleon's career had not been broken by the persistent opposition of the ambitious English, he would have established a United States of Europe under the *Code Napoléon*, the most just and intelligible of all modern systems of law.

In cases where the active elements in the horoscope occupy weak and passive signs, where there is no great driving force of any kind, this judicial temperament becomes inactive. The Libra native spends his whole time in balancing, postpones action until to-morrow, which never comes. Some of the most ineffective of all human beings are born with this sign rising; like the ass that could not decide which of two thistles to eat first, and so starved to death, they remain incapable of forcing themselves to action. The mind is so accurately adjusted that no sooner does any thought enter it than the contradictory thought is suggested automatically. This quality confers upon the Libra native an extreme breadth of mind, a universal tolerance with no prejudices. It is only the most active type that sums up hastily, formulates a plan which, while combining as many elements as possible, is in harmony with the individual purpose, and puts it to action. The contemplative mind is very commonly found associated with a body born with Libra in the Ascendant.

Another point in the character of Libra is that this devotion to balance and to harmony is also a devotion to beauty. Beauty consists in the right proportion of elements, in the just balance of one thing with another, and accordingly we find an intensely æsthetic strain in the Libra nature. This native is peculiarly disturbed by untidiness, ugliness and disorder. So acute is this feeling that he is often made actually ill by the contemplation of wrong. He is very sensitive; a disruption like war gives him the most terrible agony of spirit. He finds his consolation in one single consideration. He says to himself that the old civilization was lopsided, hideous, productive of ugliness and misery, and that, in order to change, to re-build, the building must be razed to the earth; nay, more, that the foundations must be laid anew. His final judgment in the matter, therefore, is that the war is the necessary spiritual preparation for the establishment of a new era which shall be founded according to the true laws of beauty. He will be inclined to argue that the sudden extension of the operations of science from the laboratory to field and factory was an unprepared alarm, an invasion of established civilization which was bound to distort it. He would show that the demand for new markets had become urgent, that the possibility of transportation had permitted the exaggeration of cities, and that all these things working together were bound to produce a conflict of irreconcilable elementary force. In a word, just as the thunderstorm is the result of the accumulation of intolerable potential, so the strain, commercial and political, produced by over-population, discharged itself by means of war. This line of argument is very characteristic of Libra. Every instinct of the Libra native is against violence, yet he will perceive violence as the necessary precursor of calm, and set his seal of approval upon it.

Libra is the most trustworthy of the signs for this reason, because it never allows personal considerations to interfere with abstract ideals. You will often find a native of this sign taking a highly unpopular attitude; one such, for example, might say that he thought Germany entirely right in her invasion of Belgium, but he might nevertheless fight for England on the ground that he was English by birth, thus making a complete distinction between his moral and his social being.

Libra never mixes the planes. One of the principal fallacies in philosophical and occult argument is to do so. Mystics, for example, arguing that there is no such thing as sin, will try to justify themselves when committing it; while others, arguing that we are all (men and small animals) the children of one great father, yet will complacently eat broiled rabbits. The man with Libra rising does not make this error. He does not eat broiled rabbits because he does not like them, and if he does commit sin it will be because he does like it. He will never fool himself into confusing the action proper to a body with the thought proper to a mind. He is a carnivorous animal and no argument about the sanctity of the cow will prevent him from eating a steak. In other words, he makes each department of his being attend to its own business and act in a manner appropriate to its own nature.

In regard to money matters, Libra is too broad-spirited to regard any single factor in a problem as important, and the airiness of the sign is in direct opposition to the earthiness of money. But the mathematical ability is very great, and when the Libra native is forced to deal with financial questions he is astonishingly accurate. As it is perfectly possible to use just calculation unjustly, it will depend on the development of the Libra native whether he is a clever faker of figures or an upright accountant in finances.

The native of this sign has the power of charming by his speech and writing. He is gentle, subtle and persuasive, and manages to get his own way under a great appearance of justice. He is singularly plausible in presenting his points of view and always pretends to be just a little shocked and hurt when anybody sees through him. The type is not exactly hypocritical, but Libra natives feel instinctively that all is fair in love and war and that the end justifies the means. It is one of the regular characteristics of the intriguing mind. These people make dangerous controversialists. They acquire sympathy with great skill, and their suavity often irritates an opponent to loss of temper and its consequent disadvantages, since while the native has him at his mercy, he may point out with tears in both eyes that he is being abused and ill-treated, and that the anger of the opponent is only further evidence, alas, that he is in the wrong.

The native of Libra gets on very well in his home, owing to the charm of his manners and his general capacity for doing things subtly without seeming to do them. He has, however, no particularly strong or deep-rooted attachments for his home, and though a break with his family would be comparatively rare, he does not possess the domestic sense in anything like the same degree as the native of such signs as Taurus or Cancer.

In love, the Libra native has perhaps the most interesting temperament of any in the zodiac. The influence of Libra, as a balance, comes very strongly into play. Libra as the cardinal sign of an active element is decidedly masculine; as a house of Venus, it is decidedly feminine. The temperament of this native is consequently poised between the sexes. As a rule, he is very strongly and very highly developed on the plane of sex, and this is marked sometimes by his possession of a nature intermediate between male and female, sometimes by the possession of two temperaments, one almost extravagantly masculine while the other is intensely feminine. Possessing such a range of understanding in this matter, it is natural to find the Libra native a great expert in all matters of love. He instinctively comprehends the nature of any other human being, and his adaptability is such that he is able to adjust himself without effort to the other party. He takes intense pleasure in the exercise of this power, because of his instinctive desire to master others. It comes natural to him to play a part.

These qualities often make the Libra native a good deal of a varietist, and under certain planetary combinations there may even appear a strain of homosexuality. This is not to be attributed to any real predilection, but to the fact of the delicate poise of the Libra nature between the two sexes. This type of Libra person is often intensely voluptuous, but also refined to the highest possible point. Even where there is much sensuality there is none of grossness. He does not consider love as an appetite, but as an art. It is true that he may perform acts of an incredibly gross nature, but his aim is never the satisfaction of a lust. He will take equal or greater pleasure in the similar education of others, and thereby these people are often very pernicious to their fellows. It is incomprehensible to a man with Venus in Capricorn or Scorpio that an act which they do naturally and feel to be animal should be accomplished in precisely the same manner, to all appearances, by another man in the name of art. It is, of course, exasperating to the native of Venus in Libra to find himself thus ill comprehended or ridiculed, but he will feel a singular pride and security in the idea that his soul is safe from the contamination of what he considers the vulgar.

The detachment of Libra is such that it is sometimes curious to witness the ability of the person born strongly under its influence to deal with adverse circumstances. This applies particularly to love, but may be extended to cover the whole field of his relations with the rest of mankind. He takes infinite pains to bring about a certain result, but, if he should fail, he has almost as much mental satisfaction in the analysis of the forces involved as he would have had if he had been successful. His failure is only one more factor in the problem, and he will very often take fresh hold and will succeed by virtue of the failure, in a way he could not have done if he had succeeded in the beginning.

It is difficult to be seriously angry with the type of Libra person just spoken of, for what would be unpardonable frankness of expression in others excites no resentment towards the Libra natives in those who understand them from an astrological standpoint. It is true, however, that these people, although genuinely passionate, are not really capable of love within the limitations of its definition in romantic literature. These people seldom "live happily ever after," for the idea of lifelong fidelity is not natural to them. Moreover, in marriage, such types are perhaps not altogether so happy as in a state of greater freedom and less responsibility. They are gifted with every attribute that is calculated to please, and at the same time are the possessors of immense tact, but there comes a time in the affairs of most married people when the partner is subjected to exceedingly critical analysis, which the native of Libra would make unusually searching, and which few partners could entirely pass. But under such analysis from a husband or wife of a different sign, the cleverness of this Libra type will understand the temperament of the partner and, being forewarned, will be forearmed, and therefore able to avert the full consequence of the investigation.

The native of Libra is usually fond of children and enjoys playing with them. He will treat them with justice and gentleness; he will understand their natures and never tyrannize over them. He will not spoil them, and he is likely to divine the best possible career and prepare them carefully for it. It is quite possible to take the view that this is the very best kind of parent that any child could have. It is very difficult for most parents to realize that a child is an individual soul with a nature of its own, with rights and duties corresponding to its nature. The tendency is always to try to bring up the child in the way its parent went, and not in the way that he should go. The majority of children are aborted or mutilated by this hideous attitude on the part of the parent. A child of strongly independent character, finding himself in the power of stupidly affectionate and bigoted parents, suffers the intensest agony until he fights his way out to freedom; but it is to be noticed that the child, if strong enough to keep his integrity in face of this opposition, is thereby admirably fitted for the battle of life. Unfortunately, such tremendous personalities are rare; the common result of an unhappy childhood is to break the spirit of the child and to prevent forever the development of whatever quality he may possess.

In dealing with servants, the method of the Libra native is persuasion rather than force, and his natural sense of justice wins him the respect of those employed by him. His natural tendency to laxity is, however, somewhat of a drawback in dealing with the intractable and recalcitrant; consequently, he is at times apt to be rather badly treated. In public affairs and business partnership, the situation is more fortunate for this native, for his natural instinct is to adjust all difficulties without recourse to the strong hand; but Aries being on the cusp of the seventh house, mundanely, the influence of Mars will sometimes force him to resort to open conflict, exceedingly against his will. The deeper student of history will be inclined to realize that Napoleon, from the time when he first became a conqueror, spent his life in trying to avoid war; but with Uranus retrograde in his seventh house, in opposition to Jupiter, he could hardly be expected to succeed in such pacific intentions. Fortunately for him, Mars was trined by Uranus, so that he was able for a long time to bring to successful conclusions the wars that were forced upon him.

One may also observe in this connection a striking illustration in President Wilson's attempts to avoid war. Persistently he fought against the myriad influences in his own country and abroad, which sought to drag the United States into the conflict. With an infinite patience and diplomacy, which excited rage at his alleged weakness and incompetence, he parried every stroke for over two years. But the transit of Uranus in 1916 over the opposition to his radical Mars, and the square formed by Uranus in the end of March and the beginning of April, 1917, with his radical Uranus, which was retrograding into his seventh house, succeeded in forcing him to act, in spite of his Libra instincts.

Returning to business characteristics, the native of this sign is sound and conservative, yet not in any way prejudiced against new ideas. His judgment is shrewd and his tactics ingenious, but it is rare to find him enterprising. He does not care for cutthroat competition. His mind is too catholic to absorb itself solely in the business of chasing dollars. Indeed, one is much more likely to find a Libra native engaged in professional or financial lines than in mere commerce.

In matters of science, philosophy and religion, Libra is again very excellent. It is true that bad types are often shallow and too ready to comply with ideas, not so much because they are conventional, but because they are easy to hold. When the sign is well dignified, we find a minuteness of judgment, a power of weighing evidence and a facility for reconciling apparently incompatible notions, which are extremely valuable for the purpose of progress. Libra is decidedly eclectic. It refuses to progress unless it has first summed up the past. Any person in whom this is a dominant characteristic will never be one-sided or over-specialized. It is not that he venerates the past, but that he does not wish to take a step which he might be forced to retrace subsequently through failure to take into account something that he really should have known. These people show no bigotry in religion; they are inclined to argue, but they will invariably take whatever point of view may be opposite to that of their interlocutor, in order that they may harmonize the opposing points of view. Their familiars often accuse them of inconsistency, which is really very amusing, for they see no reason why they should hold a view which they propound. The other man is there to put forward the arguments on the other side; what they really want to do is to find the Golden Mean. The love of beauty in form tends to give an appreciation of the ceremonial in religion, and when they are church-goers, Libra people are very apt to prefer the Catholic or Episcopalian creeds; they also very often belong to the Masonic fraternity.

Libra is as impatient of constraint as any sign of the twelve. To attempt to impose upon the native of this sign instantly brings all his forces into play. The Chinese character well illustrates this point. It is impossible for people of other races to control them effectively, in spite of their apparent gentleness and patience, because, without seeming to offer resistance, they find some subtle and effective way of nullifying the intentions of the other party. It is notable that, throughout history, they have always absorbed and transmuted into themselves their supposed conquerors. One must never suppose that one has gained a victory over a person whose main forces lie in Libra. While you have been breaking his lines in the front, he will have slipped round to the rear and cut your communications.

It is very necessary that children born strongly under the influence of this sign should be taught the necessity of exercising will power, of holding to their decisions, and of having a definite purpose in life. They have a certain apathy to overcome which may degenerate into indolence, unless they are kept steadily at a task until the habit of industry is formed. While their love of harmony and beauty can be an asset, provided they are given an artistic education which can be made a means of livelihood later in life, they should not be allowed to develop into dilettantes and fritter away their accomplishments or possibilities.

A great deal of affection should be bestowed upon Libra

children, even though they may not respond to it or appear to appreciate it. Unless the emotional nature can be developed, they are likely to suffer from loneliness, as their playmates may consider them cold and indifferent, and later in life they will suffer from a lack of friends and admirers. If parents of these children have formed plans for their future which do not seem to fall in with their own, it would be wise to prepare them for work for which they show a natural aptitude. It is far better for them to be successful actors, dancers, writers or painters than to be misfits in a more commercial calling. Do not try to make a dray horse out of a race horse; but rather turn their delicate susceptibilities into a channel where these traits will fit in and make for success.

People born from the 21st of January to the 20th of February, when the Sun is in the airy, humanitarian sign Aquarius, and from the 22nd of May to the 22nd of June, when the Sun is in the airy, intellectual sign Gemini, are naturally sympathetic and helpful to those born under Libra. Because their characteristics are complementary, they are good partners to the Libra-born, matrimonially or otherwise. If too intimately associated with those born from the 22nd of March to the 21st of April (Aries), 22nd of June to 24th of July (Cancer), 23rd of December to 21st of January (Capricorn), Libra people will need to exercise will power in order not to lose their individuality. Such an intimacy might result in the native of Libra first becoming too pliant and then reacting to the other extreme and becoming stubborn and unyielding. For this reason, people born under Aries, Cancer and Capricorn would not make the most sympathetic or helpful partners, either matrimonially or in a business way.

A period of about seven days—October 21 to October 28—when the vibrations of Libra are merging into those of Scorpio, and Scorpio still retaining some of Libra is known as the cusp. People born between these dates will partake of the just and artistic qualities of Libra, as well as the self-interested and materialistic side of Scorpio, or a combination of the two. As Mercury, ruling the mentality, and Venus, the love nature, are so close to the Sun, they, too, may partake of some of the qualities of the adjoining signs of Libra. This will account for some of the complex personalities so difficult of comprehension.

As with all the other signs, these deductions are drawn from the position of the Sun or Ascendant, and it is probable that some of the best friends of a Libra native may have been born under an apparently uncongenial sign. In such cases, the individual horoscopes must be consulted to discover what influences combine to produce the unexpected effect.

These indications cannot cover all the characteristics of an individual as he knows himself, as the influence of the planets must also be taken into consideration. A detailed statement or horoscope must be made to discover the whole truth.

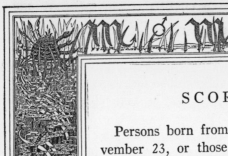

SCORPIO

Persons born from October 24 to November 23, or those who have the sign Scorpio rising at birth (which can be ascertained only through a knowledge of the hour of birth), will come under the dominion of the watery, fixed, self-interested sign Scorpio, symbolized by the Scorpion and the Eagle.

Scorpio is a comparatively simple sign with which to deal, because there is no conflict in its planetary attraction. It contains no exaltation, and its ruler, Mars, "the god of War" is not inharmonious with the nature of the sign itself. Though Scorpio is a watery sign, it is water at its greatest strength. The incompressibility of water, its unconquerable determination to find its own level, are qualities that express Mars at his strongest. He is no longer the fiery, dashing young soldier we found in Aries. He is the seasoned veteran, with a tremendous sense of the realities of war and the power to endure every kind of hardship. He has lost the illusion that war is a matter of uniform, flags, decorations, processions and bands, varied by occasional spectacular charges of cavalry. This attitude is seen clearly in the physical appearance of the native.

PHYSICAL CHARACTERISTICS

The skull is generally of the broad type, though sometimes it may run very much in the other direction, on account of the impinging Sagittarius influence. Scorpio, physically speaking, rather delights in extremes. The hair is usually dark, very strong and plentiful, sometimes wiry, sometimes crisp and curling. The face is square and may be mistaken for Leo, but for its high cheekbones and greater severity. The eyes are deep-set, with a fixed look of tremendous thought and power. One instinctively thinks of James Thomson's description of Bradlaugh: "Two steadfast and intolerable eyes." To weaker types, there is often something exceedingly sinister in the gaze of natives of this sign. The nose is sometimes short and broad, sometimes straight, sometimes even aquiline, but whatever its shape, it always gives the impression of aggressive energy and powerful will. The mouth is somewhat large and the lips tend rather to thinness; at all times they remain firmly compressed. The chin is square and strong. There is occasionally some tendency to heaviness of jowl.

The passive modification of this type may be called feminine. Here the head is usually long and the face a very perfect oval, with an expression of voluptuousness. The lips are rather full and sometimes loose, but the characteristic heaviness of the lower jaw is nearly as conspicuous as in the more masculine type. These people are usually small in stature and slim in figure, but they are slow and at times clumsy in their movements. There is a superficial resemblance to Libra, but experience will soon show that while the fascination of Libra is, in a sense, well meaning, that of Scorpio is selfish and even malign.

The masculine type of Scorpio tends to be squat and thickset, often to a quite exaggerated degree. One imagines the Herculean dwarfs of romance to have been of this type. So strong is the influence of the sign that it takes a very powerful planetary interference to modify it to any extent; the primitive characteristics remain recognizable in all disguises, however protean. The complexion, as a rule, is swarthy, and in men the beard is often exceptionally strong and thick. It is not infrequent for natives of this sign to have birthmarks such as moles. Where the planets are harmoniously balanced, the body becomes immensely strong, gifted with great endurance. It hardly ever happens that the Scorpio native is lithe and active. He spreads his energy over a long period. Quick action is not customary for him, though sometimes he has a capacity for exceedingly sudden and unexpected action. He can never run like a hare, but he can strike like a snake. His strength is never lumbering, as so often is the case with Taurus. It is exceedingly elastic; the nerves and the muscles are of tempered steel. In some respects, the native can stand a greater strain than any other type. One has only to quote the names of Sir Richard Burton, Dr. Alfred Russell Wallace, Thomas Edison, Victor Hugo, Paul Kruger, and Benjamin Disraeli, who had Scorpio rising, to make it clear how intensely powerful is the resistance of this sign to physical and mental strain. The capacity for work appears quite unbounded.

The native of Scorpio generally enjoys a very robust type of health. Older Astrologers have insisted especially upon the attribution of this sign to the reproductive system, but this is a partial and limited view. Chemistry is preëminently the business of Scorpio. The chemical process of digestion (the transformation of the food into blood) comes under the influence of Scorpio, while the function of Leo only begins after the blood has been manufactured; Virgo and Libra rule over the actual structure of their organs. The diseases peculiar to Scorpio, therefore, are not only those of the organs of reproduction. Many disturbances of the digestive system are to be traced to trouble in this sign. All toxic effects may be expected from him. All the internal secretions of the body—bile, gastric juice, semen, and so on—are under Scorpio. In the self-destroying qualities of this sign, we find also an indication that we should look for the cause of those malignant diseases in which every element of the body, even those whose function is normally protected, seem to turn against it. Finally, all forms of putrefaction and corruption, from ulcers to gangrene, are usually to be found with afflictions of this sign. The native's immense vitality assures him an exceedingly long life, unless he be overcome by one of the typical diseases referred to above. There is peculiar danger from some of the toxic complaints of infancy, but perhaps the most frequent cause of premature death is when the constitution is wrecked in adolescence or early manhood by the contraction of venereal disease.

When the native is sick from any cause, his sense of reality leads him to take immediate practical measures, and his characteristic energy urges him to employ drastic remedies. Scorpio fighting against sickness is just as efficient as in his other combats. He does not neglect his condition. He goes straight to bed when another man would keep on working, and seeks to drive out the disease by using the most powerful remedies that he happens to know of. There are no half measures with this type of man. The recuperative power is immensely strong, except in those diseases where the body turns traitor to itself. The native always chooses surgical treatment where that is possible. Its radical nature appeals strongly to him.

MORAL CHARACTERISTICS

The general physical characteristics of Scorpio are very well paralleled by the moral character. The will power of the native is so strong that at first sight it seems to put to shame people born under other signs, but this excessive strength easily degenerates into obstinacy. It lacks altogether the flexibility and tact of Libra. The native of Scorpio always goes directly to the point. He never compromises; he never beats about the bush; and he never gives in. In this sign, there is nothing of the judicial temperament which gives tolerance to Libra. The sign is tremendously selfish, far more so than even Capricornus. The undeveloped Scorpio native is the slave of his own will. He is absolutely bigoted and persists in his purpose even when he sees that to do so will lead assuredly to his own destruction. A scorpion ringed about with fire is said to drive its sting into its own body, and whether or not this is a fact of natural history, it is at least a very good description of the character of the native of this sign.

In judging the horoscope of anyone born under this sign, immense importance attaches to the uplifting aid of beneficial planetary aspects or positions, since there is no sign in all the zodiac capable of a wider difference between its higher and lower developments. If the expansive and altruistic nature of the Scorpio native be well fortified, we may find all this will power turned to noble ends. If, on the other hand, we find the constricted, selfish influences predominant, we shall probably discover a most thorough scoundrel, capable of any kind of meanness, who will brook no opposition in the furtherance of his selfish purposes.

As an example of the higher development, we may consider the horoscope of Dr. Alfred Russell Wallace. Here Mars, the ruling planet, is in the humanitarian and altruistic sign Aquarius, and even though Mars is square to Saturn, that powerful planet is in trine to a conjunction of Neptune and Uranus, and the will of the native is thus turned to the pursuit of science and the occult. Jupiter is trine to a conjunction of the Sun, Mercury and Venus, which expands, strengthens and makes gracious the religious qualities. Here, then, we find the intense will power of Scorpio, dignified in every way by the excellence of the moral nature.

In the horoscope of Disraeli, Jupiter is rising in conjunction with Venus and Neptune, a combination which expands the influence of Jupiter without directing his energies to any great height of philanthropy, while Saturn is culminating, squared by Mercury, and this gives an intense sense of reality with some lack of scruple. On the whole, Saturn is decidedly stronger than Jupiter and we may acquiesce in the verdict of posterity that Lord Beaconsfield's favorite number was Number One. On the other hand, in the horoscope of Vaillant, the anarchist, Mars in the Ascendant is sextile to Saturn, which is rising above Jupiter, both planets being corrupted by a square of Mercury and an opposition of Neptune. The altruistic side of the character may therefore be described as weak, visionary and irrational, while the strength of Mars and the bad aspects of Saturn drive that part of the character which expresses hatred to the extreme of violent action.

Contrast with this the admirable figure of Sir Humphry Davy, where Jupiter is in exact conjunction with Neptune in the tenth house, Venus being trine, while Saturn, in Scorpio, usually a sinister figure in this sign, by a sextile both with the noble conjunction in the tenth and the gracious planet in the second, loses all of his bad qualities and greatly strengthens the character. It is easy to divine, from this, a well-balanced soul influenced without any internal struggle towards the ideas of altruism yet without any foolish neglect of his own interests.

The mind of Scorpio is intensely critical and skeptical. It seeks truth with fearless and dauntless energy, once its powers are awakened, but undeveloped types of Scorpio never reach the point where such considerations apply. One of the symbols of this sign is stagnant and corrupted water, and by this the adepts of old wished to imply poisonous water. All watery signs are connected in a certain way with the past; though they might be divided by calling Cancer the past, Scorpio the present, and Pisces the future, yet the present of Scorpio remains unattached to the past unless aroused.

The skeptical attitude seems to be awakened more by personal dissatisfaction than by anything else. A child with Scorpio rising is not likely to question his religious or social surroundings as long as he gets on comfortably in them, but if his parents insist on forcing him to accept and conform with ideas that are repugnant to him, he will turn around like a trodden snake and strike. He is not going to waste any time pushing things out of the way, like Taurus, or devising plans to evade them, like Libra. Nothing will content him but the destruction of whatever has annoyed him. Merely to destroy a church would be a trifle under such circumstances; the child will simply attack religion, root and branch. From being an indifferent, perhaps even an enthusiastic member of the community, he will become a furious skeptic. Moreover, he is revengeful. An incident of this kind will make him register a resolution of perpetual hatred. He will not be merely indifferent or contemptuous, he will become a militant atheist.

Similar troubles with regard to some sex restriction may turn him into a lifelong libertine. He will wantonly destroy his own health in order to gratify his sense of hatred for the attempted control; further, he will make this one of the dominating motives of his life. Not content with ruining himself, he will leave no stone unturned to ruin others, and he will often do all this with the most absolute sincerity and even with a conviction of the noblest and most self-sacrificing altruism. A certain existing principle has hurt him, and that principle must be wiped out of existence. He considers himself as an avenging angel and he has no sense whatever of balance—"other considerations never restrain him."

In vain do you appeal to his better judgment. In all probability he sees your argument perfectly well, but no sooner does the time come for action than everything is swept away by his original impulse. Scorpio is a traitor often enough but he is never a turncoat. It is very rarely that he makes any radical change in his opinions during his whole life. When he appears to do so, it is evidence that they were never really his opinions at all, in any deep sense, but that the selfishness of the man, seeing personal advantage in going back on what he has always maintained, has determined him to go over to the enemy. In the legend of Judas, who represents Scorpio among the twelve apostles, we see this quality of mind. The interest of Judas was in the contents of the bag; he was a thief and stole that which was put therein. It was when he made up his mind that the chief priests and Pharisees were determined to get rid of Jesus that he foresaw that there would be no more money in that bag, so he naturally took his chance of getting thirty pieces of silver and being on the right side of the fence. If he was actually born under Scorpio his subsequent suicide should not be attributed to remorse. We may fairly assume that in some way or other he was cornered and saw no way out but death.

The rigidity of the mind and its incapacity to weigh one thing with another produces a curious result. The mind is, as it were, a series of water-tight compartments. The Scorpio native is capable of holding two opinions which, to a Libra man for example, would appear directly to conflict with each other, and he will hold each with equal tenacity and bigotry. Suppose, for example, that he is devoted to the idea of freedom of speech. There is nothing in him that will prevent his also taking the view that socialists must be suppressed. His state of mind will appear either comic or damnable to almost any other sign, but it will be impossible to argue with him. Any argument brought forward will be taken up by him as evidently part of one or other of his contradictory views, and even when cornered by an expert logician, the result will be not to bring him to a perception of the incompatability of his ideas, and to a resolution to reconcile their antinomy, but merely to make him angry. Taking a very mild case, we find Dr. Wallace spending his whole life defending a scientific thesis, the logical tendency of which is manifestly materialistic, and at the same time firmly believing in spiritism in its crudest form. Kruger again, an intensely sincere Christian, saw no difficulty in acting contrary to every principle of the doctrine, as it would be interpreted by the average mind. His enemies called him a hypocrite, which was not at all true.

Scorpio has an almost superhuman capacity for facing facts. The native of this sign never recoils from the investigation of the subject because it is unpleasant. On the contrary, his tendency is to think that the best way of dealing with such a subject is always to probe it to its depth. Frequently, physicians are said to be under the influence of this sign, but it is far more applicable to the surgeon. Most great investigators have some strong Scorpio influence in the horoscope. Either that sign is rising or one of the mental planets, Saturn, Uranus or Mercury, occupies it or aspects its ruler.

In his investigations, the Scorpio native exercises unlimited patience and expends unwearied energy in overcoming obstacles. His efforts suffer considerably from the destructive tendencies of his method. He is not content with removing obstacles from his path, as Taurus does, or avoiding them and even absorbing them in the way that we associate with Libra; he seeks to demolish them. For instance, a man of science engaged in classifying butterflies, who finds himself confronted by an opposing theory, is not content to try to find the Golden Mean, nor will he be satisfied with proving the other man wrong. He will make the whole thing a personal matter. He will attack the other man, not only in the matter of butterflies, but in his domestic life and his personal appearance. H. G. Wells has an excellent story called "Genus de Nova" which may be read as a most profound psychological study of the Scorpio man in controversy. A professor named Hawley disagrees with another called Pawkins about some minor scientific matter, and devotes his whole life to the crushing of Pawkins. In the process, he revolutionizes several sciences and makes for himself a European reputation; but the author makes it clear that the real driving force is hatred of Pawkins, an innocent old chap whom he has hardly ever seen and not at all the type of man to excite bitterness in an ordinary mortal. Hawley pursues him relentlessly, makes attack after attack, cruel and personal, upon the poor man, until he dies, his life probably shortened by the virulence of his antagonist. The latter, feeling that his occupation is gone, finds that he wants a rest. The emptiness created by the death of his enemy is so great that his mind, deprived of its natural sustenance of hate, begins to eat itself up, with the result that he has an hallucination—an imaginary moth of an entirely new species which after a few days begins to look to him like Pawkins. In the end, he goes mad.

One of the principal dangers of this temperament is its profound concentration upon its objects, its inability to rest. It is fortunate that this carries with it a tremendous capacity for work. The labors of such men as Burton, Wallace, Goethe and Edison would have crushed ninety-nine men in a hundred. Burton, although constantly engaged in the most terrible hardships of exploration, found time to translate or write over one hundred books, every one of them a masterpiece of observation and of scholarship—"The Arabian Nights" alone fills sixteen very large volumes—and it is well known what an enormous amount of time Edison habitually devotes to the science of his work. Yet all these men have lived to a considerable age. Burton, although he had exposed himself to every kind of fever and tropical disease in general, lived to be sixty-nine years old.

This temperament is, as a rule, singularly contemptuous of emotionalism in any form. The Scorpio native does not spare pains with himself, and as a rule he cares nothing for the sensitiveness of others. He expects everyone to be as strong as he is himself. He is, in fact, a somewhat dangerous associate, for his magnetism is so great that those who are working with him are insensibly drawn to emulate his vigorous energy, and they are extremely likely to overstrain themselves and collapse.

Scorpio, within his own limitations, is a great master of organization. He is intensely thorough in his preparation and his foresight is marvelous. In fact, it is one of the drawbacks to the immediate success of the very best types of this sign that they possess an idea so big that it is generally impossible of realization within the compass of a lifetime. We find them building for posterity, and perhaps suffering intensely in consequence of their absolute refusal to swerve from their appointed path in order to deal with temporary exigencies.

In money matters the native of Scorpio is so concentrated upon his own purposes that he will turn everything to his own account. It will, therefore, be only in the developed types that strict honesty in financial dealings may be expected, and even among these there is apt to be an exaggerated self-confidence in their own opinion of what is fair play when the rights of others are involved. It is, therefore, a good sign for the acquisition of fortune; when well dignified, this fortune may be turned to noble uses, but always along lines that satisfy the individual ideas of its possessor.

The love of power is exceedingly well marked in this type. There is an immense personal magnetism in even the most unfortunate and wretched specimen, and in one way or another, the Scorpio native finds himself able to take the lead in his own circle. Here again the faculty of self-destruction comes into play. The native possesses no tact. He will say what he thinks, even though he is sincerely anxious to propitiate the man to whom he is talking and knows that he will offend him. He will go for an interview with a carefully considered scheme of dissimulation and, before he has been talking five minutes, he will blurt out the truth. The result is that this native ends by offending everybody. He is admired and he is feared. It may be that he is most intensely loved, but hardly anybody likes him. In the building up of a career, therefore, he is rarely fortunate. People are attracted violently and then as violently repelled. The attainment of a position in this world depends very greatly upon the good will of the people with whom one is associated, and Scorpio nearly always fails to take advantage of his opportunities in this direction. He gets on well enough when he is independent of others, but he does not understand either "pull" or "push." Burton said of himself that he had every talent except that of knowing how to make use of the others. The best chance for the Scorpio native is to obtain the favor of some one powerful person and concentrate his mind on keeping it.

Scorpio has a courage corresponding to his energy, but this quality frequently degenerates into foolhardiness or cruelty. It may be regarded merely as the armor of the will, and it is evident that when the king does not sit down and take counsel as to whether with ten thousand he can meet him that cometh against him with twenty thousand, he is likely to learn a severe lesson. Scorpio will not allow any consideration whatever to interfere with his determination. The Scorpio native is rather secretive when not in action, and his sudden revolts may surprise his circle as much as antagonize it in the moment of awakening.

Ibsen drew a perfect picture of a Scorpio woman in "Hedda Gabler." The suddenness, violence, and exaggeration of her frenzies are totally incomprehensible, not only to her easy-going husband but to the clever man of the world who thinks that he has outgeneraled and mastered her; when, true to the Scorpio type, she kills herself, all the poor man can say is that people don't do that sort of thing. Such is, in fact, a very fair statement of the criticism which Scorpio almost invariably meets. Every typical act of the native is felt as an outrage, and in point of fact, every such act, though perhaps in itself easy enough to excuse, appears an outrage, because it is done in an outrageous way. Men or women with Scorpio rising will tear everything down to carry their point; wife, husband, children, home, family, friends—nothing counts against their definite purpose. If a woman with this sign rising falls in love, her family, her position, her career, all count for nothing. She does not hesitate for a moment; she shows openly her hatred and scorn for the world.

In speech, Scorpio becomes fluent only when excited and is then frank, direct and vehement. He is not, by any means, a good conversationalist, for he insists upon being the center of the gathering at which he happens to be. In writing, the style is rarely good from the academic standpoint. It is likely to be rugged and abrupt, intensely serious, possibly exalted in expression, and certainly profound. The native is likely to be a master of every detail of his subject, but the style is more impressive than pleasing. We have, fortunately, three extremely fine examples of natives of this sign who attained eminence in literature. In each of these, strong planetary aspects gave an excellence in style which supplied exactly what Scorpio lacked, but in all of them the matter was far more important than the manner.

Sir Richard Burton's "Kasidah" is a compendium of all philosophy, but it is written without those pleasing harmonies that have endeared the inferior philosophy of Omar Khayyam to the average intelligence. Burton's Venus is afflicted by the conjunction of Mars, but even apart from this we should expect more force in the presentation than persuasiveness. Goethe achieved great success even in the art of pleasing—Venus sextile to Neptune giving him a singular power of dealing with the fantastic—but the chief wonder of this great poet is in the encyclopedic extent of his knowledge. It is sometimes forgotten that he spent ten years working at the theory of light. The point is that, fine as his work was, the value of the ideas contained is even more important. If we look at the horoscope of Victor Hugo we find similar qualities. We find the same power to assimilate facts and to investigate their nature. We also note that, like the two other writers, matter counts for more than manner. Further, every one of these three men of letters spent a very large amount of energy in polemics. The hatred of Hugo was directed chiefly against the third Napoleon, that of Goethe and Burton more against ideas and systems; but the method in all three is the same—there is to be no compromise and no quarter; the evil thing is to be destroyed in such a way that it can never rise again; no consideration is allowed to any arguments which show that the evil has its good side; the thing is bad and it must go, and there is an end of the matter.

It will be fairly evident from the foregoing remarks how the native of Scorpio will behave in his home. As long as everything goes his way, all right; oppose him, and God help everybody. There is no indication that the native is likely to leave home early in life. He has no natural inclination to test the unknown. As long as he sees advantage in remaining anywhere, there he stays. Vulgar types of Scorpio are often very domesticated in a fashion. Their vision happens not to extend beyond that very small circle, and all they can do is to make themselves the engines that keep everything going. Where this native lacks imagination, as is often the case, we get a type of housewife who rules the household with an iron rod and keeps everybody on the jump. She always manages to be in the right and is very much aggrieved when a quite mild husband openly rebels or, more often, leaves her.

In love, Scorpio produces the most intensely passionate people of any sign in the zodiac, but this passion is almost invariably selfish. When undeveloped, it is likely to be coarse, gross and bestial, associated with other kinds of self-indulgence, such as overeating, and overdrinking. Incidental to his passion for work, if the Scorpio native should find his powers momentarily failing, he is apt to resort to stimulants. The native is generally consumed by a single and altogether devouring passion which takes no heed of any obstacles. He is excessively jealous and tyrannical, easy to offend, and revengeful when offended. If he forgives, it is not likely to be real forgiveness; it is rather that his passion is so strong that he cannot get along without its chosen object.

To Scorpio, also, must be attributed much of the madness of the "crime passional" and the abuses of the "unwritten law." It would hardly be too much to say that in every case of crime which shows intensity of passion, mad jealousy, and total lack of balance, Scorpio will be found prominent in the horoscope of one of the parties concerned. It is, by the way, a great trick of the Scorpio type to satisfy its selfishness and accomplish its ends by setting people at loggerheads. Even the concentrated passion of Scorpio gives little real comfort in love. When the storm has blown itself out, there is nothing left but wreckage.

Sexual excesses of various gross kinds frequently occur among people born with this sign rising, but the spirit is entirely different from that which characterizes the native of Libra in similar conditions. In Scorpio, the idea is not to refuse itself any possible intensification of pleasure.

In the matter of children, people with Scorpio rising are rather prolific in begetting children or bearing them, as the case may be, but Scorpio makes a poor parent. It is practically impossible for him to see the child's point of view or to make allowances for his natural character.

He is difficult enough in his dealings with people who are big enough to oppose him; to a defenseless child, he may become a veritable ogre. He may very often profess a passionate devotion and this devotion may even be genuine, but everything has to be done exactly as he wants it. There is no latitude, no elasticity; the home is run on the lines of a prison.

In marriage, the native is usually tyrannical and overbearing. He should not marry if any active or antagonistic planets occupy the seventh house or aspect its ruler. His only chance of finding the condition tolerable is to meet a partner who is pliable, docile and patient.

What has been said with regard to the general relations of the Scorpio native with other people applies also to friendships. The chief difference is that one is not bound to a friend so rigidly as to a family or a lover. One can maintain friendship with a native of Scorpio by keeping him at a distance. Once intimacy is established, the danger of a break is imminent.

In business partnership, very much the same thing applies. There can be no harmonious coöperation with men of the Scorpio type. What they say goes. Natives of those signs which naturally look up to a strong personality, which love to rely on others, which enjoy being "bossed" because it relieves them of some dreaded responsibility, will prove the best partners for such people. In such cases, things may go very well. Scorpio likes to have somebody to whom the routine can be delegated without his interference. In business affairs, the Scorpio native is unscrupulous and grasping. He possesses foresight, but only along the lines peculiar to his temperament. He has little power of adaptation to new conditions.

Such people often run their businesses into the ground through the lack of the power to bend. They are not blind to what is happening, but they prefer to carry on and die in the last ditch.

In the conduct of public affairs, this sign is most unsatisfactory. It is not at all probable that the Scorpio native will meet anyone whose only idea will be to knuckle under. Dealings with equals invariably require tact and courtesy, and the general spirit must be that of compromise. Scorpio has no idea at all of any of these things. He cannot see the other's point of view.

The subconscious mind of Scorpio has a very wide range. The soul of the Scorpio native, so to speak, may be intensely noble or intolerably base, but in either case it is very rare to find any conflict between it and the conscious mind. In science and philosophy, the Scorpio native is liable to the same wide range; sometimes we find him intensely bigoted and narrow; in fact, this may be called the usual tendency, but against this must be set the fact that the knowledge is so encyclopedic that bigotry is rarely based on ignorance in such cases. It springs more commonly from a perverse determination to use all facts, however recalcitrant, to buttress the idiosyncratic will toward some main idea. In religion, we find this native intensely narrow and at the same time skeptical. The combination is often exceedingly unpleasant, but there is a general power of correlating the religious instinct with the sex nature or with the subconscious will in some manner, probably unconscious. A very common type is the passionate Protestant who has no real comprehension of what more humane and developed persons consider the nobler attributes of God as described in the Hebrew

Scriptures. Their God is the jealous God, who visits the sins of the fathers upon the children, unto even the third and fourth generation, and in accordance with the general practice of that type of God, they are without mercy and without scruple. They act with lust, brutality and ferocity, and can always find a passage from Scripture to justify themselves. Chesterton, in his story of the broken sword, gives an excellent description of this type of man. It is possible that the characteristic self-righteousness of the sign is due to the complete absence of conflict between the outer and the inner will.

It has already been explained how fiercely Scorpio resents any form of constraint, but this native can be ridden much more easily than he himself supposes, provided that an exceedingly light hand be kept upon the rein. So long as he does not suspect the control, so long as he imagines that he is himself directing matters, he can be led by the nose. His own selfishness and vanity may be used by a clever hand to make him do what one wants.

The Scorpio children should be given ample opportunity to work off their surplus nervous energy; otherwise it will tend to make them impatient, contrary and difficult to manage. It would be well to reason with them and to treat them as equals or companions, rather than to give them the idea that they must or must not do a thing simply because they are told. These children have tremendous will power and are very shrewd and penetrating. It will be almost impossible to deceive them, and so it would be wise to be very straightforward and frank in your relations with them. They will have a natural understanding of mechanics and should be given plenty of mechanical toys over which to puzzle.

This sign gives its children a robust constitution and great recuperative power. Because of their inordinate amount of physical energy, they must be given ample opportunity to work it off in a normal, happy way; if suppressed, it is likely to react on their health. As selfishness, self-preservation and insincerity are so strongly marked in their make-up, they must be taught to share their toys and their pleasures with their playmates, and avoid having ulterior motives. Undeveloped types frequently make bullies and want to fight every child in the neighborhood. These children must realize that "the pen is mightier than the sword" and all types should make use of their clever mentality. It is very necessary that they should be given a broad education, in order that all the force which they possess may be wisely directed. Unless they desire to go through college, however, it would be much wiser to give them a manual, military or naval training, or a business course.

People born from the 20th of February to the 22nd of March, when the Sun is in the watery, unselfish sign Pisces, and from the 22nd of June to the 24th of July, when the Sun is in the watery and maternal sign Cancer, are naturally sympathetic and helpful to those born under Scorpio. Because their characteristics are complementary, they are very good partners for the Scorpio-born, matrimonially or otherwise. If too intimately associated with those born from the 21st of January to the 20th of February (Aquarius), 21st of April to 22nd of May (Taurus), the 24th of July to 24th of August (Leo), Scorpio natives will need to submerge their strong personality and determined will, in order not to be unduly antagonized or irritated. Such an intimacy might result in the native of Scorpio bringing to the fore the least desirable traits of this very positive sign. For this reason, people born under Aquarius, Taurus and Leo would not make the most sympathetic or helpful partners, either matrimonially or in a business way.

A period of about seven days—November 21 to November 28—when the vibrations of Scorpio are merging into those of Sagittarius, and Sagittarius still retaining some of Scorpio, is known as the cusp. People born between these dates will partake of the shrewdness and energy of Scorpio and the magnanimity and generosity of Sagittarius, or a combination of the two. As Mercury, ruling the mentality, and Venus, the love nature, are so close to the Sun, they, too, may partake of some of the qualities of the adjoining signs of Scorpio. This will account for some of the complex personalities so difficult of comprehension.

With this sign also, the deductions have been drawn from the position of the Sun or Ascendant; therefore it is probable that some friends or uncongenial associates will be found under other signs than those mentioned. In such cases, the individual horoscopes must be consulted to ascertain how the stars combine with those of the Scorpio-born, and to determine the effect of the combination of influences upon both persons.

These indications can be general only, and will not cover all the characteristics of an individual as he knows himself, since the influence of the planets modifies the signs. A detailed statement of the horoscope must be made to discover the whole truth.

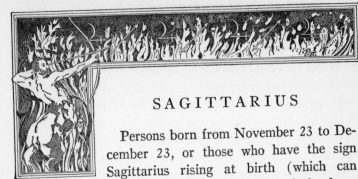

SAGITTARIUS

Persons born from November 23 to December 23, or those who have the sign Sagittarius rising at birth (which can be ascertained only through a knowledge of the hour of birth), will come under the dominion of the fiery, mutable, inspirational sign Sagittarius, symbolized by the Centaur, shooting an arrow, and ruled over by Jupiter, the "Greater Fortune."

Sagittarius, the last of the fiery signs, is not so much fire itself as the reflection of fire. The symbol of the sign is the Centaur, part man and part beast.

PHYSICAL CHARACTERISTICS

The skull appropriate to Sagittarius is finely proportioned, being rather long with good proportional breadth. The forehead is high with the hair well back from the temples. The eyes usually possess a dreamy, far-away look, though this is notably modified by planetary influence. The nose is generally long and straight, but a powerful Jupiter often lends to it the curve of his eagle's beak, while a rising Moon may make it turn up slightly. The mouth is mobile, but rather inclined to fullness, this latter trait again being accentuated by any predominance of Jupiter. Unless this same influence works to make a jowl heavy, the chin is narrow and rather pointed. As a general rule, the eyes are gray or light brown in color. The

130

hair has often a tendency to auburn. This rule has, however, many obvious exceptions, since, for some reason, the blond type of humanity is tending to disappear.

It is almost always easy to recognize a resemblance between the expression of the Sagittarius native's face and that of a horse, a deer, or one of the long-nosed types of dog, to be distinguished from the short-nosed type of man, resemblance to which is seen in Leo and sometimes in Scorpio. In many cases, this likeness is extraordinarily plain to see. A most marked characteristic is the alert and ingenuous frankness of countenance. An aquiline nose may be combined with a pointed chin, and this gives a hatchet-like profile which might possibly be mistaken for the masculine type of Cancer, should the face happen to be unusually pale. This last circumstance, however, is rare with Sagittarius. The typical complexion is rosy pink. It is, on the whole, the most beautiful and delicate of all the complexions.

The body is sometimes confused with that of Libra, owing to its gracefulness and activity, but on careful observation the difference will be seen to be well marked. The classical type of Sagittarius is Artemis or Atalanta rather than Venus. The grace is more active than passive, and there is no hint of allurement or of languor. The stature, moreover, is usually much above the average, and the limbs are athletic and admirably fitted for all active pursuits.

There will always remain a certain touch of the high-strung or nervous temperament, which completely differentiates this sign from Libra. One of the chief characteristics is indeed the restless, and, in a way, purpose-less activity of the body, which reminds one not a little of the similar mental traits found in Gemini. People with this sign rising are nearly always extremely fond of outdoor exercise of every kind, from hunting to the more ordinary sports, but it may be said that they avoid those forms of hunting or sports in which there is a serious element of combat. They do not like to put themselves in danger of bodily peril, save so far as minor accidents incidental to the sports are concerned. In this good judgment is seen the influence of the lord of the sign, Jupiter. It is the natives of cherubic signs who enjoy grappling an antagonist at even or against superior odds. Sagittarius is like cavalry; it is framed for agile movement, for participation in victory, and its symbolic weapon is the arrow. It acquires its force from its own momentum. Over short distances, it is the best of all types of activity. It lives very much upon its nervous system. Indeed, the chief dangers to health in this type arise from overactivity of mind or body, and there is apt to be depletion of life force through unnecessary scattering of energy; but there is usually sufficient vitality to overcome these dangers and, generally speaking, the sign promises a good longevity.

Herbert Spencer lived continually on his nerves, but lived to a good old age. The early death of Shelley, an even better example of the Sagittarian type, does not contradict this rule, as his accidental death was indicated by planetary afflictions. A third type of nervous delicacy of constitution is given by Samuel Taylor Coleridge, but he also, in spite of the unfortunate habits which wrecked his life, lived to the age of sixty-two.

The constitution of the native is finely poised, rather like that of Libra, but less balanced. He lives on his activity. If deprived of his outdoor recreations, he would pine; if he were forced into restraint, he would rapidly break down.

Sagittarius governs the hips and thighs, the locomotor muscles, and sympathetically, the hands and feet, the chest and lungs, the intestines and the nervous system. When the system becomes depleted or ill health overtakes these natives, they are likely to suffer from indigestion, sciatica, gout and rheumatism. The lungs and nervous system are also more or less subject to derangement. They may suffer from accidents to the hips, hands or feet, as well as dislocation of the joints. In case of fever, like the natives of Aries and Leo (both fiery signs, as is Sagittarius), they are in danger of suffering from delirium, as one extreme, or chills producing subnormal temperature as the other. In Sagittarian children, this frequently takes the form of convulsions. As a rule, however, it is well known that more octogenarians are born under Sagittarius than under any other sign.

They have great reserve force, which is partly due to the fact that they have the ability to rest profoundly, although they are very easily awakened. In extreme cases, they spend more nervous energy in daily life than does the average type, and they do not economize strength as they should. This tendency to call unnecessarily upon the store of force depletes their stock or capital, and it too often results in a nervous breakdown. Certain forms of paralysis are indicated as possibilities. Environment, however, counts for a great deal. Their love of active, outdoor life, and their impetuosity may possibly cause them to meet with accident more frequently than the natives of most other signs; but accidental troubles apart, there is every reason to expect general good health and long

life from Sagittarius. It is, however, to be said that since
he is apt to scatter his energies, he has no such power of
resistance to disease as is given by the cherubic signs;
nor is his recuperative power as great. This native is
naturally temperate in all respects, but the sign is easily
influenced and a planetary bad aspect may overcome the
original predisposition. In the case of Coleridge, we find
a conjunction of Saturn, Venus and Neptune, while
Jupiter is weakened by the opposition of the Moon and
the square of Uranus. One cannot wonder, therefore, at
his inability to resist the insidious temptation offered to
him by laudanum.

MORAL CHARACTERISTICS

The Sigil of this sign is the rainbow. Being ruled by
Jupiter, the temperament of its native is expansive and
altruistic, and it is sometimes called the prophetic sign, as
the objective and subjective mind work harmoniously
together under its vibrations. The Sagittarian is a born
idealist; he is the young man who sees visions and the
old man who dreams dreams. But there is no unprac-
ticability in his idealism, for he is capable of foreseeing
the outcome of a transaction from its very inception and
the activity and directness of his character is typified in
the ancient pictorial representation of Sagittarius as a
centaur who holds a bow outstretched, about to speed an
arrow straight to its mark.

The Sagittarian quality of ideal vision was perhaps
never better exemplified than in Abraham Lincoln, and he
illustrates equally well the significance of the other pictorial symbol wherein the centaur, guided by the divine

intelligence of a human brain, expresses his animal joy in nature through the lithe, active and robust body of a swift horse. Frank, open-hearted, honest and sincere, always truthful and intolerant of those who are not, the Sagittarian is a child of nature, whose two sides constantly manifest themselves in varying moods; for he is bold, restless, daring, and at the same time sensitive, impressionable and retiring. His likes and dislikes are very pronounced, and he is exceedingly susceptible to inharmony either in his surroundings or his associates.

Just as he is nimble and fleet of foot, so is he swift and accurate in thought. He is direct of speech and despises circumlocution in others; nothing so angers him as does duplicity, but his anger is short-lived and he never bears malice; often he will yield his point rather than enter a quarrel, although he can adhere very rightly to a position when a real principle is involved. Small annoyances give him more distress than serious difficulties, and these he is generally able to avoid by a little forethought and diplomacy—qualities with which he is well endowed. With all his pure idealism, he reasons out every question, and finds delight in facing life fairly, and frankly trying to reduce its problems to their simplest terms. An unusual degree of mental activity is one of the most marked characteristics of the sign; the alertness and directness of the bodily movements translate themselves into activity of the mind, and the native's conclusions are apt to hit the mark as swiftly and as straight as the arrow, which is a symbol of the sign. The general temper of Sagittarius is calm, buoyant and cheerful, and its natives consequently retain a certain youthfulness well into age; indeed, they never seem to be as old as their years; also, there are those among them who develop slowly, not reaching their full powers until middle age or the later years of life.

The Sagittarian vision is very clearly shown in Cecil Rhodes' dream of world empire, though in this case Saturn and Uranus, both in earthy signs, assisted him in devoting his practical energies to the actual work of building his dreams into reality, and the trine of Neptune and sextile of Uranus to his Sun so magnified the dimensions of his vision that it was far more than even his extraordinary powers could possibly achieve. "So much to do; so little done," was his exclamation when dying. Of course, Jupiter rising also solidified and made more practical the aspiration characteristic of the pure Sagittarian. We find this same element present in the horoscopes of Queen Elizabeth and Lord Northcliffe. The careful comparison of their three charts should be very instructive to the student. In each case we find a vision that may almost be called abnormal, and in each we see Jupiter rising, giving increased practical power to the qualities of his own sign. A fourth example is to be found in the horoscope of King Edward VII, whose Jupiter, just above the horizon, is squared by Uranus, while Mars and Saturn are in the Ascendant. But where the influence of Jupiter is not strong, we are apt to find the vision more imaginative and expressing itself in more spiritual terms, as in the cases of Swedenborg, Shelley and Coleridge; or in more fanciful ways, as with Lewis Carroll and Sir Edwin Durning-Lawrence.

We have already remarked that an extraordinary mental activity is the chief characteristic of the native of Sagittarius, and we have noted the insatiable curiosity and inexhaustible energy with which he reasons out every problem, finding joy in going to the bottom of things and reducing each question to its simplest terms. Thus, under favorable conditions, he not only makes rapid progress in intellectual development himself, but he is able to communicate his zeal to others; he may be an excellent teacher, usually following the Socratic method of instruction by interrogation. He is, therefore, best adapted to teach older pupils who can respond intelligently to argument and discussion. The legal profession is an excellent field for his talents, although he is likely to do well in journalism and often in literature, while the teaching of religion or philosophy is perhaps the most congenial of all occupations.

In conversation the Sagittarian is fond of argument and as he enjoys crossing swords with a good antagonist, he is apt to be a skillful dialectician. He seems to have an intuitive knowledge of the weak points in his opponent's reasoning, seldom misses his mark in his rejoinders, and excels in swift flashes of witty repartee. He is a clever cross-examiner, but, unless the emotional side of his nature is well developed, he is likely not only to disregard the feelings of others by persistent probings into their views or reasoning, but also to submit himself to such rigid examination that it kills sentiment. The best of these qualities were magnificently exemplified in Lincoln, his emotional nature being powerfully excited by a rising Neptune.

There is, in the average case, much tendency to discursive talk, with frequent interjection of the unnecessary, but full of the humor that is generally finely developed in the native of Sagittarius. An excellent example of this sort of conversation is shown in the "Table

Talk" of Coleridge. In writing, there is a very natural
turn toward the dialogue form of literary expression and
not infrequently to dramatic composition; but in this
latter field the exaltation of the mental qualities is likely
to make the plot unreal and the speeches long-winded,
while the characters have not enough of physical life to
make them seem real. The writings of Robert Brown-
ing show many of the defects as well as much of the best
quality of the Sagittarian influence.

In regard to money matters, Sagittarius is Jupiter's own
sign, and its native, unless badly limited by planetary
affliction, is well equipped for financial success. He acts
quickly and aims straight at the mark, and this is of first
importance in most financial transactions. In undeveloped
types, this may express itself in a reckless snap judgment, which may fritter away on small deals and prevent
opportunities for larger operations, but the developed
Sagittarian is apt to be a commanding figure in the financial world.

In business, the Sagittarius native is well adapted to
succeed either alone or in partnership. His intense activity
and energy, his fertility in expedient, his habit of reducing equations to the simplest terms and eliminating unnecessary details, and his general good judgment all
contribute valuable factors for commercial success, but
work of a nature that involves petty detail or business
that is made up of an aggregate of small transactions is
very distasteful to him; he is, therefore, not well adapted
to clerical duties. It will be seen easily that these same
qualities are as excellent in public affairs as in private
concerns; and his abundant self-confidence and clearness

of vision, together with his frank bonhomie, should carry him far in political preferment.

One of the two greatest faults of the Sagittarian, however, is a certain impatience and hastiness which encourage premature action. He is apt to be so anxious to pick the fruit that he cannot always wait until it is ripe. Impatient of delay, he wishes his orders carried out almost before they are given. The cultivation of patience is therefore always to be recommended.

In dealing with servants, the amiability and tact of this native are considerable assets, but he is a little inclined to presume upon his position when dealing with inferiors and to make that presumption felt. The undeveloped native may be very spiteful when crossed, and exact petty revenge on those who displease him. He may acquire the liking of his inferiors, but seldom commands their affection.

Another general characteristic, which is apt to be particularly annoying, is that, wishing to please, the native of this sign may make promises and then forget them. Sometimes one can hardly say whether he ever intends to match promise by performance. Spain is under the influence of Sagittarius, and Spain is, above all, the country of grandiose manners, combined with a perfect casuistry. The Spaniard is a master of fine speeches, which mean nothing. On meeting a Spanish gentleman for the first time, he tells you where he lives and implores you to regard his house as your own, but if you were to pay so much as a formal call on this invitation, he would think you extraordinarily lacking in *savoir faire*. It is always necessary to wait for a repeated invitation, backed by some action, before attaching any meaning to what was merely a polite phrase. Similarly, in signing a letter, the customary closing phrase is always "your servant who kisses your hand," but one has yet to experience the sensation of having one's hand kissed by a Spaniard. Where such manners are a national trait and perfectly well understood, no harm is done, but in other countries, where the ideal of social intercourse is supposed to be blunt, honest frankness, the unwary may be totally misled and horribly disappointed. It is clear how cruel a situation may be created when the inferior is in some genuine distress.

The keen delight of the Sagittarius people is to be in the open air, and in all kinds of outdoor sports and occupations the native develops a frank and hearty democratic impulse which makes him willing to fraternize with all sorts and conditions of men, and develops a genuine compassion for those who are compelled to toil under restricted or shut-in conditions. These people are often deeply interested in projects for social reform and for the betterment of the condition of the laboring class. In such work they are extremely practical, for their theories will be based upon patient research into actual conditions, and they are too clear-sighted to be easily drawn into any unbalanced radicalism.

It is quite evident that the qualities of Sagittarius are admirable in the development of friendships, for its natives are impulsive and quick to reach out to those who interest them and, as their interest is mainly excited by mental qualities, there is usually a firm basis on which to build a lasting intimacy; and they are very loyal to those to whom they become attached.

The same frank sincerity and outspoken honesty that

make the friendships of this native wholesome and genuine, when properly restrained by a due regard for the feelings of others, will be found to govern him in his love affairs; but here, even with genuine affection, these qualities will not always prove as satisfactory. If the native of this sign succeeds in finding a woman who really understands him enough to love him and trust him, his nature will expand to its highest and best and he will make a devoted and appreciative husband, but the great danger is that the average woman will not understand his frankness and he may have small success in his courtship of the ordinary romantic woman. He is also too apt to choose his wife by logical reasoning rather than by a true mental analysis of the qualities which ought to mate best with him. His impulsive and direct nature will allow him to begin easily a friendship with a woman and to enter precipitately into an engagement which, on reflection, he may find himself unable to fulfill; the native of Sagittarius finds it difficult to lie at the altar, and broken engagements are not uncommon to this type. The sign also produces many bachelors, largely from the caution and prudence that are equally characteristic of its influence. This seems regrettable, as emotional development is the most needed element in the Sagittarian nature.

In matrimony, the Sagittarian cannot tolerate restrictions or jealousy. Even though he may outwardly seem to submit, since his practicality often leads him to make the best of an existing situation, he will become irritable and sarcastic, and the union will be far from a happy one. In the undeveloped types these qualities will often express themselves in a cynical attitude toward matrimony itself; both sexes tend to grow selfish and inconsiderate, and while they seldom allow their emotion to carry them away into actual liaisons, their unconventional disregard of public opinion may often subject them to scandal.

While the native of Sagittarius is warm-hearted and friendly to humanity at large, he has, from the very wideness of his sympathies, less devotion to the home and the family life than many whose geniality is less marked and whose democratic sympathies are less pronounced; consequently they are often found to be quite detached from their relatives and household. When their immediate kindred are congenial they treat them as friends, but if the relatives do not appeal strongly to them on these lines, they are apt to be very free in their criticisms and to point out shortcomings with embarrassing frankness. Even the children will analyze the qualities of their parents, and unless the latter meet this investigation with an honest response, there is likely to be a good deal of friction in any attempt to maintain discipline. But fair treatment and truthfulness will generally find a quick appreciation and willing compliance. It is among the natives of this sign as well as Virgo that we find many examples of the small boy or girl who is almost a vocal question mark. The parents of such children should provide the growing mind with plenty of exercise and food for reflection, and they should never neglect to stimulate the emotional side of the nature. Without this, the mind may injure itself by too rigid self-examination, and the child may also develop habits of teasing which will be extremely irritating and uncomfortable later in life.

In religious belief the Sagittarian may be somewhat of a skeptic because of his activity of mind and his innate desire to examine in and reason out faith, and wherever he is brought up in religious teachings that will not bear such analysis, he is outspoken in his criticism of their shortcomings. But no sign ruled by Jupiter could be irreligious and his sense of due proportion often makes it easy for him to hold fairly orthodox opinions; indeed, Sagittarians often make excellent clergymen, far more concerned with the practical Christianity of caring for the welfare of their parishioners than for their exact adherence to the letter of the creed. It is manifest, however, that it is only a short slip from this sort of religion to philosophy, and in that field of thought the developed Sagittarius native naturally revels and excels.

In summing up, it may be said that the life and character of the greatest of ancient philosophers, Socrates, suggests Sagittarius at its best development and illustrates many of the peculiarities and even weaknesses of the sign. His method of teaching by conversational inquiry, compelling his pupil or his opponent, by clever cross-examination, to prove the truth of his postulates; his mental activity and his democratic freedom of companionship with men of every station in life; his defiance of public opinion and his uncompromising attitude toward the State; his utter indifference to the amenities of domestic life, his detachment from family ties, and his theories of marriage, as well as the geniality which made him a welcome companion outside his home; and the hopeless misfit of his marriage, in which he must have allowed his head instead of his heart to guide him, all are qualities unmistakably Sagittarian. Dr. Draper's noble defense of Xantippe points out all her commonplace virtues as an everyday wife, and we can well understand the irritation produced in a really excellent domestic woman by the very Sagittarian qualities which made the husband who seemed so impossible and trifling, from her viewpoint, a joy to his friends and a glory to the world, and we can realize the contempt which led her (although she dutifully kept and cleaned the philosopher's home) to empty her slop jar over his head.

The Sagittarius children are inherently unselfish, truthful and high-minded. They are naturally light-hearted and merry, as well as hopeful and trusting. They are fond of play, and dancing comes natural to them. Their spontaneity and enthusiasm should not be curbed, although these qualities should be wisely directed. The lack of suspiciousness in their make-up and their natural honesty make it difficult for them to believe that others are not equally open and aboveboard; for this reason they should be taught to weigh carefully what is told them before taking it as gospel.

Sagittarians are extremely fond of animals, particularly horses and dogs, and of all outdoor sports. As children they should be given pets to love and care for, and the opportunity to ride horseback if possible. They take to horses as naturally as ducks to water and are absolutely fearless, even at a very early age, when with horses. They prefer playthings that are alive or have some movement, rather than inanimate toys such as dolls or stationary objects. Unlike the Scorpio children, the Sagittarius-born are too physically active to devote much time to reading. Parents would do well to trust their Sagittarius children and to give them a great deal of freedom, treating them as chums and companions instead of dictating to them. They should be wisely guided rather than driven. It would be well to allow them to select their vocation and to educate them accordingly.

Being so well balanced and normal, they enjoy excellent health, unless they are unwisely fed or exposed to contagious or infectious diseases. Even then, they throw off disease very readily and have splendid recuperative power. It is essential that they should not be made unhappy through suppression of their feelings or through having their natural enthusiasm and exuberance of feeling checked.

People born from the 22nd of March to the 21st of April, when the Sun is in the fiery, princely sign Aries, from the 24th of July to the 24th of August, when the Sun is in the fiery, noble sign Leo, are naturally sympathetic and helpful to those born under Sagittarius. Because their characteristics are complementary, they are good partners for the Sagittarius-born, matrimonially and otherwise. If too intimately associated with those born from the 20th of February to 22nd of March (Pisces), 22nd of May to 22nd of June (Gemini), 24th of August to 24th of September (Virgo), Sagittarians will need to check their impatience and curb their tendency to be too frank; such an intimacy might result in the native of Sagittarius becoming too sarcastic, too brusque, and too disregardful of consequences. For this reason, people born under Pisces, Gemini and Virgo will not make the most sympathetic or helpful partners, either matrimonially or in a business way.

A period of about seven days—December 21 to December 28—when the vibrations of Sagittarius are merging into those of Capricorn, and Capricorn still retaining some of Sagittarius, is known as the cusp. People born between these dates will partake of the magnanimity and impulsiveness of Sagittarius and the conservatism and seriousness of Capricorn, or a combination of the two. As Mercury, ruling the mentality, and Venus, the love nature, are so close to the Sun, they, too, may partake of some of the qualities of the adjoining signs of Sagittarius; this will account for some of the complex personalities so difficult of comprehension.

The position of the Sun or Ascendant only has been considered in drawing these deductions; therefore it is probable that persons born under other signs than those mentioned will be congenial or uncongenial to the Sagittarius-born. The combinations of influences indicated by the individual horoscopes will make clear the reason for such variations.

These indications can be general only, and will not cover all the characteristics of an individual as he knows himself. A detailed statement or horoscope must be made to discover the modifications made by the planets.

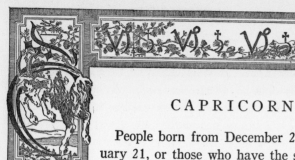

CAPRICORN

People born from December 23 to January 21, or those who have the sign Capricorn rising at birth (which can be ascertained only through a knowledge of the hour of birth), will come under the dominion of the earthy, cardinal, conservative sign Capricorn, symbolized by the Goat.

Capricorn is a very uncompromising sign. It is ruled by Saturn, and Mars is exalted in it. It is an earthy element, but it is active because it is a cardinal sign. The essential idea of earth is one of passivity and repose; for earth to be active is completely out of character. Earth in activity is not a symbol of fertility, of solidity, of ease, but of destruction. Consider how even nature, as known to the uninitiated, confirms this view. Active earth means the avalanche or the earthquake. The idea is a synonym for destruction. It is not surprising, therefore, that the Tarot card attributed to this sign should be called "The Devil." We see, therefore, that earth itself in this sign is traitor to its own nature.

Saturn is a superb planet when he receives help from forces that transmute the gross into the subtle, but without such assistance he represents all that clogs and weighs down humanity. Unhelped, he stands at his very best only for common sense. The sign is overbalanced upon the side of severity. Also, there is little to lift it from the material plane.

147

PHYSICAL CHARACTERISTICS

As a general rule, the skull of the Capricorn native is long rather than broad, but this trait may easily be modified by planetary influence. The presence of the Sun or Jupiter in the Ascendant would unquestionably broaden both cranium and features. The forehead is high, the eyes rather small and piercing, the nose long and bony, the mouth thin and closely compressed. The bony structure is prominent. The native is probably about the average height and is inclined to be lanky and angular. The bones are big and the limbs rather disproportionately long. There is usually a lack of gracefulness in the whole presence. The hands and feet in particular are likely to be ungainly. The figure is spare and sinewy, rather than muscular. Women with this sign rising are often troubled with superfluous hair.

The expression is intense, with something of bitterness or sadness. Very often the complexion is actually leaden. There is often little flesh on the face and wrinkles appear early in life. Joviality is conspicuously absent; sometimes we find a settled melancholy or gloom in the appearance.

The degraded type characteristic of this sign exaggerates all these features in the worst way. The body is frequently small and possibly deformed, though occasionally still possessing the characteristic strength and endurance. In such cases we usually discover an element of nervous timidity, superadded to the bitterness or gloom.

The greatest possible difficulty arises in judging specimens of this rising sign from the appearance, because earth, even in its most active form, is easily molded. In fact, its great fluidity in this nascent condition seems to permit the planets to affect it very strongly, very much as arsenic will not combine in the ordinary way with hydrogen, but will do so with nascent hydrogen. The most extreme departures from type are therefore seen quite frequently.

Some points of the type will remain pretty constant even under adverse conditions. An intense, erratic agility, very easy to distinguish from the swift and direct activity of Sagittarius, characterizes the bodily motioning. Nothing seems to destroy the power of endurance and the general impression of resolution.

To show how extremely this type may be modified, let us look for a moment at the horoscope of Nell Gwyn who had Capricorn on the Ascendant. Here we have Venus rising in Aquarius, squared by Jupiter, who in his turn has the Moon trine, this luminary being in Cancer. It is clear how this combination must soften the natural asperity and ruggedness of Capricorn, for Jupiter and the Moon in watery signs will both tend to plumpness. Again, Saturn is in the airy sign of Gemini, which will modify the skeleton and reduce the height, especially as it is in trine to a rising Sun. Again, Mars is in Pisces trine to both Jupiter and the Moon, so that the muscles assume the most gracious possible form. All these dispositions, so utterly contrary to the original indication, suffice to overwhelm it entirely.

In the case of Gladstone, the Sun on the cusp of the Ascendant in exact conjunction with Mercury is quite sufficient to broaden and dignify the type, which is given a certain grace by the trine of Venus and Jupiter, this also counteracting any tendency to excessive leanness. It is, however, easy to see the rugged characteristics of Capricorn underlying the more pleasing planetary modifications.

It is of the utmost importance that the student of astrology should study many examples of a rising Capricorn, so that he may learn to recognize the underlying characteristics in spite of any of the planetary modifications which are often the most notable features in this type.

One of the most hard-bitted types in the zodiac is presented by Capricorn. The capacity of the native for work is inexhaustible. His muscles are of steel. He is exempt from that growing menace of all civilized people—nerves. His senses never fail; at eighty his eyesight is apt to be as keen and clear and piercing as it was at twenty; his hearing will usually be as acute as ever.

Capricorn rules the bones and sinews, together with that principle in the muscles which hardens them. Capricorn also rules the knees, and, sympathetically, the head, stomach and kidneys, and the ovaries (in the case of a woman); rheumatism of the joints is one of its greatest dangers. A much afflicted Saturn in the nativity is likely to cause deformity in the skeleton; many hunchbacks have this sign rising. One may also class under this sign diseases involving spasm, such as cramp and infantile paralysis; indeed, all forms of paralysis which are not nervous in origin may also be classed here. It is interesting to note that nervous troubles in the native of any other sign rarely culminate in paralysis, unless Capricorn or its ruler be afflicted by directions or transits.

There is danger among the lower types of Capricorn of great intemperance and many drunkards are found among its natives. In a large measure, the melancholy of Saturn in this sign is a motive for alcoholic excess.

MORAL CHARACTERISTICS

The mind of Capricorn is very conservative. It runs in grooves and, though constantly in action, seldom moves out of the beaten path. His idea seems to be one which is perfectly true in a vast spiritual sense, but by no means so if we are reckoning time in terms of ordinary centuries. This idea is that the order of the Universe is immutable and eternal. He lives in the present, yet he acts in many respects like the native of Cancer who founds his basic ideas upon antiquity. Capricorn knows that to acquire any new aptitude is very difficult, that it is much easier to proceed within existing forms than to invent new ones, that it is much simpler to appeal to authority than to prove your proposition by the exercise of reason.

The energy of the native of Capricorn is very great, but he is not going to waste any of it, for the Saturnian influence makes him a miser of time. It is much less trouble for him to work within the limitation of his environment than to seek to change or transcend it. He is intensely ambitious. He must ever be climbing, but he is going to do so in the conventional way. He knows how much disorder and confusion are caused by even small breaches of routine. He is meticulous in observation of outward form. Suppose he is in a business office. He will not seek promotion by upsetting the ideas of everybody in the place. He is the man who is never a minute late in fifty years, who never makes an error of a single cent in an account, who is always there when he is wanted, with the precise piece of information required. He believes that diligence, probity and accuracy are the essentials of business. He wishes his employer to feel that he is a perfect machine, absolutely reliable in every respect, to be trusted never to run off the rails. One always finds him steady and industrious, every capacity in him bent inexorably to the task in hand.

He proceeds assiduously with his appointed task; he never considers what may be the goal for he imagines that the goal must be the logical consequence of the steps to it. He seems to forget that life is full of chances and adventures and any such incidents are intensely resented by him. His thought lacks consideration of those interferences from other planes which lend diversity to life. The mind of the average German professor is usually of this type. He sees a theory and becomes completely obsessed by it; even really eminent men like Max Müller and Ernst Haeckel share this tendency to walk in blinders. With lesser men, the most absurd conclusions are maintained with bitter obstinacy. One need only instance Freud with his theory of the influence of the sex instinct upon dreams, a theory which he has carried to such an extreme.

This limited viewpoint, combined with extreme determination to get on, is of the greatest use to the Capricorn native in his chosen career. One is constantly reminded of his magical image of Totem, the Goat. See how surefooted is the ibex as he leaps from crag to crag and on what sparse grass he manages to find nourishment. In just the same way, the native of Capricorn, contented with far less than any other type in the zodiac, goes through his life. He has little of the dreamer's vision to distract him; pleasures do not appeal to him as they do to most people. Even the idea of reward is not strongly implanted in the majority of people born with this sign rising. Their own groove of work seems to them an appointed thing. They do not complain, but pursue their path with matchless perseverance.

It is rare indeed to find imagination illuminating the path of the pure Capricorn type. Self-centered and complete in his own channel, he never seeks to overflow his banks, or even to perceive the possibility that those banks do not really exist. One might think *a priori* that certain pursuits at least could not, by any possibility, be followed by persons who lacked imagination, but it is not so. Consider the case of Swami Vivekananda, whose chosen path was that of saintship, the most dangerous of all the roads that the feet of man may tread. Yet in spite of his amazing scholarship, in spite of his extraordinary attainment of those things which he had set out to seek, we find in him few original tendencies. His teachings added no new feature; he is a perfect classic, but he said nothing that the Seven Rishis had not said before him.

In Pope Alexander VI we find an extraordinary, narrow ambition carried out without scruple. He did not even bother himself too seriously about new methods of poisoning, but rather clung to the conventional procedure of antiquity. In the career of Gladstone we find a similar instance. In his youth he was called "the hope of the stern, unbending Tories," and although he found it convenient to his ambition to label himself Liberal, a stern, unbending Tory he always remained.

Another great statesman, Mazarin, also had this sign rising. We find precisely the same quality. Mazarin did nothing that Richelieu would not have done, but Richelieu would have done it a great deal better. The Italian could not perceive that the times were changing. He could not understand why the old methods would no longer work, and therefore, despite his extraordinary cleverness, he came near to wrecking the monarchy which it was his object to sustain; indeed, his policy did prepare the ground for the seeds of the Revolution, which were to bring forth their red harvest, a little more than a century after his death.

Even in such spiritual matters as music and art, the Capricorn native seems to be unable to get beyond comparatively narrow barriers. Schumann, for example, although his Saturn is conjoined with Neptune, and although Uranus is on the Midheaven, confined himself to practically one branch of music. Turner, with the Moon rising, sextile to Mercury and trine to Uranus, as well as trine to Saturn, a combination of stupendous power, although possessing in such full measure the great qualities of imagination and color, does not seem to have had much versatility. Great as he is, in his own line, it would be stupid to compare him with Velasquez.

All this proves that Capricorn rising is the sign of the specialist.

It is a singular defect in the native of this sign that he does not push obstacles aside like Taurus, slay them in battle like Leo, destroy them utterly like Scorpio, or turn them to his own advantage like Libra. He merely leaps over them, and it is this detachment that makes him unsympathetic.

In dealing with money, this native is scrupulously faithful, but his lack of imagination makes him "penny wise and pound foolish." He is the best man in the world to intrust with money for safe investment; he will handle it carefully and intelligently; he will render an account of it to the last cent; but he will be too cautious to make big coups with it. Unless the Capricorn native be uplifted by good dignities, these qualities are apt to degenerate into penuriousness. Mazarin is a notorious example. In emergency, where loyalty and devotion were more necessary to him than anything else in the world, he would disgust his followers by giving them insignificant rewards for great services done. He was constantly making people draw comparisons between himself and his predecessor. Richelieu, they would say, was terrible, perhaps even hateful, but as for Mazarin, he was contemptible. During his ministry he stole some forty million dollars, which was a large sum for those times. Yet, ambitious as he was and greedy of power, he never used the money to get it. He was always trying to make one crown do the work of ten.

In speech and in writing, the native of this sign will be direct, sometimes eloquent, but there will be no originality either in matter or in style. This tends to be dry, but is sometimes very ornate and elaborate in a conventional way. This native is very fond of allusion; he interlards both speech and writing with classical phrases and artificial images or metaphors, or rococo effervescence, which has in it very little of spontaneous growth. The style, even when most impassioned, is academically perfect. Gladstone and Macaulay are good examples of this kind of expression at its best. There is always a certain aridity which does not make for permanence; one always gets the effect of artificiality and strain. It is too painfully clear that the native has said exactly what he meant to say, whereas the Scriptural injunction is "take no thought how or what ye shall speak, for it shall be given you in that same hour what ye shall speak, for it is not ye that speak, but the Spirit of your Father which speaketh in you." In modern language, the native lacks inspiration. The native never loses consciousness of himself as distinguished from other people. He does not understand that he can only realize himself by losing himself in the beloved. It is this quality which the mystic instinctively recognizes as the supreme evil.

Capricorn is rather domesticated than otherwise; being born into a family, it does not strike him to leave it. Whatever rules happen to be current, he accepts as part of the natural order of things and he works within those limits. He may be harsh and uncongenial, but there is in him no tendency to break up an existing situation.

In love, the native is very self-centered, not understanding that this sentiment must be mutual. He does not feel even true jealousy—he is not wounded by infidelity; he is merely robbed. He is quick and unrestrained in appetite, with little appreciation of delicacy. It is almost safe to say that one never finds real sexual perversion or inversion with this sign. If degeneracy exists, it is purely animal. Where good planetary influences exist, the rule is that the native becomes the conventional, domesticated citizen.

Capricorn is overbearing, and often tyrannical in his

treatment of children. He is not actively or consciously cruel; he is merely cold and unsympathetic. The individuality of the child is offensive to the parent, who makes rules which may perhaps be in accordance with righteousness or good discipline, but which are so rigid that only the most poor-spirited children can conform to them without suffering.

This native is severe in dealing with inferiors. He may be just and exact in paying the agreed wage, but he is not generous. As a business partner, Capricorn is reliable but unsympathetic. He is apt to be grasping and tyrannical. He understands this and usually prefers to work alone.

Capricorn is so materialistic that problems of the subconscious mind disturb the native little. He always takes life seriously, and he takes things as they are, or rather as they appear at first sight. This sign does not possess the imagination required for great scientific discovery, but the native has at least one quality profoundly necessary to all research, the quality of patience. A chemist with this sign rising might continue for half a century in working out the compounds of one substance. In a subordinate position, he makes a perfect laboratory assistant. He is unsurpassed, whenever attention to detail, untiring perseverance and rigid accuracy are the principal essentials; but, if he once happens to leave the track, he has no means of readjusting his position.

India is under Capricorn, and it is doubtful whether India has ever produced anything original. The Taj Mahal was designed by an Italian. Nearly all of the great Indian masterpieces are due to persons of Chinese influence. You can give a suit of clothes to an Indian tailor and he will copy it so exactly that it cannot be told from the original. If the seat of the trousers happens to be patched, he reproduces the patch with the most scrupulous fidelity. An Indian cook learns one way of cooking potatoes. Tell him that you want a change and show him a new way. He learns it and goes on with the new way, night after night. You can proceed to teach him forty ways, but all he will do is to follow the way that you taught him last, so that a new order must be given every night if you are to have variety in diet. Characteristic of this sign, too, is the patient, laborious, uncomplaining life of the average native. His caste system is entirely rigid, giving no scope for ambition, save in the peculiar trade or profession into which the man happens to be born.

Capricorn is intensely solitary and almost incapable of building up a lasting friendship. This native does not react strongly against constraint in the ordinary sense. He takes it as natural, part of the condition in which he exists. We see this again in the character of the population of the Indian peninsula. Again and again, they have been conquered, from the time of Alexander the Great to that of Clive, but there is that singular quality that the submission itself is a mode of victory; it is not too much to say that the Indian has imposed the caste system upon all his conquerors. It is impossible to turn him from his traditional groove of thought, and the attempt to hurry a Hindu has proved fatal to many a Sahib. It is the apotheosis of passive resistance.

Capricorn children are inclined to be very old for their age, and too serious in temperament. They are very self-conscious, introspective and fearful. They should never be told stories that would have a tendency to implant fear in their natures, and they should be given a great deal of praise and affection. They are inclined to be solitary and to have very few friends of their own age. They are not only industrious in their school work, but delight in helping out at home by running errands or in serving their elders. It would be advisable to give them a college education if possible, or to encourage them to obtain one, even if they have to work their way through college. One of the advantages of a college education for these children is the close contact with other young people of their own generation, which will help them to overcome their shyness and self-consciousness. Their education should be along practical lines, rather than the purely academic.

People born from the 21st of April to the 22nd of May, when the Sun is in the earthy, practical sign Taurus, and from the 24th of August to the 24th of September, when the Sun is in the intellectual sign Virgo, are naturally sympathetic and helpful to those born under Capricorn; because their characteristics are complementary, they are good partners for the Capricorn-born, matrimonially and otherwise. If too intimately associated with those born from March 22nd to April 21st (Aries), 22nd of June to the 24th of July (Cancer), and 24th of September to 24th of October (Libra), Capricorn natives will need to avoid being too self-centered and too morbid. Such an intimacy might result in the native of Capricorn becoming too introspective and self-conscious. For this reason, people born under Aries, Cancer and Libra would not make the most sympathetic or helpful partners, either matrimonially or in a business way.

A period of about seven days—January 21 to January

28—when the vibrations of Capricorn are merging into those of Aquarius, and Aquarius still retaining some of Capricorn, is known as the cusp. People born between these dates will partake of the personal, conventional Capricorn and the humanitarian, impersonal Aquarius, or a combination of the two. As Mercury, ruling the mentality, and Venus, the love nature, are so close to the Sun, they too may partake of some of the qualities of the adjoining signs of Capricorn. This may account for some of the complex personalities so difficult of comprehension.

With this sign also, these deductions are drawn from the position of the Sun or Ascendant, therefore it is probable that among the best friends of a Capricorn native, or those with whom he is uncongenial, will be found some who were not born at the times mentioned. The individual horoscopes must be consulted to ascertain how the stars combine with those of the Capricorn-born, and thus determine what effect the combinations of influences have upon each other.

These indications are only general, and will not cover all the characteristics of an individual as he knows himself, since those born under the sign Capricorn are subject to modifications by the planets. A detailed statement or horoscope must be made to discover the whole truth.

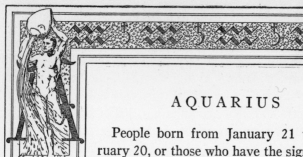

AQUARIUS

People born from January 21 to February 20, or those who have the sign Aquarius rising at birth (which can be ascertained only through a knowledge of the hour of birth), come under the dominion of the airy, fixed, humanitarian sign Aquarius.

The symbol of Aquarius, a man pouring water from an urn, indicates graphically the childlike tendency to give, of those who are undeveloped, and the love of imparting knowledge by those who have reached self-control under this sign.

Aquarius, being the cherubic sign attributed to air, represents that element in its most static form. In this sign Uranus rules unchallenged. In the attributes of the cherubim, Aquarius represents The Man, and this quality, blended with the attributes of its ruler, establishes a strong sympathy between the native of the sign and the interests of humanity at large. There is nothing eccentric about Aquarius; the static air of the sign calms Uranus, whose humanitarianism inspires the native to become the advance guard of mankind.

PHYSICAL CHARACTERISTICS

People of this sign seem to be a little ahead of their fellows in an all-round way. It is natural to them to live on a slightly higher plane, and the effect of all this upon

161

their physical appearance is to give them a look of remoteness. The average man is impressed by the appearance of the Aquarian. It is too much to say that an instinctive reverence is felt for the type; the feeling is better expressed by saying that people seem to recognize in him an elder brother.

The skull is broad in proportion to its length, unless modified by some planetary action. The hair is rather remarkable in possessing a peculiar glint suggesting the play of sunshine upon it; it tends to be curly, and often becomes gray even in youth. The face is long and oval, with flat planes, like those of other cherubic signs. The forehead is very broad, with an expression of benevolence, and the power of profound thought. In general, the eyes are set widely apart; they are hazel in color, or perhaps gray, with a slight tendency towards blue, but their expression is totally different from that of the gray-blue eye characteristic of Mercury, which is so hard and cold. These eyes, on the contrary, are large and luminous, full of understanding, with exceedingly quick apprehension and liveliness, and in most cases they positively beam with kindness. The nose is not extreme in any respect, neither too long nor too short, neither too thin nor too broad, but occasionally we see the type of nose which we recognize instinctively as inquisitive. The mouth is of medium size with a tendency to be somewhat thin-lipped, and the chin is the regular cherubic chin; not so heavy as Scorpio, not so aggressive as Leo, not so determined as Taurus, but keeping a somewhat happy mean between these various extremes. Moderation is indeed characteristic of Aquarius in every respect. It is rare to see marked departure from the main type. It has a kind of quiet strength which resists any but the most powerful planetary influences. This is perhaps more the case than with any other sign.

The body presents little opportunity for description, being moderate in every way. We do not find immense strength or robustness and we do not find many examples of puniness. Everything is well proportioned. The same remarks apply to the actual strength developed. The capacity for physical endurance is not so great as that of any of the other three cherubic signs. Aquarius, more than they, lives by moral rather than by physical assistance. The native seems to be actually ill when he is not hard at work. Such work, however, must always be inspired by an idea. One cannot think of this native as toiling, even with the mind, for no good beyond material reward. It would require some extraordinary affliction of Saturn to bring an Aquarian to the level of earth. At the same time, he does not shirk physical toil, unless he is weakened in some way. Venus rising might do something of the sort, as in the case of Alfred de Musset, or the Moon and Neptune rising, as in the case of Robert Louis Stevenson and W. B. Yeats. Even the Moon alone might produce a certain fragility. We do not find exceedingly virile or effeminate types in this sign. The tendency is rather to modification of the sex, so that Aquarian men have a considerable flavor of femininity; Aquarian women, of masculinity.

Aquarius rules the calves of the leg, the ankles, teeth, and circulation, and, sympathetically, the heart, throat and organs of generation; he also has influence over all vessels of the body which contain fluid, particularly the lymphatic system. One may say indeed that the lymphatic temperament is characteristic of this sign. Generally speaking, the native experiences very little trouble in the matter of health. His tendency is to lead an equable, temperate life, so that he is not likely to do anything which might sow the seeds of any fatal malady. If Stevenson seems to be an exception to this rule, the Moon, lady of the sixth house, rising in conjunction with Neptune in Pisces, shows his congenital predisposition to tuberculosis. But the Sun, in conjunction with Mars, gave him his indomitable energy to combat his physical weakness, and his Aquarian, temperate habits undoubtedly prolonged his life against serious odds. There may be a general liability to diseases of the bladder which is not, of course, one of the vessels above referred to, but because the bladder is under the rule of Scorpio (a sign which is squared by Aquarius), and possibly to such maladies as phlebitis and aneurism (the heart being under Leo, the opposing sign to Aquarius).

MORAL CHARACTERISTICS

To understand Aquarius, we can hardly do better than take the other three cherubic signs and harmonize them. The Aquarian has all their powers and qualities to some extent, but never to excess. He has the kindness of Taurus, without its blind devotion, the courage of Leo without his combative and challenging qualities, the scientific spirit of Scorpio without the passionate intensity. Aquarius is essentially the all-round man. One cannot put one's finger upon a definite lack in his character, and at the same time, one cannot say that he markedly excels in any one feature, save that of being armed at all points.

This completeness of mind must be most carefully distinguished from a superficially similar quality in Gemini, for the mind is not detached from the earth and from the heavens, like that of Gemini. Aquarius is at home on all planes and never either separates them or muddles them. In fact, the great drawback of the Aquarian is his inability to specialize in this way. He rarely becomes expert in pure mathematics, because the aridity of the subject is distasteful to his humanity. Scorpio makes a much better surgeon, because Aquarius finds it difficult to regard the operation as a mere matter of cutting and tying; at the back of his mind there is always a feeling that there is a human being on the operating table. We commonly find him far more distinguished as a physician, where he can combine the patience of Taurus and the courage of Leo with the insight of Scorpio.

The genius in every department of progress is bound to be a revolutionary, for nature progresses by excesses, but Aquarius always tries to progress without upsetting existing conditions. He has a great sense of realities and does not shut his eyes to facts; but his tendency is to bring existing facts to flower by submitting them to the operations of a kindly wisdom, rather than by challenging things as they are and by breaking new ground. Thus there is never anything of the fanatic in this type. Its tolerance is both broad and deep. Its common sense can only be described as stupendous. Knowledge of the world seems natural to it, not being painfully acquired by experience, as in so many other cases. But in the imperfect condition of the human intelligence, we hardly recognize any other means of progress than by the warfare between absolutely opposing views; so controversy goes on, pitting extreme against extreme, until true causes come to light and are found to be composed of various elements taken in proper proportion. Aquarius never leaves the balance.

People of extreme types of mind, particularly Scorpio, are thoroughly annoyed by the calm and moderation of the Aquarian method, and, indeed, human prejudice is so ingrained in the majority of people that it must be conceded that the world is not yet ripe for the Aquarian methods. Aquarius is too practical to be visionary, but the native often fails to command the appreciation of the average impulsive human being. There is nothing people hate so much as good advice. The natural man always wants to rush to extreme action. In fact, it is only very sensible people, people with some touch of Aquarius in their own composition, who naturally appreciate the quiet virtues of good sense.

People who fail to understand the Aquarian temperament are apt to describe them as inefficient and lacking in concentration. This is very far from being the case. The illusion is caused by the fact that the conclusions of this native are upon so broad a base. He leaves out nothing, and the rash observer is apt to suppose that he has got nothing done. If one enlarges a statue of a man by slightly increasing the entire surface of his body in due proportion, it will not seem much bigger; but if the whole of this additional material is added to the head only, the difference is very obvious. Most people like to make their advances in the latter way. One remembers the old fairy story of the people who had three wishes. The good woman used the first in wishing for some black pudding; her husband, angry at her stupidity, wished it would stick to her nose, and they were obliged to use the third wish in wishing it off again. This story is very characteristic of most men and women. The Aquarian never makes this particular kind of a fool of himself.

But there is a defect in the temperament in that it finds difficulty in coping with emergencies when they really arise. There are occasions in life when the most violent action is absolutely necessary. The natural inclination of the man with a stomach ache is to adopt some violent remedy which would probably make him worse. His Aquarian counselor will save him from all this folly by telling him to be careful with his diet, to rest, to use mild correctives, to give the thing a little time. Even if the man's complaint happens to be appendicitis, this plan will usually be as good for him as anything else, but there is an occasional case of appendicitis where the man will die if he is not operated upon within a few hours, and it is very doubtful whether any Aquarian would give so drastic a counsel. The same applies to nearly all the troubles of life. The Burmese settle divorce in a very simple way. When the woman comes to the elders of the village with a complaint against her husband, they reply, "Why, certainly, this is an outrage. We shall immediately draw up the papers of divorce; kindly call around for them in three days' time." Of course, she seldom returns. But in a case of an assault upon a wife, which may end in murder if not immediately restrained, all the wisdom of the world would fail to save the situation by counseling delay and moderation.

In undeveloped types, this defect is really a serious matter, for where wisdom is not based upon the very widest possible experience, almost every circumstance is new. The uneducated or semi-educated, with no knowledge of history and with little experience of their own, are helpless in quite ordinary emergencies, even of quite trifling domestic kinds. As a rule, the mind of the Aquarian is not rapid in its action, and this may become a tendency to let things slide. The native is perfectly active and competent where he has a situation in hand, but there is no doubt that new things are apt to confuse him.

This is not by any means to say that this native is opposed to new ideas; on the contrary, he receives them gladly, but he does not go so far in his acceptance of them as the enthusiast. He tempers everything with his natural discretion. It is easy to see how the native, in spite of his exceedingly sympathetic nature, may often be unpopular for the ordinary people like the Billy Sundays and the yellow newspapers and the shrieking sisterhoods. The average man cannot appreciate anyone who does not react instantly to impression without a moment's reflection. At the same time, one is bound to admit that, in many cases, rash and even foolish action is really wiser than the wisdom of deliberation. This is not the fault of the wise, but of the foolish. We live in a world where we often have to answer a fool according to his folly. The habit of deliberation, which is right, may easily become the habit of temporizing, which is wrong. Even where this has not occurred, deliberation may sometimes look like temporizing, or even like cowardice, and Aquarius may sometimes do better to remember that "a stitch in time saves nine."

The Aquarian native's breadth and balance, while alienating him in a sense from the petty interests of men and women, bring him closely in touch with the high ideals of humanity. He is much more interested in the cure of consumption than in the cure of consumptives; in the alleviation of some economic wrong than in the relief of individual distress. He is habitually kind, make no mistake on that point, but the general welfare is so fixed in his mind that he finds it difficult to regard the particular example as anything but a special case. Sometimes, of course, an exaggeration and distortion of this quality may lead to a complete moral catastrophe, as exemplified by Robespierre, whose Ascendant, Aquarius, is corrupted by Saturn rising in Pisces, squared by Mercury, and just above Uranus and Venus. This square of Saturn and Mercury seems to have made him academic in the worse sense of the word. His moral principles, his plans for the regeneration of France, were undoubtedly sincere, but they caused him to lose sight completely of the fact that France was a country inhabited by human beings. In his zeal for humanity, he cut off many heads. This difficulty in reckoning with the individual is a very common failing of people with Aquarius rising. In previous signs, we have met people who could not see the wood for the trees; the Aquarian only too often cannot see the trees for the wood.

There is undoubtedly a certain coldness in the type. The native seems to say to himself, "most human troubles come from selfishness and exaggeration of personal feeling"; which is quite true, but humanity at large does not recognize this and is not going to recognize it for a very long time yet. Aquarius instinctively recognizes that humanity at large has not progressed to his viewpoint, and yet he often speaks and acts as if it were in the same rank with him. Occasionally, error of judgment may result; for one thing, Aquarius is far too optimistic to suit the average mind. It would not matter so much if it were the optimism of enthusiasm, for people like fireworks; but it often occurs that the native wishing to give all possible sympathy to someone who is in distress is understood by that person as merely offering vague generalities; in short, as being rather heartless. The exact contrary, of course, is the case. The fact is not only that the heart is too big to narrow itself down to a single, trivial instance, but also from his broader vision the Aquarian knows the deeper significance of sorrow or misfortune, in that, often through suffering, the soul is perfected, and he hesitates to interfere with the workings of fate.

In dealing with money, the native of Aquarius is exceptionally trustworthy. He realizes that money is only a means to an end, and values it principally for its use in facilitating those transactions which make for the welfare of the human race. He is neither generous nor mean in the ordinary sense of those words. He never flings his money about and he never hoards it, but he is usually willing to spend money when he feels that he is doing real good with it, and when he seems overcautious in dealing with it, the true reason is that he wishes to conserve his power of using it wisely. The greatest danger in the sign is its tendency towards too great optimism.

We have some remarkable instances of the Aquarian temperament among authors. The style is fluent and pleasing and, therefore, likely to be popular. It is not marked by the explosive and eccentric force which must always be characteristic of the very greatest masters of thought. In England, we have Robert Louis Stevenson and John Ruskin, both men most highly endowed with the gift of adorned expression; and in the realm of poetry, William Butler Yeats. In each case, we find a singular felicity of expression, a pleasant optimism, an art of decorating every subject and of pervading it with a soft and genial glow, but in no case do we find any aptitude for searching deeply into the nature of things. The philosophy of all three is gentle, poetic, optimistic, and throws a veil of glamour over any subjects that are, in their superficial aspects at least, rather unpleasant to the average man. Stevenson never loses his essential airiness, while deeper in the background is that deep-seated humanity which flowered at its fullest in his letter in defense of the memory of Father Damien.

Aquarius seems to be too superficial to produce the epoch-making writer. In general it produces the commentator on the matters of the moment, which is best fitted to make life livable, but it does not create revolutions or establish new principles. The same remarks apply to casual speech and correspondence. The conversation of the Aquarian native is pleasant, informing, dealing with subjects of real interest to well-educated minds. It is helpful in matter and cheerful in manner. One will always get up from a conversation with the native of this sign feeling much the better for it; but though there is no avoidance of the serious problems of life, and they are always treated with sound common sense and informed of the wisdom which is based on experience, there is none of that desperate restlessness and acute agony of thought which seems always to preoccupy the minds of the very greatest thinkers.

We must refer for a moment to the matter of the stage, for we have a magnificent example of Aquarius in this department of life in Ellen Terry. One cannot but remain lost in admiration of the extraordinarily fine influence exercised for more than half a century by this one

woman, whose position in England was unique and supreme. Her influence was to elevate the stage to an entirely higher plane; at the beginning of her career, ac-
tresses were considered little more than courtesans, and
the average play was of the basest possible type. Ellen
Terry did nothing eccentric, nothing revolutionary; she
simply lived an age ahead of the rest and brought up the
rest of the theater to her standard without apparent effort.

This sign provides us on the whole with the best of the
domestic types. The devotion of Taurus is sometimes unwise, overdone. Aquarius develops a proper feeling of
independence; it does not slop over. It maintains a high
standard of conduct without exacting unwished-for sacrifices on the one hand, or offering embarrassing sacrifices
on the other. The Aquarian native respects himself. He
respects others, and he expects others to respect both
themselves and him. Such a basis for domestic life is
much better than sentimentalism. The native is not eager
to leave his home, nor does he cling to it like a lizard
to a rock. He develops his independence early, but he always tries to maintain the most amicable relations with
his people.

The universality of spirit characteristic of this sign
does not permit the Aquarian native to fall in love easily.
He finds it hard to concentrate what was meant for humanity upon the individual; he is too advanced, he is too
sensible; romanticism appears to him rather silly and
unworthy of a highly developed soul. He is apt to be
much more in love with a school, a hospital, or a science,
than he can ever be with any individual. This is not to

say that he is insensible to love in the ordinary sense of the word, but we shall find that his attitude in this respect will depend very much upon the position of his Venus, or some other planetary influence. He is likely to feel affection as strongly for one sex as the other. When he loves, his general amiability leads him to do all in his power to gratify the feelings of the other party, and his efforts in this direction are much more sincere and satisfactory than is the case with a somewhat similar quality in the native of Sagittarius.

Aquarius makes an altogether admirable parent, though the sign is not exceptionally prolific. There is, however, no better person to be in charge of children. The influence is gentle and reasonable; the native encourages independence in thought and action, and respects the individuality of the child, while at the same time correcting faults with sweet reasonableness and just the right amount of firmness. We may again refer to Stevenson and Ruskin in regard to the works which they wrote, especially for the young. "Sesame and Lilies" and "Virginibus Puerisque" should always remain classics of their kind.

The strongest point in the whole make-up of the Aquarian is his capacity for friendship. He is much better here than in love or marriage, because there is no limit to the number of objects to which he can devote himself. This is not, by any means, to say that he is "Hail fellow, well met," with the world at large. On the contrary, he always preserves a fine sense of the dignity of human intercourse. The native never forgets that the object of friendship is not merely to pass away the time pleasantly; he knows the importance of it as facilitating the interchange of ideas, and he does not lose sight of its true purpose in making life easier by consideration for others and the extension of help to those in real need.

As a partner in marriage or business, Aquarius is all that can be desired. He never causes trouble, and his good sense and practical wisdom may be relied on to avert it. This native can be relied on never to quarrel or to do anything to break up an existing situation. The only difficulty arises from his extremely advanced intellectuality. His partner may find it difficult to live up to his standard. There are some natures that experience the most extreme irritation at being treated reasonably. Aquarius, however, can hardly be considered as having any very strong impulse toward matrimony.

The Aquarius native shows no exceptional capacity for business; he conducts it with intelligence and perhaps a certain mild enthusiasm, but the mere matter of money-making does not appeal to him strongly. He always looks beyond materialism. One would never find this native engaging in a questionable business; indeed, the nearer the nature of the business comes to his ideals, the better he will succeed in it. Nothing gives him a greater incentive than some genuine, ultimate value to humanity.

In the conduct of public affairs, the native is again excellent. None is better able to avoid friction, to compose quarrels. He understands a situation better than any other zodiacal type, and his measures for dealing with it will always be thoroughly sensible. He will never yield to fanaticism, or allow himself to be rushed into a violent decision.

There is a certain conservatism in the people as an aggregate which corresponds to common sense in the individual. The common people, those whose voices are never heard, represent a substratum of practical wisdom and it is to these people that the Aquarian always appeals. He will never satisfy extremists, but will express the subconscious feeling of the great mass of humanity. His only danger lies in the fact that he is a little likely to mistake the ideal for the real, to imagine people a bit better than they are, or, as he would say, than they seem to be. Virtue and good sense, for the most part, lie silent in the heart. It is upon this that Aquarius depends for the formulation of his judgments, but there are times of stress in human life when conscious pain or anger overwhelm the deeper feelings, and at such moments Aquarius ceases to be popular. Shakespeare says, "Beware of entrance to a quarrel, but, being in, bear't that the opposed may beware of thee." Here we see that once the Rubicon is crossed, Aquarius must give way to his opposite, Leo. His function begins once more, only when the battle is fought, and the true necessity is to calm the violence of partisanship.

The subconscious mind of Aquarius is generally of profound importance in informing his objective consciousness. The two are usually found to harmonize in a very gentle and natural way. There is no conflict between the two minds, and it may be said that in the ordinary way Aquarius is far more accessible to the promptings of the inner self than most other types. In science and philosophy, the Aquarian native is not likely to make deep research; indeed, with this temperament he does not need to do so. In his religious beliefs, Aquarius is tolerant and sensible, not exactly indifferent, but anxious to relieve religion of its great handicaps, atavism, superstition, and bigotry. The fanatical Christian or Mohammedan will describe him as a heretic, infidel, miscreant, atheist, and any other nasty word he can think of, but the native of Aquarius will only pity his assailant for his narrowness.

Aquarian children can be more interesting and yet more difficult than those born under any other sign. Because of their unusual intelligence and understanding of life for their age, it is most essential that they should be treated as chums or companions; their parents should allow them to share their confidences and their conferences, realizing that these children must be given a reason why they should or should not do certain things, and then they are both willing and happy to coöperate, as they are naturally obedient and have a desire to do the right thing. Parents, however, should study their Aquarius children and be wise enough to draw the line between reasonable leniency and too much license. Otherwise, these children become overconfident of their ability, have too great self-assurance, and develop into perfect bores.

The ordinary toys or childish plays do not usually appeal to these children; they read and understand books far in advance of their years, and their parents should not attempt to push them in their school work, as it is more important to watch their physical condition and to encourage outdoor sports. Animals make a strong appeal to their protective and humanitarian instincts, and nothing will so delight them or bring out the best in their natures as having a pet to love and care for. Children of their own age, unless equally intelligent and far in advance of their times, do not especially attract them, as they seldom have much in common with the average child, preferring their elders or those of unusual intelligence. These children should have special attention given to their teeth and their tonsils, as infection is easily aggravated with them. They are much more active mentally than physically. These children desire to have a good education, and every effort should be made to give them the opportunity to obtain one; they look up to those who have accomplished great things in life, and have less regard for mere material worldly possessions. Travel and association with men and women of distinction will mean much to them.

People born from the 22nd of May to the 22nd of June, when the Sun is in the airy, intellectual sign Gemini, and from the 24th of September to the 24th of October, when the Sun is in the airy, artistic sign Libra, are naturally sympathetic and helpful to those born under Aquarius. Because their characteristics are complementary, they are good partners for the Aquarius-born, matrimonially and otherwise. If too intimately associated with those born from the 21st of April to 22nd of May (Taurus), 24th of July to 24th of August (Leo), and 24th of October to 23rd of November (Scorpio), the Aquarius-born will find it necessary to guard against those who would take advantage. Such an intimacy might result in the native of Aquarius becoming too nervous and irritable. For this reason, people born under Taurus, Leo and Scorpio would not make the most sympathetic or helpful partners, either matrimonially or in a business way.

A period of about seven days—February 19 to February 26—when the vibrations of Aquarius are merging into those of Pisces, and Pisces still retaining some of Aquarius, is known as the cusp. People born between these dates will partake of the practical, concentrated Aquarius and the emotional and visionary Pisces. As Mercury, ruling the mentality, and Venus, the love nature, are so close to the Sun, they, too, may partake of some of the qualities of the adjoining signs of Aquarius. This may account for some of the complex personalities so difficult of comprehension.

As these deductions are drawn from the position of the Sun or Ascendant, it is probable that among the best friends of the Aquarius-born, or those with whom he is uncongenial, there will be some who were not born at the times mentioned. The individual horoscopes must be consulted to ascertain how the stars combine with those of the Aquarius native, and to determine the effect of the combinations of influences upon each other.

These indications will not cover all the characteristics of an individual as he knows himself, since they do not take into consideration the influence of the planets. A detailed statement or horoscope must be made to discover the whole truth.

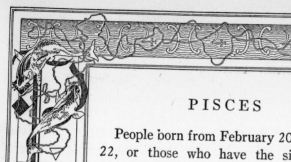

PISCES

People born from February 20 to March 22, or those who have the sign Pisces rising at birth (which can be ascertained only through a knowledge of the hour of birth), will come under the dominion of the watery, mutable, emotional sign Pisces, symbolized by the two fish, and ruled over by the psychic, impressionable planet Neptune.

Pisces, symbolized by two fish swimming in opposite directions, was the pictorial representation given by the Ancients to this sign. These people are natural wanderers and lack concentration and directness. They are restless physically and inattentive mentally. They should not have too many conflicting interests, and should strive to overcome a tendency to scatter their forces.

Venus is exalted in the sign, and the Moon seems to have a strong influence upon its natives, as is indicated by the fact that in the Tarot the card representing the Moon is attributed to Pisces. The sign is, indeed, the most feminine and receptive of any in the zodiac. The God of the Sea, that world of waters which is so exact a physical symbol of the emotional psychic plane, was hailed in ancient times as "the saviour" and Pisces is preëminently the sign of salvation, the true hearth of body, soul, and spirit as united in man, which is attained only through the evolution of the emotional or psychic body. The ocean, even when calm, is never absolutely still; ebb and flow and unseen undercurrent are perpetually in motion; it answers to every breeze with a quiver of response, and while it mirrors the sky above, its waters rest upon the solid earth.

This thought is connected with action through emotion, and it is by the gradual evolution of the emotional qualities that a man at least learns to choose his pleasures rightly, since through their agony lessons of spiritual growth are brought home to his inner self in wrongdoing. We shall see that the planet Neptune is considered in esoteric astrology as typifying the soul in man, and there is something eminently fitting in his rule over a sign which, free of contradiction in its undeveloped natives, nevertheless represents the struggles and defeats through which an aspiring soul in bondage must come into its full fruition, whether here or in another life. Moreover, though Neptune may be masculine, his force is that of a finer vibration of the Venus rays, and his dominion over the sign is therefore unmarred by any lack of harmony between the lord and the exalted lady, or with the Moon which, as we have suggested, has strong influence therein.

PHYSICAL CHARACTERISTICS

The physical type of so mutable a sign depends very largely on planetary influence, and there is, therefore, a great deal of variation in the type. The shape of the skull in particular will depend to an immense extent on Saturn's position, and the general stature on the strength or weakness of Jupiter, but the Pisces face is very easy to recognize. Its lines are of singular softness. Everything in it is rounded, but particularly the cheeks, which are usually very prominent, one might almost say bulging. The eyes are unusually prominent, in most cases suggesting the fish totem, and generally with a sleepy expression. The lips are full and there is a decided tendency to double chin. The neck is short and thick and the Pisces native generally has round shoulders. The hair is usually brown and the complexion is normally florid, but in some cases the influence of a rising Moon or similar planetary configuration may cause an extreme pallor. The more masculine types may be mistaken for a weak Leo; the more feminine types for the passive form of Cancer.

When there is no strong planetary indication to the contrary, the stature is rather below the average; the frame is weak—weaker than in any other sign. Generally speaking, women with this sign rising are better formed than men. There is sometimes a good deal of sensuous beauty, the gracefulness in repose of the Persian cat, but this is very likely to degenerate into slackness of body. The legs are apt to be short and fat. Weak specimens of this type hardly exist for themselves or by themselves, but great care must be taken to distinguish this recessive type from that in which Neptune asserts himself to the full— the type in which we find the great, jolly face; the boyish, genial manner—yet even in such cases the expert Astrologer can trace the stigmata of weakness manifested in softness, luxury and self-indulgence.

Pisces governs the feet and, sympathetically, the hands, the arms, the lungs and nervous system; gout is the characteristic disease of this sign. Being a torpid and cold-blooded sign, its peculiar relaxing and softening action upon the tissues explains its manifest connection with tuberculosis and many diseases involving the secretions. The constitution is not strong; it does not resist attack

or infection of any kind, but the native is so adaptable
to his circumstances that he is not easily upset. When
ill, he takes great care of himself and responds readily to
treatment, but as he is so suggestible, it is of the highest
importance that his doctor should have a strong personality and the gift of communicating confidence. The type is
not very long-lived in any case. A great many die in infancy, while adults are almost sure to fall a prey to some
disease caused by slackness and self-indulgence. He is
particularly susceptible to the influence of toxins, and
drugs and drink have a strong fascination for him; if he
is not addicted to morphia, he is pretty sure to indulge
in excess of some kind. This tendency manifests itself
in the higher type by an intense passion for love or religion or psychic manifestation, with little self-control in
its pursuit. Pisces is wholly sensuous in all these matters.
His chief interest in religion or art, for example, is the
spiritual exaltation which he derives from it, and such
sensuousness is only a short step removed from sensuality.
His spiritual emotion is apt to be orgastic.

MORAL CHARACTERISTICS

Pisces is the weakest of all the signs in its reaction to
material and mental affairs. Its strength lies wholly on
subtler planes, which will be discussed in the proper place.
This is one of the so-called double-bodied signs, in which
we find so curious a division of interests. In really weak
cases, this amounts almost to negation of any moral character. Edgar Allan Poe had some pretty good planetary
aspects, Venus just above his Ascendant being in exact
trine to Uranus and a few degrees below Venus, the Moon

in conjunction with Jupiter, but Neptune, the ruler of the Ascendant, is square to this configuration, thus accentuating the weaker side of the sign. Hence we cannot be surprised to find a sensitive nature with a will unable to transcend the influences of the moment.

Speaking generally, the native of Pisces receives almost all impressions that may reach him. He not only reflects them like a mirror, but absorbs them like a sponge. He has usually no standard of truth in what may be called the essential structure of the mind. It may be remarked that this subconscious mind, which is typically Neptunian, seems to have no conception of mundane morals. Truth, to the native of Pisces, means that which he feels for the moment. All watery signs seem to have this quality to some extent when the type is a weak one. "Unstable as water, thou shalt not excel." The undeveloped native of Pisces would hardly go so far as to explain or analyze his moral deficiencies; he would simply fail to understand that there was anything wrong.

The type is so impressionable that it reacts immediately to any influence; it cannot stand alone. This sensitiveness extends to all planes. The Pisces native is singularly open to suggestion, being always very psychic. He appears to possess no power of discrimination, no capacity of resistance to any set of thoughts. His character, therefore, is really negative; but if he leaves the sheltered life, where he has been exposed during the whole period of it to one set of impressions only, he will remain perfectly undisturbed and therefore pass for a general adherent to that particular class of views. One may, therefore, like Lord Roberts, be a quiet, conventional Christian, a gentleman and a soldier, happily married and the father of just the right kind of sons. Such may be the natural development where the career is simple and straightforward, beginning at the public school where the headmaster has the baton, and graduating in the school of war where he ends by getting a baton of his own. With a different environment, one may get a Cléo de Mérode.

There is something biologically admirable about the character of the Pisces native. His adaptability to circumstances is his best guarantee of survival. There is, therefore, no reason to expect anything particular *a priori* from the Ascendant of the native. We shall discover that he is much better if we examine the parts of the horoscope that refer to the people with whom he is brought in contact. For example, Edgar Allan Poe's best help came from friends, as indicated by an exact conjunction of the Sun and Mercury very strong in Capricorn in his eleventh house, whose lord Saturn is in conjunction with Neptune, thus indicating the origin of the friendships in artistic sympathy. Where the personality is itself strong, it is indicated by planets in the Ascendant or powerful aspects of Jupiter.

Hitherto we have been compelled to follow the general reaction of Pisces to external impression, but there is in the Pisces native something much deeper than this. Within himself, he is mysterious and sublime. The Tarot trump called "The Moon," which is attributed to Pisces, gives us a very clear representation of what is here meant. At the top of the card shines the waning Moon of illusion. She sheds her light upon a winding path which leads between two towers, and on either side of the path are jackals. The pilgrim is the prey of illusion, of prejudice, of obsessing force, but at the bottom of the card is a pool in

which is a beetle, representing Kheperer, the Egyptian
Scarab, symbolizing the Sun at midnight. The true soul
of the sign lies in this secret place of reflection where the
lord of life is born, but this pool is silent and unstirred.
It does not manifest, as a general rule, in the external
life. It is going too far to say that the native is a natural
poet or mystic, but in his sensitiveness and in his interior
silence, we find the passive half of genius. There is always the possibility of its coming to birth where there is
an active or creative principle at work in the nativity.
But even so, the form that genius will take seems to depend upon the environment.

Poe was powerfully influenced by the peculiar form that
mysticism was taking at his period. He did not make a systematic study of the business. Scholar as he was, it does
not seem to have occurred to him to investigate the classics of the subject and to compare them. He took the
quaint volume which Glanville wrote about the witches.
He was profoundly interested in the phenomena of hyp-
notism, which were just becoming well known in America,
and on these slender data he meditated and produced a
charming little philosophy of his own, with hardly any
other aid than a trace of Plato, natural enough to one of
his education. One is really reminded of the fish, perfectly happy in his own environment, displaying his
golden sails on golden sand, but becoming rapidly black
if he happens to reach a pool with a muddy bottom.

In all cases, however, we find that this extraordinary
flexibility and adaptability seem to select the subtle and
interior nature of the forces which are at work upon it.
The developed native has an almost divine power of sep-
arating the subtle from the gross, and using only the for-

mer. Nature itself seems plastic in his hands. We may see this very strongly manifested in a very unusual department in the case of Luther Burbank, in whose hands even living things changed their nature as though under the manipulation of a magician. The transmutation of life is no less wonderful, but rather more so, than that of metal.

Pisces responds not to the surface of things, but to the soul in them. The Pisces native seems to have an intimate apprehension of the spiritual forces in any phenomenon. We do not find Poe investigating mesmerism in the scientific sense, despite the fact that he had a remarkable gift, both for pure mathematics and for close observation, as is witnessed by his analysis of Maelzel's chess-player and the similar power displayed in some of his stories. He preferred to go behind the phenomenon, to deal with causes rather than with effects.

The supersubtlety of Pisces often leads to most serious danger for the native. He is only too apt to take the shadow for the substance. He too easily confuses the material and spiritual planes. He has no rational idea of the correlation of cause and effect and may often be quite absurdly superstitious. Pisces will always act on an impression rather than on rational judgment. He delights to feel himself in communion with the subtle worlds, and unless well developed, he has no power to discriminate between the world of true causes upon higher planes, and that of dream, glamour and illusion. Such people may often be abominably untrustworthy; they will say, "I know something or other," when all they mean is that they dreamt it.

Another point connected with the extreme sensitiveness of the Pisces native is his exaggerated reaction to those physical influences which hardly disturb the mind of the stronger type of humanity. Alcohol is exceedingly dangerous to natives of this sign, and the temptation to employ the subtler and stronger drugs is even more pronounced. The immediate effect is extraordinarily bad, throwing the native off such balance as he may possess, and there is an appalling strength in the temptation to indulge habitually and to excess. Drugs do for him exactly what he is in his own nature only too prone to do without their aid. They translate him to a subtler world. This world, always dangerous, is invariably fatal when created in such artificial manner.

In dealing with matters of money, this native is exceedingly careless and is likely to spend profusely and with little judgment. He cannot be called untrustworthy in managing the affairs of others, but he is certainly not reliable. He is generous, but not wisely so. He helps other people indiscriminately without consideration as to what may be genuinely useful; though his charity gives temporary pleasure to the recipient, it does not assist him to get permanently out of his condition of distress.

In speech and writing, the native is very fluent and voluble. His words seem to flow forth from him in a torrent. He is extremely genial and may be the life and soul of a party. He is inclined to see everything through rose-colored spectacles. His style is usually very pleasant to hear; the poetry of Poe, from the point of melody, is the most musical ever written in the English language.

The Pisces native, being essentially lazy, is one of the most domesticated persons to be found. He does not give much active assistance in the home, but he always makes himself pleasant and is very often the pet of the family.

He has the great art of making those around him happy. The exception will be if any of them are of a stern, uncompromising type, who object to his character as such. He will never leave home of his own initiative, for circumstances which irritate other people, the narrowness and restraints upon ambition, do not affect him at all. He lacks ambition and he is very happy where he is.

In love, this native is of an exceptionally pleasing type. The devotion displayed exceeds even that of Taurus, but it is much more placid in character. It is almost a parasitical phenomenon. There is little tendency to infidelity of the active sort, but on the other hand, there is no likelihood of much resistance to any pressure that may be exerted by some new admirer. Both men and women of this type exact the most constant attention, particularly the women.

Women with this sign rising are usually very fertile. Both fathers and mothers are devoted to their children, but are too indulgent to make good parents.

The Pisces native may get on very well with servants because of his natural tendency to be indulgent toward them and his manifest appreciation of their devotion to him.

In marriage, the woman of Pisces makes an ideal wife from the Oriental standpoint. The woman of the harem typifies very exactly the sensuous nature of the Piscarian's enjoyment of emotion in her indolence, her devotion to the sweetmeats of life, and her complaisant response to the invitation of passion. Such a disposition is not well suited for marriage in countries where the wife is not kept secluded and under lock and key, since if the undeveloped woman of Pisces is left too much to her own resources, her

natural sensuality will assert itself, for there is little
chance of her working it off by active interest in intellectual amusements. In the more developed type these
tendencies manifest themselves in devotion and loyalty,
though still with much taste for indolence and the sweetmeats. Where the Pisces native is a man, he will be very
devoted and pet and spoil the wife, but he will be little
good for the practical duties of the home. Comfort will be
his first consideration, but he will not take very active
steps to secure it. He is the worst kind of husband for a
woman of any activity. Mr. Mantilini in "Nicholas
Nickleby" is a good picture of the undeveloped type of
Pisces.

As a business associate, very similar objections apply
to him, though he makes a splendid sleeping partner. If
a man is needed to put his money into a business and let
it lie there, it would be well to look for a native of Pisces.

In the active conduct of public affairs, Pisces will be
utterly hopeless, if he is ever intrusted with anything
of the sort, which he hardly ever is. An amusing example
is offered in the case of a man who, through family influence, was intrusted with the conduct of a railway in
Central America, the men to whom he was responsible
being far away in New York. His idea of carrying out
their instructions was to throw all their letters unread
into the waste-paper basket, because it saved him trouble,
and when somebody came down and threw him out, he
remarked that that saved him trouble too, because the
job was rather a bore after all.

The subconscious mind of this native is the best part
of him; in fact, he may be said to live in that mind and
by virtue of it. To him this world which we can see and

touch is not the world of reality. The same man who so ridiculously failed in Central America is in his real life a far-seeing mystic of an erratic type, with what seems to be a genuinely prophetic gift. There is, however, nothing in the temperament itself that enables the native to make a bridge between the subconscious and the ordinary mind, so that in many cases he is a voice crying in the wilderness. His marvelous ability does not even benefit him in the majority of cases, since he does not naturally have the gift of action. However, assisted either in business or in public affairs by harmoniously balanced active partners, his insight and intuition may make him a veritable power behind the throne.

The native may reach great eminence in science through his appreciation of the subtle forces behind phenomena. In philosophy, he may prove admirable from the same cause, but in both philosophy and science, his work will almost infallibly be one-sided. The man is likely to make new discoveries, but not to have anything like a complete intellectual understanding of the subject as a whole.

In religion, the Pisces native may be a mystic of the devotional type; he will, in all probability, be highly gifted with clairvoyance. Religion being altogether a matter of faith and inspiration, he is enabled to dispense with even the pretense of rationalism. Very low types of this sign will be conventionally and sentimentally religious to an inordinate degree. Even when the native is a mystic, he is unbalanced; there is no intellectual backbone, no idea of maintaining psychic balance by any corrective skepticism.

The native is extremely warm in his friendships, sometimes even unpleasantly so. He is always trying to drain the last drop of any honeyed cup. Most people prefer friendships to be something in the nature of an offensive and defensive alliance. The native of Pisces tries to make it a romance. However, there is no better man to dine with when you are tired and have the blues. He understands very well the art of entertainment, and his desire for fullness of everything never allows him to forget a single ingredient that makes for pleasure.

Pisces yields immediately to any kind of constraint without resentment or any tendency to revolt. He becomes immediately part of the existing system that is imposed upon him. He has not the slightest desire to make trouble for anybody.

Neptune represents the unifying principle of the solvent, as against the differentiating and analytical tendencies shown by Mars. The latter impulses drive man's energies into the physical; the power of Neptune and Pisces turns the native away from the physical plane and gives a longing for union with the divine. At the first indications of this aspiration manifest in a yearning for emotional experience, we can see how it is that the undeveloped types show on the surface so little of the divine and so much of the fleshly. But as the true strength of the Piscarian is in his ideals and inspirations, in its more advanced types the natives of the sign live by inspiration, and in their supreme moments may attain to a realization of the essential unity of all things, so that their life, their speech or their writings may approach almost to the divine. Many among the saints and mystics of the early church give evidence of the dominations of this planet and sign, especially St. Francis of Assisi, whose most famous hymn illustrates his feeling of kinship with the Sun and the Moon; and whose life was a long record of ceaseless love, devotion and self-sacrifice.

The instincts of Pisces children will be towards good, and because they expect people to be honest like themselves, they may be inclined to place too much confidence and trust in others. They will be more grieved and confused than resentful at an injury. The sins of this sign are those of omission rather than commission. These children lack initiative and are too willing to take a back seat, often being taken advantage of by their playmates. Later in life, they find it difficult to assert themselves and push their way to the fore. Everything should be done to teach them self-confidence and to fight their own battles; they must not, on any account, be coddled. While they should be sympathized with, they must not be made "soft" or content to hold the least place in any contest with their friends. If they are made to realize that they must fight in order to gain a standing and hold their own, this will help to give them confidence in themselves and change their outlook for the future.

It will be necessary to give these children a good education and to send them to college, if practicable. They are so impressionable that they naturally fall into the habits of those with whom they are associated; unlike their Taurus and Leo brothers, they are lacking in will power; knowledge and the realization of their own importance and potential value to the world will help to make them more self-reliant and strengthen their will.

The Pisces-born, as a rule, have a strong sense of the ridiculous and can see a funny situation even at the expense of hurting the feelings of their close associates and best friends. For this reason they may often be considered hypocrites, when in reality they are merely indulging this side of their nature, with no intent to hurt. Even though their intention may not be unkindly, they must realize that the other person does not understand their motives, and is therefore justified in being hurt. They are often misjudged and mistrusted for this reason, as well as for others.

Because of their absentmindedness or inattentiveness, they lose their possessions very easily, and are constantly dropping things and forgetting to pick them up.

They must guard against falling into the habit of feeling terribly sorry for themselves. They are often selfishly unselfish, and unconsciously cause others annoyance by their insistence in giving their time and strength when it is really unwelcome.

People born from the 22nd of June to the 24th of July, when the Sun is in the watery, maternal sign Cancer, and from the 24th of October to the 23rd of November, when the Sun is in the watery, self-reliant sign Scorpio, are naturally sympathetic and helpful to those born under Pisces. Because their characteristics are complementary, they are good partners for the Pisces-born, matrimonially or otherwise. If too intimately associated with those born from the 22nd of May to the 22nd of June (Gemini), 24th of August to 24th of September (Virgo), and 23rd of November to 23rd of December (Sagittarius), Pisces natives will need to practice self-preservation. Such an intimacy might result in the native of Pisces becoming too vacillating and lacking in ambition and will power. For this reason people born under Gemini, Virgo and

Sagittarius would not make the most sympathetic and helpful partners, either matrimonially or in a business way.

A period of about seven days—March 21 to March 28 —when the vibrations of Pisces are merging into those of Aries, and Aries still retaining some of Pisces, is known as the cusp. People born between these dates will partake of the impressionable, unselfish Pisces and the domineering Aries.

As we have said before, these deductions are drawn from the position of the Sun or Ascendant, therefore it is probable that among the best friends of a Pisces native, or those with whom he is uncongenial, will be found some who were not born at the times mentioned. The individual horoscopes must be consulted to ascertain how the stars combine with those of the Pisces-born, and thus determine what effect the combinations of influence have upon each other.

These indications are only general, and will not cover all the characteristics of an individual as he knows himself, since those born under the sign Pisces are subject to modifications by the planets. A detailed statement or horoscope must be made to discover the whole truth.

PART II

THE PLANETS

THE SUN

THE SUN

The Sun, the star to which the visible planets belong, is the parent body of the solar system. The Sun rules over the sign Leo, both by day and night, and his exaltation is in 19 degrees of Aries. He has no latitude, being always in the ecliptic, and is never retrograde. He seems to coöperate sympathetically with all the planets except Saturn. He is considered temperately hot, dry, masculine and diurnal; and when well dignified, equal to one of the fortunes. He is said to be good or evil, according to the planets in configuration with him.

It cannot be too clearly understood that in Astrology, as in Nature, the Sun is the center and the giver of All Life, and as it were, the backbone of the whole system. The Moon is the giver of form; consequently the conjunction or opposition between the Sun and the Moon is malignant on the physical plane, or the same when in parallel of declination. It is most apparent that the relationship of the Sun and Moon very largely determines whether life can be expressed harmoniously or the reverse. If the aspects are friendly, our personality and individuality coöperate and we are not confronted with the many oppositions and conflicting conditions present when the Sun and Moon are unfriendly or in parallel to each other. The author has found, in her extensive research work, that many of the Joan-of-Arcs of the past have been born at the full Moon, and in nearly every instance they have been forced to play the part of the martyr; even if they were not burned at the stake as was the original Joan of Arc, they suffered in some degree in attempting to put over their message.

When the Sun is strongly placed, particularly if his own sign, Leo, is rising, the native has a large, bony, strong body; piercing eye and well-made person; broad, high forehead; light, sandy, curly hair, which will fall out while he is still young, leaving him bald.

If the Sun be well dignified, the disposition is noble, proud, magnanimous and generous, humane and affable, a faithful friend and a generous enemy. It causes one to be overfond of magnificence. If the Sun is ill dignified, the native is foolishly proud or vain, arrogant, troublesome, stubborn, superficial, restless and uncharitable.

Where the Sun is a dominant influence in the life, the will is strong and the character masterful, and the confidence given by self-respect and a cheerful outlook toward life will cause the native to attract much good fortune. He may find it necessary to guard against being too frank and outspoken and to cultivate caution and secretiveness. He must not allow his fondness for display to encourage the "exhibition complex." He is qualified to look into the mysteries of life, to make a study of nature's finer forces, and is given the power to rise above the station to which he is born; others will just naturally turn to him for counsel and assistance, but he must always bear in mind that "there is danger in another's duty." Many holding government positions or those of a purely executive character are born strongly under the influence of this luminary, and it all depends on one's sphere as to the degree and type of success attained.

The native of the Sun is easily led, but can be very stubborn and difficult to manage if he feels that he is being "bossed" or in any way imposed upon.

The Sun represents the constitution, the life principle, and the character of the native. Where the Sun is strong, it does not, of itself, imply more than the vigor of powerful animal life, which enables the native to reap the rewards of favorable planetary aspects and, conversely, to suffer and endure the buffets of adverse influences. Where the Sun is weak, no amount of benefits from the other planets will counteract that affliction. A moment's reflection will disclose the soundness of this proposition, since it is evident that no matter what capacity a man may possess, he will not be able to employ it profitably if his life is too short for him to develop it or too broken by spells of illness for him to prosecute it with that continuity which is necessary to success.

The Sun governs the back, the heart, the arteries and eyes; also the retentive faculty or memory. His diseases are faintings, palpitation of the heart and weak sight. It must ever be borne in mind that the Sun rules organic troubles and the Moon functional disorders.

THE MOON

Just as the Sun stands for the individuality, or Life Force, so the Moon expresses the personality and has rule *over the sign Cancer. The Moon performs her synodical course, or the period between her conjunctions, in twenty-nine days, twelve hours, forty-four minutes. She is a cold, moist, watery, phlegmatic, feminine, nocturnal luminary, and fortunate or otherwise, according to the way she is configurated.

The pure type gives a fair stature, fair, pale complexion, round face, gray, full eyes, short arms, thick hands and feet, smooth, corpulent and phlegmatic body. If combust or approaching to a conjunction of the Sun, the native is likely to be very delicate during the first four years of the life.

The Moon being so easily influenced by every other force, it is of prime importance to investigate everything that may, by any possibility, react upon her. She is more sensitive to the influence of the signs of the zodiac than any of the planets. Indeed, the horoscope of two children, born only a few moments apart, would be to all intents and purposes identical, except for the degree on the Ascendant and the position of the Moon. This slight change would produce the greatest difference in the two lives, owing to the Moon having moved, say from Taurus into Gemini, and the Ascendant from Capricorn to Sagittarius. This is the reason why twins are often so unlike each other.

Not only do the signs themselves affect the Moon tre-

THE MOON

mendously, but also their subdivisions into the decanates. This refinement, however, is too subtle to treat of in this volume.

If the Moon is well aspected, the native will be mild, soft, kind, ingenuous and polite, but timid and thoughtless, unsettled and fond of rambling about, yet peaceful and wholly averse to disputes or trouble of any kind. If ill dignified, he is apt to be idle, stupid, beggarly and fond of drinking.

The Moon governs the brain, the stomach, the bowels, the bladder and the left eye. It also seems to have much influence over the fluids of the body, the saliva, lymphs, glands, and in the case of a woman, the breasts. Her diseases are rheumatism, consumption, colic, vertigo, palsy, apoplexy, scrofula, smallpox, dropsy, and lunacy in its various forms. A badly aspected Moon is one of the most unquestionable threats to the health and is the cause of most of the functional disorders.

If the Moon is the Star of Destiny, it is necessary to consider the curiously double quality of this planet, for its vibrations can either produce extreme purity and devotion to the higher things, or it can make one a slave to the emotions. It is important that people born strongly under its impressionable influence should choose well their associates and adopt some line of life in which discipline is rigid, otherwise they are in danger of being "everything by turns and nothing long." They are extremely sensitive and naturally absorb all kinds of influence, so they must try to discriminate between the true light and the false, between things worth while and those which are useless. There seems to be no middle path for those born under the influence of Luna; she either stands for "Isis, Guardian of the Mysteries," or for the "Mother of Illusion."

Their extreme adaptability can give them charm, make them versatile and help them to take advantage of opportunities or cause them to be simply straws to indicate which way the wind blows. Turner, the artist, Stevenson, Bernard Shaw, Bulwer Lytton, as well as the late J. Pierpont Morgan, were all born when this luminary was in the Eastern sky, proving that its force can be stabilized provided one exercises sufficient will power to overcome the tendency to diffuse one's forces. It can give the *wanderlust* (like Mercury), a desire to change one's occupation or place of residence too frequently, or, if one lives a more restricted life, may cause one simply to enjoy rearranging the furnishings in one's home.

When the Moon is the dominant force, one rarely follows the vocation chosen early in life, although it is often the stepping-stone that leads to one's true work later on. It brings many changes of position and fluctuations of reputation. Such people are not destined to lead an obscure or uneventful life, and should so govern their affairs that any publicity which comes may be conducive to success and happiness. This planet often brings an opportunity to play an important part in public affairs, politics or clubs. As the Moon rules the populace, many who enjoy great popularity and who influence the masses are born strongly under it. In a more personal way, it frequently brings about either scandal or prominence of a better sort, through being connected with distinguished people or those involved in public affairs.

As the Moon governs the home, the women born under its beams make excellent wives and mothers, but, because of their love of novelty, change and sensation, they frequently find it necessary to have a large circle of friends and acquaintances and to be given great freedom; otherwise they chafe and become restless and discontented with their domestic life. The masculine natives of the Moon are more often the "mothers" of the family, as they are likely to attract for wives a masculine type. Unless they cultivate will and grow more self-assertive, they are likely to develop into being "henpecked husbands."

Although the Moon is negative in influence, she is of extreme importance, because she represents the Sensorium. Whatever qualities a man may possess, whatever may pertain to his ego, whatever, in short, goes to make up what a German philosopher would probably call "the him-in-himself"; all these things can only come into manifestation through the medium of the senses. For example, a man might have a genius for music, but it would be only potential unless to some degree he mastered the art. Art consists of two things, genius and technique. No matter how great a man may be in himself, he must have material with which to work and the whole of this material comes to him through the senses; the whole of the possibility of a man's employment of his original gift depends on the accuracy of the information conveyed to him through these channels. Part of the quality of the work of a great artist depends on his outlook on the Universe. There is, for example, a tremendous difference between the conception of women shown by Titian and that exhibited by Burne-Jones, but this difference is the difference in the soul of the two painters; their eyes were equally normal. Taking two other painters, J. J. Henner and Eugène Carrière, we find nothing very individual or remarkable in the point of view of the artist in either case. The pictures of both are rather conventional, but they gain a distinctive character, through the very peculiar formation of their arts. Henner saw everything with a blurred outline; Carrière saw everything in a mist. It is hoped that the distinction between soul and sense is sufficiently obvious. If not, it can be made so by taking an extreme case of a painter who becomes blind. However great he might be, the affliction would put a stop to his painting, just as much as if he were dead.

Regardless of other aspects in the chart, it must be borne in mind that an afflicted Moon cuts one off from the ability to make use of all that might be promised by the remainder of the horoscope, so that, although one may have plenty of corn ready for grinding, no meal can be expected where the mill is not in working order. Just as the Sun, if too badly afflicted, cuts off the life, so that its inherent qualities can never develop, so any affliction of the Moon inhibits these qualities owing to faulty conditions for operation. For a concrete example, take the actual horoscope of a congenital idiot: with the Sun and Moon in trine to Neptune, which should make him spiritual and illuminated; with Jupiter in the seventh house, which should mean a fortunate marriage; and with Venus in conjunction with Mars, which should make him violently passionate. None of these things have developed, because of a Moon which has very bad afflictions, and which afflicted the Sensorium sufficiently to prevent any real impulses from reaching his Ego from without.

In order to attain perfection, all things must work together for good. The intricate machinery and tremendous
engine power of the *Titanic* were of no use to her when
she had a gash in her hull.

The influence of the Moon has been described at length,
partly because, being of swifter motion than the planets,
she forms more aspects and is found to indicate minor
incidents, circumstances, changes, and all actions of
daily life, and is therefore responsible for the mundane
happenings which interest the average man or woman.
We must look to the Sun and the planets for the great,
broad and epoch-making events.

At a later date, the author hopes to consider the Sun
and the planets in an even more exhaustive manner.

MERCURY

Mercury, the "Winged Messenger of the Gods," also known as Hermes, symbolized by the Caduceus (two serpents curled around a staff and looking in a mirror), is never more distant from the Sun than twenty-eight degrees and performs his orbit in eight-seven days, twenty-three hours. He is considered as cold, dry, earthy, masculine or feminine, diurnal or nocturnal, good or bad, lucky or unlucky, according to the planets with which he is configurated, and he has domain over the signs of Gemini and Virgo. Just as mercury, or quicksilver, is wholly dependent on temperature for its rise or fall, so with the temperament of those who have this planet as their Star of Destiny. We may liken it to the pencil, which needs support in order to stand erect and immediately topples when its prop is taken away. Mercury takes on the vibration of whatever sign and house it is placed in or whatever planet it is aspected by.

In the old mythology, Mercury was supposed to take delight in tricking the gods, and to a greater or lesser extent, this planet plays the same part in the affairs of men. He is sometimes referred to as the god of thieves, merchants and lawyers. It naturally depends on whether Mercury is supported by friendly aspects or is ill dignified as to what prompts the motives back of the actions of all those born strongly under its influence. There is said to be honesty even among thieves!

The pure type of the Mercury-born is tall, straight figured, has a deep forehead, straight nose, thin lips, narrow chin, thin, narrow face, long arms, hands, fingers, thighs, legs and feet. If Mercury be oriental, it tends to make the type shorter and of a more sanguine complexion and disposition, but if occidental, more lean, shallow and pallid.

If well dignified, the mind is strong, active and subtle, the memory retentive and the native eager in the pursuit of all kinds of knowledge, a good orator, eloquent, witty and pleasing in disposition. If in conjunction with the Sun, it then makes one more qualified for trade than for learning.

If ill dignified and badly afflicted, the native will be of a mean, shuffling, unprincipled character; even prone to become a liar, thief, talebearer and gambler, void of any kind of useful knowledge or ability, but very conceited.

If Mercury be void of aspect with Saturn, it is very essential for its natives to be concrete in thought, and to avoid making promises without carefully considering just what it will mean to carry them out; also, to visualize as perfectly as possible any new project or personal interview before attempting it. By doing this, they will add fifty per cent to their efficiency, and will avoid embarrassment and expense. They find it difficult to realize that others are not as frank and sincere as themselves, and are therefore in danger of making mistakes through being too trusting and optimistic. It might be wise, therefore, for them not to be too credulous, and even to look askance at those with whom they have business dealings until the latter have proved themselves worthy of their confidence. This type of mind will meet with more success where inspiration, brilliancy of thought or quick action are

MERCURY

called for rather than concentration, method or persistency.

Mercury governs the thought centers of the memory, speech, the nostrils, the hands, feet, lungs and nerves. His diseases are consequently vertigo, apoplexy, convulsions, stammering, lisping, dumbness, stoppage of humor in the nose or head, nervous cough, hoarseness, and gout in the hands and feet. Many mental diseases result from an afflicted Mercury. To quote from Regulus, "This planet has without doubt chief rule of the nerve forces and mental faculties of mankind. . . . When Mercury is strong and well supported at birth, his natives are led to choose, and they become distinguished or eminent in, the intellectual and literary pursuits; but when badly afflicted at birth, the natives are likely to prove mean and unprincipled in character, full of deceit and low cunning, promoters of lies, swindlers, forgers and thieves."

Mercury is the most truly sensitive of all the planets. Venus and the Moon are more easily affected, it is true, but for them a better term is "impressionable." Mercury responds to every impression as does the weathervane, which is a very different thing from the receipt and reflection of every impression. In slightly different language, Mercury is not modified by the signs as are the more passive planets; rather, each excites him to give a special expression of opinion. Mercury is, as we have already indicated, the mind; and while the contents of the mind are determined by the food of the mind, yet different minds deal quite differently with identical foods. It has been well said that thousands of people before Newton saw apples fall from trees, but their only impulse was to eat them. The proper and best influence upon

Mercury is Saturn, and without his steadying hand to hold him in tutorship to a profounder wisdom, Mercury may be frivolous and vain. It is only when Mercury is overpowered by Venus that the mental qualities become subservient and slavish, so that one may say of the native that "he has no mind of his own."

Again, like mercury in the thermometer rising and falling according to temperature, Mercury is still Mercury, and so whatever aspects may exist will not alter the essential character of the planet. The main point to remember is the delicate sensitiveness of the mental ruler and the fact that such impressions as are made on him are not like seals upon wax, but like the rise and fall of the column of quicksilver at every change in the atmosphere.

The desire for knowledge, the longing for change, and the cosmopolitan spirit of those born strongly under this planet will cause them to feel the *wanderlust*, and consequently to take many journeys and make many changes. Their keen intuition and ability to sense what people are about to say often causes them to interrupt in conversation and to change the subject so quickly that at times it is difficult to follow them. It will all depend on their environment and mental development whether their inquisitive nature will cause them to be curious over petty things or those of more importance. They should realize that their restiveness and tendency to be too easily bored is caused by their own mercurial nature and is not the fault of people or circumstances. Lack of decision and a tendency to allow the attention to wander are two of their outstanding characteristics, which may prevent their permanent success.

The mind of these people is never at rest, and for this

reason they require more sleep and fresh air than does the average person. They should guard against being too introspective and should associate as much as possible with spiritually minded people.

The reader is referred to the occupations ascribed to Gemini and Virgo to ascertain those in which the person with Mercury as his Star of Destiny will excel.

VENUS

Aphrodite, or Venus, "Goddess of Love and Beauty," is never above forty-eight degrees distant from the Sun, and has for a period two hundred and twenty-four days and seven hours. She is a feminine, nocturnal, temperate planet, considered as the "Lesser Fortune," and is the Star of Destiny of those born under Taurus or Libra. It may at first sight appear difficult to differentiate between the action of Venus and Jupiter, which is considered the "Greater Fortune." Both represent the expansive and altruistic vibration, but Venus is the handmaiden of the Sun and consequently is attached to the vital force, even as Jupiter is more closely an emanation of the other extreme of the system—Neptune, or the soul. Altruism in Venus, therefore, commonly means love in a quiet, conventional, often selfish sense; her expansiveness is often mere amiability, possibly assumed, in order to gain some end associated with the instinct of self-preservation; and finally, Venus is altogether more personal and, so to speak, more material than Jupiter. The more material a planet is, the more easily it is influenced. The vaster planets are not radically disturbed by zodiacal stress; for example, Uranus, which is more mystic than material, operates in Aries in much the same manner as in Libra, whereas Venus in Gemini operates wholly differently from Venus in Sagittarius.

The pure Venus type is usually elegantly formed and extremely beautiful, with sparkling, dark, hazel eyes,

round, smooth face, light or chestnut hair, dimples in
the cheek or chin, a wandering eye denoting desire, sweet
voice and very engaging address. If the gift of pleasing
be indeed, as Baudelaire says, "the brightest and rarest
of all the benefactions of the fairies," then the native
of Venus is endowed beyond his fellows. It must be remembered, however, that the amount of influence this
planet will contribute towards bestowing all the above
qualities on the native of Venus depends largely on its
position with regard to sign, house and aspect. For instance, if Venus is friendly to the degree on the Ascendant, or to Jupiter, it enhances the beauty, whereas if it
is unfriendly to the Ascendant or to any of the planets,
it tends not only to mar the beauty, but to interfere with
the harmony of the character. Venus, even at her best,
tends to make one pleasure-loving, rather superficial, and
inclined to go along the line of least resistance; unwilling
to make the sacrifices and do the hard plodding that are
essential to great accomplishment. These people are the
dilettantes of the world, dabbling in this, that or the
other thing; with them, more than most people, "necessity
is the mother of invention," and they are frequently too
fortunate to be fortunate.

A badly afflicted Venus will often cause the native to
be profligate, indolent, without shame, and wholly aban-
doned, and open to every species of lust and depravity.
As a rule, however, the natives of this sign are mild, in-
offensive, and their sins are more of omission than commission. It would be well for them to realize that, in the
eyes of the world, "birds of a feather flock together," and
it is therefore most essential that they show discretion in
the selection of their intimates.

VENUS

When Venus is the dominating influence, a great deal of good fortune in the way of favors, kindness and patronage are bestowed on the native; he will have powerful friends who will assist in making his path in life easy and pleasant. It frequently brings friendships or attachments with people in high positions, or even with those holding titles. The element of love will play a very prominent part in the destiny and directly or indirectly be the source of much happiness. Gifts and favors will be showered upon them, as their own love of pleasing naturally attracts kindness and consideration from others.

While persons born strongly under Venus might feel as did Charlotte Cushman, who remarked that, although she had had the world at her feet, she considered her life a failure because she had not enjoyed the devotion of any one man, they must realize that, by contracting a too early marriage, they are in danger of "marrying in haste and repenting at leisure." As a rule, when a marriage is contracted by these people before twenty-eight or thirty, the strong, motivating force is generally due to sex, and, in consequence, when this physical attraction wears off, there is nothing lasting to hold the partnership together. The more mature mind realizes that, in order to have a lasting marriage, there must be first of all real companionship, congeniality of tastes and mental understanding.

As Venus has domain over the signs Taurus and Libra, it would be well to refer to either of these signs for more detailed information regarding this planet.

Venus rules jewels, perfumes, gewgaws and pastel shades in colors, as well as beauty of form, both in human and still life. Consequently, those who have this planet for their Star of Destiny will have a marked tendency to over-expression of ornamentation. It will all depend, however, on their training and environment whether they will select diamonds, emeralds and rubies, have a faint aroma of delicate perfume, and clothe themselves in a refined symphony of color, making a harmonious whole, or adorn themselves with cheap gewgaws, exhale a cloud of musk perfume, wear extremes of colors, and look like a "Christmas tree" generally.

MARS

Mars is the planet which precedes Jupiter in the heavens, and performs his course in one year, three hundred and twenty-one days and thirty-two hours. It is a hot, dry, fiery, choleric, nocturnal, violent planet, and is called the "less-in-fortune," just as Saturn is the "great-in-fortune."

Mars is exalted in twenty-eight degrees of Capricorn and rules the signs Aries and Scorpio. His place in a nativity always stirs to action that which is ruled over by the sign and space of heavens in which it is operating.

The color of Mars is fiery, and when in perigee he appears like a flame or bright spot in the heavens. It is generally observed that at this time the weather is warmer than usual for the season, particularly if Mars happens to be in aspect to Jupiter. Murders are more frequent and of a more atrocious nature, when this planet is nearest the earth; robberies and innumerable calamities mark the whole period when he is retrograde, particularly if Jupiter be near his apogee at the same time, and when Mars retires to his apogee they will gradually diminish. When he is in conjunction with the Sun he tends to produce about the same effects.

The true Martial type gives a strong, well-set, but short body, bony, lean and muscular; complexion red, rather than ruddy; sharp hazel eyes, violent countenance, light brown, flaxen or red hair. When Mars is rising, the hair is often Titian and a scar is frequently to be found on the head or face.

MARS

The disposition, when Mars is well dignified, is fearless, violent, irascible and unsubmitting, fond of war and contention, but in other respects prudent, rational and even generous and magnanimous.

If ill dignified, the native is prone to violence, quarrels, treachery, robbery, and many species of cruelty and wickedness. The real disposition of Mars people is to anger, violence and an apparently eager wish to be in quarrels and mischief. They expect and exact universal submission, and, although often generous and magnanimous, they are rarely kind or sociable. Such dispositions, however, are seldom seen, as the aspects of other planets alter the influence of Mars very materially.

Mars governs the parts of the body ruled by the signs Aries and Scorpio; i. e., the head and face and sympathetically the stomach, kidneys and knees; also the groin, bladder and organs of generation and, sympathetically, the heart, throat and circulation.

The illnesses most menacing to those born under Mars are those of an inflammatory kind and those resulting from wounds or burns, especially if afflicting the face or organs of generation. Tumors, abscesses, and fevers of all kinds, smallpox, toothache, headache, diabetes, strangury, jaundice, measles, shingles, hot eruptions, carbuncles, etc., are also afflictions caused by this planet.

It must be borne in mind that Mars simply represents physical force and that it wholly depends upon the individual whether this is utilized in a constructive way. It can either furnish the native with vitality, courage, "pep" and ambition, or make him unreasonable, intolerant, too hasty in arriving at decisions, cause him to take hazardous or foolhardy risks and an attitude that antagonizes and brings to the surface the most undesirable qualities of those with whom he may be thrown.

If the native of Mars is to be happy, he must be "full of business" and feel that he is conquering and overcoming obstacles. He must avoid taking offense too easily and carrying a "chip on his shoulder."

Mars not only causes fevers and sudden attacks of illness, but also is responsible for the majority of accidents. While it is perhaps more difficult to avert accidents because of the quick and unexpected action of Mars, many accidents can be avoided by maintaining the equilibrium, by keeping the temper even, and by not becoming confused or absent-minded.

Just as Saturn sometimes interferes with accomplishment, through too great caution or introspection, Mars can have much the same effect, through a failure to formulate definite plans; for the actions of the Martian native will be futile unless reflection and visualization precede them. Deeds have no endurance unless they proceed from intelligently directed thought; therefore the native must take time to think out clearly his course of action and not act on impulse. The more he tempers his anger or resentment with mercy, and the more sympathetic and tolerant he is toward the shortcomings of others, the greater will be his success, popularity and happiness. Just as in the affairs of the nation, "the pen is mightier than the sword," so in the life of the individual, counsel and patience are mightier than coercion.

The reader is referred to the occupations listed under the signs Aries and Scorpio, to ascertain those in which the native born with Mars as his dominant influence will excel. Mars rules iron and sharp instruments; therefore metal workers, carpenters, barbers, butchers, as well as soldiers, military men, surgeons, chemists and dentists will all be included in the occupations for which a native of Mars should have the greatest aptitude.

JUPITER

Jupiter is next in orbit to Saturn and is of a beautiful, clear brightness. His period is eleven years, three hundred and fourteen days, twelve hours, twenty minutes and nine seconds. He is considered a hot, moist, airy, sanguine, masculine, beneficent, social planet, the author of temperance, justice and moderation. He is known as the "Greater Fortune" and rules over the fiery, magnetic sign Sagittarius. His exaltation is in fifteen degrees of Cancer.

When a native is born under Jupiter's influence unmodified, he will be tall, well made, erect and free in carriage, handsomely proportioned, robust, ruddy, with a sober, commanding aspect, oval face, high forehead, full gray or blue eyes, soft, thick brown hair, wide chest, long feet, and be firm and frank in his manner. We rarely, however, find a pure Jupiter type.

If Jupiter is well dignified, the person born strongly under his influence will be wise, magnanimous, jovial, affable, just and good, mild in manner, temperate, moderate and inclined to be religious. If ill dignified, the native will be prodigal, indifferent, conceited, careless, of shallow abilities, easily led astray, and a fanatic in religion. He will be too dependent upon luxury, inclined to be lazy and too self-indulgent.

The real character of Jupiter is to make one just, good-natured, a lover of freedom, and to give a disposition that would be most uncomfortable in doing or contriving to do wrong; the native could never, under any circumstances, be what is considered a bad character. His sins are apt to be more of omission than of commission, and he is often his own worst enemy. His prepossessing appearance and frank countenance cause him to enjoy the confidence of others, and everyone feels happy and secure in his society.

When one is strongly under the influence of this beneficent planet, it increases one's chances of success and helps to mitigate any threatening indications from any less favorable aspects. It adds to the executive ability, makes the sympathies broad, the judgment sound, and gives unusual vision.

Jupiter is often called the "eleventh-hour" friend, and he who is born strongly under his rays will always be given the strength to bear any misfortune which may overtake him; he will afterwards realize that the experience he may have gained through the suffering has been worth the cost. "There is no royal road to wisdom." The greatest misfortune in life of the native of Jupiter will come as the result of forcing issues or neglecting to take advantage of the opportunities which come to him naturally.

Jupiter governs the lungs, the liver, the veins, blood and all the viscera; the diseases to which the native of this sign is subject are those which are seated in these parts, or which arise from plethoric habit or corrupt blood. When afflicted at birth, particularly by Saturn, the greatest care is required to keep the liver from being torpid and to be sure that waste substance is freely eliminated.

The sign in which Jupiter is placed and also that portion of the heavens which he occupies at birth, are the

JUPITER

sources from which the greatest good fortune of the native proceeds. The reader is referred to the occupations which are listed under the sign Sagittarius to ascertain those in which the native born with Jupiter as his dominating influence will excel.

As Jupiter is the symbol of wisdom and is the largest planet of our solar system, it very naturally exerts a powerful influence not only over man but over everything in existence. Its effect is, however, very much modified by its position and aspects to other planets. For instance, if Jupiter is in aspect to Mars, it gives tremendous executive ability, but a little more grandeur in the influence than will be the case if in aspect to Saturn, which has a subduing influence and restricts optimism and faith.

Jupiter, in a general classification, may be said to be the precise contrary of Saturn. The latter constricts and conserves; the former expands and spends. The one is egoism, the other altruism. In religious symbolism Saturn is Jehovah. Jupiter is the instinct of creation, of generosity and hospitality and of the religious emotions generally. He represents these qualities in the cosmos as bestowed upon the man and hence, "Good Fortune." His actions, however, with regard to this scope, depend very largely upon its aspects of Neptune and Uranus. Unless these planets lend their more subtle influence, a good Jupiter will be no more than a luck-bringer in business or profession and will contribute toward making the character noble, generous and easy-going.

Three forceful and passionate poets, Shelley, Baudelaire and Swinburne, were born under a conjunction of Mars and Jupiter. They are in a class by themselves with regard to the intensity of their fire. They may not be so truly great as others in some ways, but they exceed them all in this one respect, the devouring brilliance of the flames that consume them.

In the religious world we have Martin Luther, mighty enough to destroy the power that had held Europe enthralled for twelve centuries. We had J. P. Morgan, and still have J. D. Rockefeller, in finance, the most dominant figures of all America's sons, and, on the whole, the most constructive, as marked examples of the effect of Mars and Jupiter in conjunction.

In politics we have Kruger, who built up the Transvaal Republic so powerfully that it was able to defy the armed might of England—a handful of sixty thousand farmers against four hundred thousand soldiers—for three years.

There is also Winston Churchill, one of the most successful politicians that England has produced in the present generation.

The soft delicacy and beauty of Venus combine well with Jupiter's large sight, power and beneficence. Unless these planets are strengthened by a third of more robust and severe character, however, there is a tendency to softness, which, so long as it finds expression in art, is altogether to be praised, but if applied to life may be inadequate to the stern conditions of that ordeal.

The greatest men who have Jupiter and Venus in aspect will always be found to have some stiffening influence in their composition from such a planet as Uranus, Mars, the Sun or Saturn.

These suggestions will be sufficient to give the student a hint of how all the planets must be combined in order to obtain an intelligent means of interpreting the various planets and their aspects.

SATURN

Saturn is the most distant from the Sun of all the planets, with the exception of Uranus and Neptune. He is twenty-nine years, one hundred and sixty-seven days and five hours in finishing his revolution, which is the duration of his year.

Neptune and Uranus being forces so spiritual, and therefore so powerful, it is to them that we look for those qualities which make a man a genius. We must not expect that Saturn alone will produce more than a unique and individual character. An isolated Neptune and Uranus means far more to genius than a Saturn dignified by the whole host of heavens. Such a combination would only be subsidiary to the soul and the personality. Neptune answers the question, "Who is the man?" in the deepest sense of the word. Uranus answers, "Why is the man?" "What is his true purpose?" From Saturn and the other planets we get a reply to this question only, "How will this man fare?"

For this reason the Astrologer will occupy himself, when considering Saturn, more with the action of the planet on the man and less with the action of the planet in the man. Let us, however, consider this lesser phase first. The Saturn portion of any man represents his wisdom; that is to say, his innate and accumulated experience. In this respect, so far as Saturn implies obstacle and delay, he does so because he signifies prudence and caution. His is also the force of isolation and concentration. One is not

SATURN

to confuse the two former qualities with stress of circumstances, or to mistake the latter two for will power. The exact meaning will become clearer as we study the effect of the planet in its various positions.

When, however, we consider Saturn as acting upon the man as part of his environment, we are entitled to consider him as generally unfortunate. He means delay, which is the enemy of the will: "Hope deferred maketh the heart sick." He is the element of Time itself and he is the slow fire that chars the brand of Meleager. He is the force of age and of all that wastes and clogs. It is to be observed that in some respects these two qualities of action are fundamentally opposed. For the same force that conserves a man's energy in his character also opposes to that energy in mundane affairs the restricting stagnation of inertia. The planet is, therefore, a good indicator of the amount of success in life which depends so much on these two factors.

The question then arises, "Is it better to have a strong Saturn, or a weak Saturn which can do little harm?" The answer is easy; weakness is always evil and delays are not always bad in the long run. Greater energy is generated by the crash of two suns than by the rubbing of two dry sticks. It is undeniable that the greater a man is, the greater are the obstacles which he must overcome. A genius without such obstacles is inconceivable. So that the stronger Saturn is, the better. It is, of course, well that his aspects should be favorable, but unquestionably it is not good to find Saturn in his fall or even in his detriment; it requires very good aspects to mitigate so obviously malefic an influence.

The influence of Saturn is most powerful during the

first thirty years of life, and after the sixtieth year. This point may well be carefully noted, since during the most active years of the ordinary mortal's life, the influence of Saturn upon mundane affairs is apt to be materially lessening, which, of course, in some cases, will quite change its significance. Here is another very important significance of Saturn, which should not be overlooked. We have said that Saturn is the force of age and of all that eats and clogs. So also on the physical plane he represents diseases which proceed from cold and obstructions, such as melancholy, agues, epilepsy, black jaundice, toothache, cold defluxions, catarrh, phthisis, atrophy, fistulas, palsy, apoplexy, dropsy and leprosy.

As the sign indicates a specific section of the human body, the position of Saturn in the zodiac will show clearly which portion of the body will be most sensitive to diseases resulting from poor circulation, such as chills or from accumulation of pathogenic bacteria caused by inhibition of the excretory functions. Thus in Aries, Saturn indicates sensitiveness of the head, with danger of catarrhal troubles; consequently deafness is often found with natives in this position. In Taurus, the illness would be apt to be adenoid growths, tonsilitis, diphtheria, or glandular swellings upon the neck. In Gemini, the danger is through bronchial tubes, chest or lungs. From these suggestions, the student will easily determine the threat to the health that is implied by Saturn's affliction in any one of the twelve signs.

When one is born under the sign Capricorn, or Saturn dominates the horoscope, the life will be one of discipline and experience; the motto should be: "No cross, no crown." Those born strongly under Saturn will have much to endure and much to overcome, but the austerity and dignity of Saturn will impart the moral strength to attain great reward. Self-sacrifice and service should be the keynotes of the life, and the sooner the natives understand this, and the more cheerfully they acquiesce, the less will they suffer. If they meet the blows halfway, the impact will be less. They should not let failure dishearten them; they should learn to "rise on stepping-stones of their dead selves to higher things." As they grow older, this attitude will come more easily, and the asperities of life will be materially softened, provided they have manfully battled against circumstances. But if they fail to realize that their thorny path is, after all, just as truly a road to the great goal as one strewn with rose petals, and allow themselves to be beaten in the struggle, they may fall into melancholy and take a jaundiced and bitter view of life. Only when confidence and courage cease to support them can they be considered among those who have failed.

The hermit in his cell may be as much the master of circumstances as the king upon his throne; patience, diligence and austerity bring their reward as surely as those more obvious and shining traits of children of a supposedly happier fortune. Those under Saturn should guard against taking life too seriously and assuming too much responsibility regarding the destiny of others. They should try to select for friends, partners, or business associates those who are naturally more optimistic and less seriously minded than themselves, for with such associates they will be a greater force in the world. The child of Saturn will do well to try to feel, "My wealth consists not in the abundance of my riches, but in the fewness of my wants."

Until those born strongly under Saturn learn to cultivate patience, they are likely to encounter one obstacle after another. Their successes will usually come only after hard work and much delay. They will often endure difficulties rather than make a change, fearing that they may meet disappointment. They are wedded to old customs and conditions, although, in a large way, they are progressive and optimistic. They are also sympathetic with elderly people, and the older they grow the younger they will be in their feelings. They may find it difficult to get comfort from others because of their tendency to live within themselves, although they crave love and sympathy.

The influence of Saturn often inclines persons born strongly under its influence to give up at just the moment when the tide would naturally turn, and unless they overcome their timidity and self-consciousness, they will often have their feelings hurt when nothing of the kind was intended. Because they magnify the importance of obstacles, they will miss opportunities and keep much good from coming to them.

Where Saturn has a strong bearing on the marital relations, or business partners, it tends to cause the partner to be older in years or one who will shirk responsibility but will expect to share equally in the profits. When Saturn is elevated, it invariably causes persons to rise in life and be in a position to wield power; but, if a selfish use is made of their authority, they will meet with downfall. Napoleon is a striking example of how a "Waterloo" may come for those having Saturn in this position. The more secure these people seem to be at any time, the more cautious they must be to make no false step. They must not disregard the best interests of those whose trust they hold. They must avoid being too ambitious for power, enjoy what they have, realizing that no matter what they may attain they will still crave for more kingdoms to conquer. Saturn elevated often denies benefits through parents and usually takes one or both of them out of the iife early.

The self-made man and woman is usually found to be born strongly under Saturn, and their early efforts are generally attended by obstacles and delays. Their success does not usually come until after the age of thirty.

The developed Saturnian is always economical, thrifty and provident, having a natural aversion to wastefulness and all undue extravagance. He will ever strive to succeed through his persistency, perseverance, punctuality and great attention to detail. He has overcome all the tendency to be argumentative, too critical, and has learned the value of silence and the wisdom of meditation. Many men who have either attained great power during their lifetime, or who have been lauded by historians, were born strongly under the beneficent influence of this planet.

Gladstone is a marked example of the Saturn nature at its best. He loved power, he was ambitious, but because of the influence of Jupiter with Saturn, his every act was tempered by mercy, combined with justice. He considered himself a divine instrument and that he was peculiarly adapted to solve the problems of the British Government.

His tremendous self-control and concentration made it possible for him to play the important part he did in the politics of his day.

Many of these same qualities were possessed by Woodrow Wilson, but the fact that Saturn afflicted his Moon was doubtless responsible for his failure to realize his hopes, and his ultimate breakdown which resulted in his death.

The undeveloped Saturnian holds a very narrow outlook on life generally and is not above deception or not unwilling to take advantage of his less fortunate fellows. Until he realizes that we take out of life just in proportion to what we put into it, and that it pays to be honest, even from a selfish standpoint, he is likely to meet with one misfortune after another, as he cannot escape the law of cause and effect. While Saturn may be a corrosive, hindering and retarding influence, it is also a crystallizing, building and constructive force when used unselfishly. Although Saturn gives a strong sense of self-preservation and those under its influence appear selfish, these people can be more intelligently sympathetic with pain and misfortune, because of their own unfortunate experiences, than many who are born under planets that give more noble qualities. We must realize, therefore, that Saturn's good influence bestows qualities which make it possible for us to reach our highest goal, whereas its malign influence tends to encourage carelessness, indifference, suspiciousness, fear, frequently amounting to cowardice, melancholy and laziness. Unless those who are strongly under Saturn transpose this depressing influence to a higher plane, they may sink to such depths and court such misfortune that they may have a very sad and lonely old age, and even end their life by suicide.

The reader is referred to the sign Capricorn for a list of the occupations in which the person with Saturn as his Star of Destiny will excel.

URANUS

Uranus, which is the most distant planet, with the exception of Neptune, was discovered by Sir William Herschel on the thirteenth of March, 1781. It passes through one sign of the zodiac in about seven years, and completes its circuit around the Sun in eighty-four years and twenty-seven days with a velocity of 250 miles per minute.

This planet having been known to astrologers only one hundred and forty-six years, we have no record from the Ancients as to its nature, its electric or magnetic emanations or its extraordinary influence on human life. Modern astrologers, however, have determined quite definitely its general nature and major attributes.

Considering how baffling this lack of knowledge concerning Uranus (and also Neptune) was in former times, and how many difficulties must have arisen on this account in making any astrological calculations, it is not surprising that all students of this science in the past met numerous difficulties; and yet there are people so extremely unreasonable as to require from the astrologer what they demand from no one else—infallibility.

This occult, revolutionary, unconventional planet, which has its greatest influence in the sign Aquarius, stands for the interior, subconscious, magical Will of persons born strongly under its influence. At one time the native may be in complete harmony with his surroundings and he will naturally describe himself as "lucky." At another time he will be entirely out of unison and consider himself as one of the unfortunate ones. Either view is, of course, unintelligent and unworthy of a philosopher. There is, however, no doubt that Uranus, more than any other planet, produces the most extraordinary vicissitudes. Sometimes he may occasion death, but not often by disease; his force is too vital, and one might almost say too spectacular, to bring about anything so banal as the mere fall of the curtain. Where he does bring death, it is usually of a catastrophic and tragic kind, but for determining the time when critical events in the career will occur and the effects thereof, Uranus has no equal among the planets. The influence of Neptune is so subtle and obscure that, even though it be more truly profound, it does not affect the destiny in the same way. The tragedies of the soul are usually invisible except to the eye of the poet, philosopher and mystic.

Both Uranus and Neptune might be considered as outposts, moving in an opposite direction, and therefore do not really belong to our solar system in the effect they have on humanity. For this reason, both Uranians and Neptunians are usually going in an opposite direction from the masses, both in thought and action. By the time any custom, fashion or idea has become popular, they have outgrown it or lost interest in it. The other planets treated of in the preceding chapters are much more mechanical and calculable in their actions. Perhaps it would be useful, as an explanation of certain difficulties in interpreting the action of the two greater planets (Uranus and Neptune), to suggest that they are not so simple and constant in their movements as are the others. It is quite conceivable that, from time to time, they receive new and varying influxes of the force from the higher

URANUS

planes, or from planets not yet discovered; and, if so, however far we may advance in the science of Astrology, pure and simple, there would always be a possibility of our calculations being upset by some such cause and disturbance. This hypothesis is, to a certain extent, supported by the already discovered characteristics of both these planets. In such cases, there is a peculiar uncertainty about their action which we, living as we do, mostly upon the material plane and upon a planet comparatively close to the Sun, are apt to call tricky, or at least unaccountable.

The vibrations of Uranus transcend the ordinary dimensions of length, breadth and thickness, and go over into what is known as the fourth dimension. This is often called the Planet of Destiny and indicates that, when persons are born strongly under its influence, Fate plays a large part in their existence; it gives an individuality which has something of the divine in it. Few but the Uranian and Neptunian are able to understand those marvelous lines of Baudelaire's, "I am the wound and the steel, I am the buffet and the ear, I am the limbs and I am the wheel, Victim and Executioner." If Uranians are children of Fate, they are also children of Opportunity; therefore, opportunism is indicated as their best strategy —they have the ability to be "all things to all men." Freedom is essential to these people—they cannot work in harness; they will rebel at what appears to them to be the stupidity of others, and they should use the wisdom of the serpent to avoid expressing their thoughts in this respect too freely.

Uranians are more or less ducklings in a brood of chickens, just as Neptunians are pheasants in a barnyard.

Their family and their friends may consider them most impractical, too readily resentful of opposition, and so out of tune with the commonplace affairs of life that it is difficult or impossible to coöperate harmoniously with the average mortal.

The action of Uranus is sudden and unexpected, at one time conferring great material benefits, when least expected, and again causing too great independence, too great impatience, and so opposing routine or prescribed methods as to court the opposition and misunderstanding of associates. Until Uranians learn to value the law of non-resistance and to realize that nothing happens by chance, they will experience most unusual happenings, suffer from estrangements, and be considered odd or even eccentric. The moods of Uranus change so rapidly and are so different at times, that those born strongly under its influence may find it difficult either to be understood or to understand themselves. They should make the most of each opportunity and live one day at a time, forming few definite plans too far ahead. This caution will save them much nervous strain and unnecessary disappointments. The mission of this planet is to prepare mankind for an advanced state of spiritual knowledge and to make people more impersonal and less possessive in their attitude toward life. Its influence can be reactionary, if one lives in an uncongenial atmosphere or with people who are too materialistic. Like the X-ray, Uranians penetrate and understand what appears to the ordinary individual to be impossible.

The occupations or avocations which seem in sympathy with this strange planet are progressive, inventive, exploring, and of a humanitarian nature. The influence of

Uranus is the least personal, and the most universal in the zodiac; consequently any endeavor for the betterment of humanity is favored by those who are strongly responsive to its vibration.

Uranus does not seem to favor occupations for which one gets a stated income or to help one accumulate wealth; for this reason, when one who is under its influence has a "run of luck," a wise provision should be made for less favorable periods. This explains why any money made during a good aspect of this planet is rarely saved; the same tide that brings it in is almost sure to carry it away; and the successful operator, even in Wall Street, should bear this law in mind. The moment he begins to lose should be a sign that the tide has changed, and, for a time, inaction is the only safe course.

Many astrologers, scientific research workers, investors, and those who make a study of the undiscovered, are born strongly under the influence of this planet. Uranus stands for the higher octave of Mercury, and, in order to court its most favorable vibrations, it is essential to be impersonal, unprejudiced and without any ulterior motive. Too often the force of this mighty planet becomes very destructive and malefic, because it no longer operates on the universal plane, having become personal and self-interested. Like the sign Aquarius, over which it rules, it is the planet of Universal Brotherhood, and it is essential that it remain on this lofty pinnacle.

Highly developed natures under Uranus aim at great and noble things, are fond of philosophical studies, have strong intuition, and desire to rise above the material. They are romantic, unsettled, and prophetic, not only as regards personal matters, but also in national and race questions. In short, they are extraordinary characters.

Unless one understands the finer force of nature, the influence of Uranus is apt to make one eccentric, abrupt and brusque in manner, altogether out of tune with every-day people and affairs, and, if under restraint, reckless, headstrong, and even rebellious, with a great desire for rule and authority.

Uranus is the controlling planet in governmental bodies, large corporations, and public enterprises. During recent years, our nation has been plunged into political unrest, commercial anxiety, and business chaos, because of the influence of this mystical planet. When Uranus is seriously afflicted, mundanely, it may cause strikes, rioting, rebellion, resistance to authority, inharmony between master and man, or superior or inferior, as well as explosions and accidents.

It seems probable, however, that Uranus has other and more important national functions to perform than these. Uranus is somewhat aristocratic in its tendencies, or at least autocratic and also individualistic, whereas Neptune appears rather to be democratic and socialistic. Looked at in this way, it should be noted that, during the years when Uranus was in the sign Scorpio, Morocco, ruled by this sign, was the scene of frequent mutations, attended by bloodshed; that Norway, also ruled by Scorpio, shook itself free from Sweden (ruled by Aquarius, a sign in which Uranus has its greatest power) and is now a separate kingdom, and lastly, that the Transvaal, the scene of the Boer War, was also ruled by Scorpio.

Uranus rules the nervous system and, when afflicted, has a very malign influence upon the cerebrospinal axis of man, and often superinduces such strange symptoms of a psychic character that the regular practitioner will find them difficult to diagnose or cure.

In the few years during which Uranus has been under observation, it has been found that, if afflicted, it is the source of incurable organic diseases, collapse of fortune, and individual as well as national destruction. It is demonstrable that, in inharmonious nativities, evil Uranian influences, both rough transits and directions, have brought about headlong destruction from bad habits, misdirected affections, illicit connections before or after legal marriage, according to the signification of the place or radical affliction in the horoscope.

It is necessary that the appetites and passions be under subjection to the will, that every step be taken in obedience to enlightened reason, and that the mind rest in the repose of an unfaltering trust in the Divine Spirit, if the evil vibrations of Uranus, when threatening the bodily or mental health (which are in effect one), are to be overcome.

Where Uranus operates strongly in a horoscope in the marital relation, its effects are generally very disastrous. The great danger seems to lie in the fact that Uranus gives so much individuality to the character that it is not easy for a husband or wife to merge the life in that of the other. A strong safeguard would be for each party to have a definite interest in life, leaving the other free of conventional restrictions, because of absolutely mutual confidence.

Where the Uranian force operates on the material plane, it causes its natives to be overconfident, too ambitious and inclined to go into hazardous undertakings and schemes which often result in heavy and sudden losses, unless great caution and the best of judgment are exercised. These people are likely to be very enthusiastic about a thing to-day, but to-morrow absolutely indifferent; so they should realize that this variation in feeling is due to the influence of this strange planet. They should not make sudden changes or depart from legitimate activity without serious thought, otherwise they will certainly have strange vicissitudes of fortune and great ups and downs in their lives.

Uranus is often termed the "emancipator" and brings about some new current of thought, possibly of a very original character. It increases intuition, stimulates the telepathic faculties and elevates the mind to a higher state of consciousness, particularly during sleep. Those born strongly under the influence of this planet may find that problems which have perplexed them before retiring will solve themselves by morning. A good rule to follow when undecided will be to concentrate without worry on the subject in question, while falling asleep, and then trust to the thoughts which come upon awaking.

Uranus being very slow, as well as irregular in motion, is stimulated to activity only about once in twenty-one years, and this always marks an epoch in the life. Just as it is the herald of movements that are in advance of the times, so with the individual, it stirs to activity departments of the mind as yet not awakened, and pushes out one's boundaries into the unknown beyond anything experienced hitherto. At such times, those who come under its sway should not set their will against the Will of the Universe, but rather make the most of the opportunities which Fate presents, and not be surprised if they almost attain many things which, at the last moment, elude them. Uranus is perfectly in accord with the higher natural law, and appears to be a violator of man-made laws only in the eyes of those conventional souls who have not the courage of their convictions or who cannot think independently.

Uranus gives tremendous occult force which, if used constructively, can make Uranian natives powers in their own sphere and enable them to be the vehicles through which comes a message to mankind. That message may be uttered in terms of art, science or philosophy. The artist who understands the law of vibration in relation to color, the physician who looks beyond ordinary physical symptoms for the causes of disease, the scientist who is willing to admit that there may still be new theories that will explode the old and accepted, the chemist who is still looking for the "Philosopher's Stone" and who realizes that the Ancients had a deeper motive than simply changing base metal into pure gold, the inventor who is more interested in discovering something to save life than something to save labor, the astrologer who is more interested in the spiritual interpretation of the message of the stars than in predicting events, and the preacher who is also a teacher and priest, are all true children of Uranus. It is safe to predict that, in the not-too-distant future, we shall see a financier whose motive for amassing a huge fortune will be that he may give it to a great human cause, and a statesman who is all that that word implies. From an astrological point of view, it will only be *then* that we shall reach the culminating point in which discord, inharmony, anxiety, and commercial and political chaos will no longer hold sway. The masses will then come

more and more into their own, through the evolution of
humanitarian impulses, which will induce realization of
the fact that in the welfare of each lies the happiness and
security of all. "Each for all and all for each" will become
less of a mere platitude and more of a conscious realization.

The occupations in which a native of Aquarius is likely
to excel are those that appeal most strongly to one whose
Star of Destiny is Uranus.

NEPTUNE

Neptune is so vast, so slow, so mystical, that, in order to study his action in the zodiac, we shall do best to consider him not so much as an influence on individuals but rather as an indication of the tendency of the period, a barometer of the Zeitgeist, the spirit of the times.

Neptune requires about one-eighth of a generation to move through a single sign. To give account of his effects would be to write the history of the world. One can gauge him to some extent by consideration of comparatively recent events. Practical matters are usually directed by men of between forty-five and fifty-five; and the consensus of their influence may be divined from the place of Neptune at their birth.

Thus, the Revolution of 1848 was brought about by men influenced by Neptune in Libra—they struggled for freedom and justice, but their policy lacked virility and directness. Similarly, the French Revolution was begun by people influenced by Neptune in Leo, and prepared for by people with that planet in Cancer and Gemini. Cromwell's Neptune was in Leo. The late Great War was doubtless due to the influence of Neptune in Aries; and the rebuilding of civilization is now falling upon those laborious and initiated Free Masons for whom Neptune works through Taurus.

The scientific advance of the nineteenth century was due to pioneers stimulated by Neptune in Capricorn; and the fruit of their labors was gathered by men born under Neptune in Aquarius. Neptune was in Pisces, influencing

NEPTUNE

the artistic, psychic decadent generation of the nineties. Times when skeptical thought attacks tradition by purely intellectual methods and makes constructive work possible are those influenced by Neptune in Gemini. Immanuel Kant, who destroyed the old philosophy, Voltaire, who destroyed the old religion, and their contemporaries were of such a generation.

Neptune being the planet of Spirit, is always revolutionary. Forever he increaseth new life, the material varying according to the signs through which he works. We may, therefore, tabulate very simply Neptune's whole zodiacal course as follows:

Aries—Political upheaval of a military character. (Julius Cæsar—Religious revolution headed by initiates of the Gnosis, the founders of Free Masonry.)

Taurus—Constructive program of civilization.

Gemini—Great increase in learning. Reaction against previous sign. More intellectuality of thought. (Shakespeare.)

Cancer—Principally digestion of previous more active signs.

Leo—Revolutions of a national character, constructive in type. (Christ, Robespierre, Cromwell.)

Virgo—Great lawgivers. Completion of previous sign. (Napoleon—Declaration of Independence.)

Libra—Political upheaval of the people led by humanitarians. (Shelley.)

Scorpio—Skeptical and realistic thought. Realization of previous influences. (Kant, Erasmus, Albrecht Dürer, Michael Angelo.)

Sagittarius—Artistic revival. New religious ideas. (Wagner, Luther.)

Capricorn—Materialistic, scientific, skeptical thought. (H. Spencer, Huxley, Pasteur, Blavatsky.)

Aquarius—Scientific thought applied. (Edison.)

Pisces—Absorption of and reaction against last signs. Revival of art, religion, and the like in a weak and deciduous form. (Oscar Wilde, Swedenborg.)

INFLUENCE OF NEPTUNE ON THE INDIVIDUAL

Neptune, the outermost planet of our solar system, was discovered by Adams of Cambridge (1845) and by Leverrier of Paris (1846). This discovery is considered the most triumphant achievement of mathematical astronomy, as both of these men determined its position from no other data than certain perturbations of Uranus. It makes a revolution around the Sun in one hundred and sixty-four years, at a velocity of about three and one-half miles per second.

Neptune, this mystic, romantic, irresponsible planet, the hermit of the solar system, might be considered the planet of the fourth dimension to an even greater degree than Uranus. It represents the forces of nature too undifferentiated to be understood by the average mortal, or to be utilized on the material, practical plane. One born strongly under its influence is generally possessed of a highly organized nervous system and most acute sensibilities, a very fascinating and elusive magnetism, and such a one exerts a peculiar influence over others. People who seem too obvious, those who say just what they mean, or mean just what they say, soon bore the Neptunian. They seem to anticipate the thoughts of others before expressed, but must endeavor to hide their impa-

tience. Unless they allow their companions an opportunity
to finish their line of thought, it causes confusion and is
likely to end in misunderstanding. Because of their ability
to broadcast so far and to visualize the complete picture,
persons who are born strongly under Neptune can fore-
see the outcome of events and are rarely surprised at
whatever may happen. They must overcome their tendency to be too vague on the practical details of a plan,
and should depend on someone less creative and more
objective to do this for them; otherwise, they will undertake impossible tasks and be accused of being visionary
or impractical.

The Neptunian influence on the physical plane is
strangely disorganizing, often manifesting itself in obscure nervous troubles and heart complications. These
appear to be valvular, but the source, in reality, is purely
nervous and psychic. Its diseases are always of an unusual kind; sometimes of a slow wasting nature, and
sometimes just the opposite. Under great excitement, this
influence produces psycho-hysteria. Neptune does, however, give very young arteries, and generally causes one
to be older in youth and younger after middle life. It
causes those born strongly under its influence to hear, see
and feel things which are not registered by those less
sensitively organized. It gives a love of experience and
the ability to get the meat out of the coconut, while the
average mortal is attempting to crack its shell.

The Neptunian influence causes people to be so remote from the average individual that they may feel
themselves somewhat solitary figures among their contemporaries. They have a hunger for love, sympathy and
happiness, but not the same as the craving of the or-

dinary mortal. They realize so clearly that "all the world is a stage and all the men and women merely players" that they find it difficult to take life seriously. It is always present to them—at least, subconsciously—that the curtain will soon ring down:

> "The cloud-capp'd towers, the gorgeous palaces,
> The solemn temples, the great globe itself,
> Yea, all which it inherit, shall dissolve;
> And, like this insubstantial pageant faded,
> Leave not a rack behind: We are such stuff
> As dreams are made on, and our little life
> Is rounded with a sleep. . . ."

This planet being the ruler of the sign Pisces, it necessarily follows that the description of the sign and the planet must be read in combination, in order to get a complete understanding of the character and its possibilities. Many psychics are born under powerful Neptunian influence, and to this vibration may be attributed second sight, warning dreams, clairaudience, clairvoyance, and similar phenomena.

It is usually easy to recognize persons born strongly under the influence of Neptune. Even at the first glance, it is apparent that they are not as others. The impression they convey is difficult to define, but it is unmistakable. They seem, in some way, peculiar, strongly individual, but not with any common kind of strength. The eyes have a peculiar magnetic quality, the effect of which is often weird and startling. They are often coldly penetrating, and when the type is undeveloped they are frequently shifty and secretive, with a slight hint of perversity or madness in them. So characteristic is this appearance that only a few observations of people who possess it are necessary to familiarize the student with it. This indication from the eyes is often especially valuable when the hour of birth is not accurately known; for, if Neptune happened to be rising, there can be no possible doubt, and the figure may then be cast for the appropriate hour with perfect confidence.

The moral and mental characteristics of people with Neptune dominant are singular and subtle. The action of Neptune, taking place as it does, in the remotest fastnesses of the soul, causes deep-seated upheavals of the personality. Nothing so upsets the normal indications drawn from the sign and ruler as the presence of Neptune. It does not modify them; it introduces an entirely new influence from a finer and more powerful plane. The first result of the Neptune influence is that the person often betrays a contradictoriness, a whimsicality, a perversion, or introduces some fantastic element of mockery or masquerade. In some natures, this will be very profound and far-reaching; in others, shallow, even superficial.

This question must be determined by consideration of the relative strength of Neptune, essential or accidental, to the rising sign, its ruler, and in multitude of aspects it forms with the Sun, Moon and planets. We may, however, mention a few of the practical observations which have been made, especially characteristic of Neptune's effect. In younger souls, which have not freed themselves even partially from the gross influence of the physical, a yearning of the spirit, that Neptune represents, is likely to manifest itself in seeking after strange gods. The use or abuse of drugs which break down the limitations of time and space and seem to develop the individual, though only temporarily, at the expense of his environment, is frequent. For exactly the same reason, abnormal vices are resorted to by the Neptunian. The common satisfactions of life appear to him banal—he has not yet developed that mastery of his soul which brings the seeker after the hidden mysteries of life back to sanity. The advanced soul knows that life is a dream, but he knows also that it is a divine dream. He no longer mixes the planes. In the beginning of his search, inspired by a sense of dissatisfaction, he imagines quite naturally that, by reversing the established order of things which he has decided to be bad, he will attain to good. Indeed, this state of thought is probably necessary for everybody at some time or other. However, by following this path, he comes to the conclusion that after all, things are no better upside down than they were the right way up. He will then sensibly enough take the easiest way—he will become content with life, no longer in the unthinking way which is characteristic of the lower animals, but through his having gained a divine wisdom. No doubt, he and everyone else in the world are but players on the stage, shadows in a dream, but he sees also that in this play, he should make the best of his part. In his dream, he should not invoke the powers of the nightmare.

For these reasons, as well as because of our own understanding of the divine tolerance which pours the smiles of the Sun and the tears of the rain alike upon the just and the unjust, we must not blame younger Neptunians for these peculiarities which seem to our elder judgment to be destroying his soul. In extreme cases, it may be necessary that the soul should be allowed to attack itself, for only through destruction lies redemption. Our attitude, therefore, should be sympathetic. We should endeavor to understand these wonderful impulses. It will be useless for us to endeavor to suppress them. They are divinely ordered, but we may advise the control of these passions, where they seem to us to be doing more harm than good. It will be well to remember that the source from which they spring is irrepressible. It comes from depths which are the very seat of character, and any attempts to deal harshly with them are foreordained to prove futile. Our efforts would only excite opposition, and that opposition would be justified, for to our worldly wisdom it would array in battle the army of the All-wise Providence.

There is one characteristic of the native of Neptune which is excessively annoying to the person possessing it. This has been described by Edgar Allan Poe in his story, "The Imp of the Perverse." The mind of the individual may be perfectly made up, his judgment may be sound and his desire unhampered, but at the moment of putting his will into execution, he balks. Ibsen has pictured the same quality in his description of "Troll in Us," but perhaps the clearest and most succinct of all the accounts of this curious quality is given by St. Paul in his Epistle to the Romans.

This is not to be confused with the war of the flesh against the spirit, which takes place constantly in all of us, or with doubt, hesitation, vacillation and a conflict of impulses, or the difficulty in striking a balance of judgment. It is pure perversity.

The quality of aspiration to things beyond the limits of life is common to all Neptunians, and in elder souls which have passed through the purifying fires, in those sane minds which possess knowledge and understanding of the Cosmos and have learned how to deal with passion and emotions, it assumes the less devastating form. There is still the determination to attain to the Bournless Beyond, but the method which appeals is carefully reasoned instead of being instinctive, and common sense takes care that health, reason, fortune or social relations are not endangered. A person thus gifted may study strange philosophies and sciences, but he will not go astray in them; will devote himself during his spare time to prayer and meditation, but will not become a fanatic; will adopt mystical practices which might appear entirely foolish to the average man, but will probably keep his own counsel in the matter.

The gamut of Neptune's influence is thus seen to extend from the darkest abyss of Hell to the crown of Heaven's everlasting, shining mountains, but the underlying impulse is always the same. It is the hunger for the Infinite. The drug fiend, the psychopath, the lunatic and the saint are all members of the same family, and that which divides them is not the result of any differentiation in the soul, but rather in the degree of knowledge and experience. It is his mentality which separates St. Francis of Assisi from the Marquis de Sade; and, in judging any particular horoscope, the characterizations of a native must be determined by those houses and planets which govern the mind.

To recount a few of the less important Neptunian qualities, the same impulse which causes an Ignatius Loyola, Gilles d'Rais, an Indian Yogi, or a Napoleon to determine to be something extraordinary makes unpractical persons, with less sense of actuality, determine to pretend to be something extraordinary; hence, we find people who assume titles to which they have no right, who love to wear extraordinary clothes, who smother themselves in exotic perfumes, or who make up their faces to a fantastic degree. This idea may again express itself in a different kind of action; such, for example, as a love of intrigue, of playing practical jokes, of hoaxing their friends or the public, or of playing some part upon the stage of life, which is not altogether natural. Better balanced persons will probably manifest this tendency by actually going on the stage, where the impulse finds a legitimate and accepted expression.

In all these matters, it is rare to find a true creative tendency. Mimicry and imitation are the rule, but there is usually a certain spice or originality invoked. As an example of a whole period under Neptunian influence, we may cite the time of Molière, when everybody masqueraded. It was not merely the valets and maids who pretended to be their masters and mistresses, but the nobles themselves could not conduct the most ordinary flirtation without pretending to be shepherds and shepherdesses of the time of Virgil. It has been necessary to elaborate on this masquerading quality of Neptune, lest the student confound it with the coarseness, quite inexcusable, of snobbery.

The Neptunian is usually a somewhat irresponsible person. He is very inconstant and his moral character appears weak, because it is based on what seems mere impulse or whim, rather than on judgment, inspired by self-interest. He usually knows that he is making himself ridiculous by his antics, but the elfishness of his spirit leads him to continue with them, and a hint of opposition will often cause him to exaggerate the errors of which his friends complain. Neptune also gives a disposition to wander, a discontent with the place where one happens to be. We would refer the reader to Baudelaire's prose poem, "Anywhere, anywhere, out of the world," which gives the most eloquent picture of the spirit of which we are speaking.

It follows from all that has been said that the purely Neptunian type lives almost entirely in and through the psychic nervous system. Very often his body is frail, delicate and flower-like, but the soul in him burns strong and may easily wear out the bodily scabbard. At any time when the physical functions are depressed and the nerves cannot obtain that supernormal energy which they so insistently demand, the result is likely to be hysteria and nervous breakdown. Persons who suffer in this way are perhaps fortunate, for the warnings of nature in such cases are insistent and demand absolute rest and quiet. Where the body is stronger and responds with more elasticity to the extravagance of the nervous system, the result is likely to be worse; for, then, insidious and often incurable disease obtains a hold before the patient is aware of it. Such troubles as locomotor ataxia, general paralysis of the insane, softening of the brain and other obscure lesions may perhaps be caused, in part, by this influence. Worry and all its attendant illness are very often Neptunian in origin, as are also certain other wasting diseases whose nervous origin is not yet understood by the less advanced schools of orthodox medicine.

PART III

TABLE OF ASCENDANTS

TABLE OF ASCENDANTS AND HOW TO USE THEM

In the following table will be found the rising sign (Ascendant) and its approximate degree for each hour of every fourth day in the year. The rising sign for the intervening days and any fraction of an hour may be found by simple proportion. This table may be used for any place having about 41 degrees North latitude; it has been computed from Dalton's "Spherical Basis of Astrology."

The degree of the rising sign or Ascendant for the hours from 1 A. M. to noon are given in the left-hand column, and from 1 P. M. to midnight in the right-hand column.

If the birth of the person whose Ascendant is desired took place since the spring of 1916, at which period Daylight Saving Time was instituted, it is necessary to subtract one hour from clock time, provided Daylight Saving Time was operating in the locality where the birth took place. The short list given below is correct for England, France and Belgium, as these countries have universal Daylight Saving Time. Unfortunately, in the United States and Canada, Daylight Saving Time is *not* universal, and therefore it will be necessary to ascertain definitely whether the locality has adopted this summer time.

Legal Dates (in each case 2 A. M.)

1916.	May 21 to October 1.
1917.	April 8 to September 17.
1918.	March 24 to September 30.
1919.	March 30 to September 29.
1920.	March 28 to October 25.
1921.	April 3 to October 3.
1922.	March 26 to October 8.
1923.	April 22 to September 16.
1924.	April 13 to September 21.
1925.	April 19 to October 4.
1926.	April 18 to September 19.
1927.	April 10 to October 2.

The characteristics and influence of the signs and their corresponding ruling planets have been comprehensively dwelt upon in Part I and Part II of this book. At the beginning of Part I are tabulated the twelve signs of the zodiac, their symbols and ruling planets, for quick reference.

JANUARY —1—

A. M.					P. M.				
1 o'clock	20°	of	Libra	♎	1 o'clock	11°	of	Taurus	♉
2 "	1	"	Scorpio	♏	2 "	1	"	Gemini	♊
3 "	13	"	Scorpio	♏	3 "	17	"	Gemini	♊
4 "	25	"	Scorpio	♏	4 "	2	"	Cancer	♋
5 "	7	"	Sagittarius	♐	5 "	15	"	Cancer	♋
6 "	19	"	Sagittarius	♐	6 "	27	"	Cancer	♋
7 "	2	"	Capricorn	♑	7 "	9	"	Leo	♌
8 "	18	"	Capricorn	♑	8 "	21	"	Leo	♌
9 "	6	"	Aquarius	♒	9 "	2	"	Virgo	♍
10 "	27	"	Aquarius	♒	10 "	14	"	Virgo	♍
11 "	22	"	Pisces	♓	11 "	26	"	Virgo	♍
12 Noon	16	"	Aries	♈	12 Midnight	8	"	Libra	♎

JANUARY —5—

A. M.					P. M.				
1 o'clock	23°	of	Libra	♎	1 o'clock	16°	of	Taurus	♉
2 "	5	"	Scorpio	♏	2 "	6	"	Gemini	♊
3 "	16	"	Scorpio	♏	3 "	21	"	Gemini	♊
4 "	28	"	Scorpio	♏	4 "	5	"	Cancer	♋
5 "	10	"	Sagittarius	♐	5 "	18	"	Cancer	♋
6 "	23	"	Sagittarius	♐	6 "	0	"	Leo	♌
7 "	7	"	Capricorn	♑	7 "	12	"	Leo	♌
8 "	22	"	Capricorn	♑	8 "	24	"	Leo	♌
9 "	11	"	Aquarius	♒	9 "	6	"	Virgo	♍
10 "	4	"	Pisces	♓	10 "	18	"	Virgo	♍
11 "	29	"	Pisces	♓	11 "	29	"	Virgo	♍
12 Noon	24	"	Aries	♈	12 Midnight	11	"	Libra	♎

JANUARY —9—

A. M.					P. M.				
1 o'clock	26°	of	Libra	♎	1 o'clock	22°	of	Taurus	♉
2 "	8	"	Scorpio	♏	2 "	10	"	Gemini	♊
3 "	19	"	Scorpio	♏	3 "	25	"	Gemini	♊
4 "	1	"	Sagittarius	♐	4 "	8	"	Cancer	♋
5 "	14	"	Sagittarius	♐	5 "	21	"	Cancer	♋
6 "	26	"	Sagittarius	♐	6 "	3	"	Leo	♌
7 "	11	"	Capricorn	♑	7 "	15	"	Leo	♌
8 "	27	"	Capricorn	♑	8 "	27	"	Leo	♌
9 "	17	"	Aquarius	♒	9 "	8	"	Virgo	♍
10 "	9	"	Pisces	♓	10 "	20	"	Virgo	♍
11 "	5	"	Aries	♈	11 "	2	"	Libra	♎
12 Noon	1	"	Taurus	♉	12 Midnight	14	"	Libra	♎

JANUARY —13—

A. M.					P. M.				
1 o'clock	29°	of	Libra	♎	1 o'clock	27°	of	Taurus	♉
2 "	11	"	Scorpio	♏	2 "	14	"	Gemini	♊
3 "	23	"	Scorpio	♏	3 "	29	"	Gemini	♊
4 "	5	"	Sagittarius	♐	4 "	12	"	Cancer	♋
5 "	17	"	Sagittarius	♐	5 "	24	"	Cancer	♋

A. M.					P. M.				
6 o'clock	0°	of	Capricorn	♑	6 o'clock	7°	of	Leo	♌
7 "	15	"	Capricorn	♑	7 "	18	"	Leo	♌
8 "	2	"	Aquarius	♒	8 "	0	"	Virgo	♍
9 "	22	"	Aquarius	♒	9 "	12	"	Virgo	♍
10 "	16	"	Pisces	♓	10 "	24	"	Virgo	♍
11 "	13	"	Aries	♈	11 "	6	"	Libra	♎
12 Noon	7	"	Taurus	♉	12 Midnight	18	"	Libra	♎

JANUARY —17—

A. M.					P. M.				
1 o'clock	2°	of	Scorpio	♏	1 o'clock	2°	of	Gemini	♊
2 "	14	"	Scorpio	♏	2 "	18	"	Gemini	♊
3 "	26	"	Scorpio	♏	3 "	3	"	Cancer	♋
4 "	8	"	Sagittarius	♐	4 "	15	"	Cancer	♋
5 "	20	"	Sagittarius	♐	5 "	28	"	Cancer	♋
6 "	4	"	Capricorn	♑	6 "	10	"	Leo	♌
7 "	19	"	Capricorn	♑	7 "	21	"	Leo	♌
8 "	7	"	Aquarius	♒	8 "	3	"	Virgo	♍
9 "	29	"	Aquarius	♒	9 "	15	"	Virgo	♍
10 "	24	"	Pisces	♓	10 "	27	"	Virgo	♍
11 "	20	"	Aries	♈	11 "	9	"	Libra	♎
12 Noon	13	"	Taurus	♉	12 Midnight	21	"	Libra	♎

JANUARY —21—

A. M.					P. M.				
1 o'clock	5°	of	Scorpio	♏	1 o'clock	7°	of	Gemini	♊
2 "	17	"	Scorpio	♏	2 "	22	"	Gemini	♊
3 "	29	"	Scorpio	♏	3 "	6	"	Cancer	♋
4 "	11	"	Sagittarius	♐	4 "	19	"	Cancer	♋
5 "	24	"	Sagittarius	♐	5 "	1	"	Leo	♌
6 "	7	"	Capricorn	♑	6 "	12	"	Leo	♌
7 "	23	"	Capricorn	♑	7 "	24	"	Leo	♌
8 "	12	"	Aquarius	♒	8 "	6	"	Virgo	♍
9 "	5	"	Pisces	♓	9 "	18	"	Virgo	♍
10 "	0	"	Aries	♈	10 "	0	"	Libra	♎
11 "	25	"	Aries	♈	11 "	12	"	Libra	♎
12 Noon	18	"	Taurus	♉	12 Midnight	24	"	Libra	♎

JANUARY —25—

A. M.				P. M.			
1 o'clock	8° of	Scorpio	♏	1 o'clock	11° of	Gemini	♊
2 "	20 "	Scorpio	♏	2 "	26 "	Gemini	♊
3 "	2 "	Sagittarius	♐	3 "	9 "	Cancer	♋
4 "	14 "	Sagittarius	♐	4 "	22 "	Cancer	♋
5 "	27 "	Sagittarius	♐	5 "	4 "	Leo	♌
6 "	12 "	Capricorn	♑	6 "	16 "	Leo	♌
7 "	28 "	Capricorn	♑	7 "	27 "	Leo	♌
8 "	17 "	Aquarius	♒	8 "	9 "	Virgo	♍
9 "	11 "	Pisces	♓	9 "	21 "	Virgo	♍
10 "	7 "	Aries	♈	10 "	3 "	Libra	♎
11 "	2 "	Taurus	♉	11 "	15 "	Libra	♎
12 Noon	23 "	Taurus	♉	12 Midnight	27 "	Libra	♎

JANUARY —29—

A. M.				P. M.			
1 o'clock	12° of	Scorpio	♏	1 o'clock	15° of	Gemini	♊
2 "	23 "	Scorpio	♏	2 "	0 "	Cancer	♋
3 "	5 "	Sagittarius	♐	3 "	13 "	Cancer	♋
4 "	17 "	Sagittarius	♐	4 "	25 "	Cancer	♋
5 "	1 "	Capricorn	♑	5 "	7 "	Leo	♌
6 "	15 "	Capricorn	♑	6 "	19 "	Leo	♌
7 "	3 "	Aquarius	♒	7 "	0 "	Virgo	♍
8 "	24 "	Aquarius	♒	8 "	12 "	Virgo	♍
9 "	18 "	Pisces	♓	9 "	24 "	Virgo	♍
10 "	13 "	Aries	♈	10 "	6 "	Libra	♎
11 "	7 "	Taurus	♉	11 "	18 "	Libra	♎
12 Noon	28 "	Taurus	♉	12 Midnight	0 "	Scorpio	♏

FEBRUARY —2—

A. M.				P. M.			
1 o'clock	15° of	Scorpio	♏	1 o'clock	19° of	Gemini	♊
2 "	26 "	Scorpio	♏	2 "	3 "	Cancer	♋
3 "	8 "	Sagittarius	♐	3 "	16 "	Cancer	♋
4 "	21 "	Sagittarius	♐	4 "	28 "	Cancer	♋
5 "	4 "	Capricorn	♑	5 "	10 "	Leo	♌

A. M.					P. M.				
6 o'clock	20°	of	Capricorn	♑	6 o'clock	22°	of	Leo	♌
7 "	7	"	Aquarius	♒	7 "	4	"	Virgo	♍
8 "	0	"	Pisces	♓	8 "	16	"	Virgo	♍
9 "	24	"	Pisces	♓	9 "	27	"	Virgo	♍
10 "	20	"	Aries	♈	10 "	9	"	Libra	♎
11 "	13	"	Taurus	♉	11 "	21	"	Libra	♎
12 Noon	3	"	Gemini	♊	12 Midnight	3	"	Scorpio	♏

FEBRUARY —6—

A. M.					P. M.				
1 o'clock	18°	of	Scorpio	♏	1 o'clock	23°	of	Gemini	♊
2 "	29	"	Scorpio	♏	2 "	7	"	Cancer	♋
3 "	12	"	Sagittarius	♐	3 "	19	"	Cancer	♋
4 "	24	"	Sagittarius	♐	4 "	1	"	Leo	♌
5 "	8	"	Capricorn	♑	5 "	13	"	Leo	♌
6 "	24	"	Capricorn	♑	6 "	25	"	Leo	♌
7 "	13	"	Aquarius	♒	7 "	7	"	Virgo	♍
8 "	5	"	Pisces	♓	8 "	18	"	Virgo	♍
9 "	1	"	Aries	♈	9 "	0	"	Libra	♎
10 "	27	"	Aries	♈	10 "	12	"	Libra	♎
11 "	19	"	Taurus	♉	11 "	24	"	Libra	♎
12 Noon	8	"	Gemini	♊	12 Midnight	6	"	Scorpio	♏

FEBRUARY —10—

A. M.					P. M.				
1 o'clock	21°	of	Scorpio	♏	1 o'clock	27°	of	Gemini	♊
2 "	2	"	Sagittarius	♐	2 "	10	"	Cancer	♋
3 "	15	"	Sagittarius	♐	3 "	22	"	Cancer	♋
4 "	28	"	Sagittarius	♐	4 "	5	"	Leo	♌
5 "	12	"	Capricorn	♑	5 "	16	"	Leo	♌
6 "	29	"	Capricorn	♑	6 "	28	"	Leo	♌
7 "	19	"	Aquarius	♒	7 "	10	"	Virgo	♍
8 "	13	"	Pisces	♓	8 "	22	"	Virgo	♍
9 "	9	"	Aries	♈	9 "	4	"	Libra	♎
10 "	4	"	Taurus	♉	10 "	15	"	Libra	♎
11 "	24	"	Taurus	♉	11 "	27	"	Libra	♎
12 Noon	12	"	Gemini	♊	12 Midnight	9	"	Scorpio	♏

FEBRUARY —14—

A. M.					P. M.				
1 o'clock	24°	of	Scorpio	♏	1 o'clock	0°	of	Cancer	♋
2 "	5	"	Sagittarius	♐	2 "	13	"	Cancer	♋
3 "	18	"	Sagittarius	♐	3 "	26	"	Cancer	♋
4 "	2	"	Capricorn	♑	4 "	8	"	Leo	♌
5 "	16	"	Capricorn	♑	5 "	19	"	Leo	♌
6 "	3	"	Aquarius	♒	6 "	1	"	Virgo	♍
7 "	24	"	Aquarius	♒	7 "	13	"	Virgo	♍
8 "	18	"	Pisces	♓	8 "	25	"	Virgo	♍
9 "	15	"	Aries	♈	9 "	7	"	Libra	♎
10 "	9	"	Taurus	♉	10 "	18	"	Libra	♎
11 "	29	"	Taurus	♉	11 "	1	"	Scorpio	♏
12 Noon	16	"	Gemini	♊	12 Midnight	12	"	Scorpio	♏

FEBRUARY —18—

A. M.					P. M.				
1 o'clock	27°	of	Scorpio	♏	1 o'clock	4°	of	Cancer	♋
2 "	9	"	Sagittarius	♐	2 "	16	"	Cancer	♋
3 "	21	"	Sagittarius	♐	3 "	29	"	Cancer	♋
4 "	5	"	Capricorn	♑	4 "	11	"	Leo	♌
5 "	20	"	Capricorn	♑	5 "	22	"	Leo	♌
6 "	9	"	Aquarius	♒	6 "	4	"	Virgo	♍
7 "	0	"	Pisces	♓	7 "	16	"	Virgo	♍
8 "	26	"	Pisces	♓	8 "	28	"	Virgo	♍
9 "	21	"	Aries	♈	9 "	10	"	Libra	♎
10 "	15	"	Taurus	♉	10 "	22	"	Libra	♎
11 "	3	"	Gemini	♊	11 "	3	"	Scorpio	♏
12 Noon	20	"	Gemini	♊	12 Midnight	15	"	Scorpio	♏

FEBRUARY —22—

A. M.					P. M.				
1 o'clock	0°	of	Sagittarius	♐	1 o'clock	8°	of	Cancer	♋
2 "	12	"	Sagittarius	♐	2 "	20	"	Cancer	♋
3 "	25	"	Sagittarius	♐	3 "	2	"	Leo	♌
4 "	9	"	Capricorn	♑	4 "	14	"	Leo	♌
5 "	25	"	Capricorn	♑	5 "	25	"	Leo	♌

A. M.				P. M.			
6 o'clock	14° of	Aquarius	♒	6 o'clock	7° of	Virgo	♍
7 "	7 "	Pisces	♓	7 "	19 "	Virgo	♍
8 "	3 "	Aries	♈	8 "	1 "	Libra	♎
9 "	28 "	Aries	♈	9 "	13 "	Libra	♎
10 "	20 "	Taurus	♉	10 "	25 "	Libra	♎
11 "	8 "	Gemini	♊	11 "	6 "	Scorpio	♏
12 Noon	24 "	Gemini	♊	12 Midnight	18 "	Scorpio	♏

FEBRUARY —26—

A. M.				P. M.			
1 o'clock	3° of	Sagittarius	♐	1 o'clock	11° of	Cancer	♋
2 "	15 "	Sagittarius	♐	2 "	23 "	Cancer	♋
3 "	29 "	Sagittarius	♐	3 "	5 "	Leo	♌
4 "	13 "	Capricorn	♑	4 "	17 "	Leo	♌
5 "	0 "	Aquarius	♒	5 "	28 "	Leo	♌
6 "	20 "	Aquarius	♒	6 "	11 "	Virgo	♍
7 "	14 "	Pisces	♓	7 "	22 "	Virgo	♍
8 "	10 "	Aries	♈	8 "	4 "	Libra	♎
9 "	4 "	Taurus	♉	9 "	16 "	Libra	♎
10 "	25 "	Taurus	♉	10 "	28 "	Libra	♎
11 "	13 "	Gemini	♊	11 "	10 "	Scorpio	♏
12 Noon	28 "	Gemini	♊	12 Midnight	21 "	Scorpio	♏

MARCH —2—

A. M.				P. M.			
1 o'clock	7° of	Sagittarius	♐	1 o'clock	15° of	Cancer	♋
2 "	20 "	Sagittarius	♐	2 "	27 "	Cancer	♋
3 "	3 "	Capricorn	♑	3 "	9 "	Leo	♌
4 "	18 "	Capricorn	♑	4 "	21 "	Leo	♌
5 "	6 "	Aquarius	♒	5 "	2 "	Virgo	♍
6 "	28 "	Aquarius	♒	6 "	14 "	Virgo	♍
7 "	22 "	Pisces	♓	7 "	26 "	Virgo	♍
8 "	18 "	Aries	♈	8 "	8 "	Libra	♎
9 "	12 "	Taurus	♉	9 "	20 "	Libra	♎
10 "	1 "	Gemini	♊	10 "	1 "	Scorpio	♏
11 "	18 "	Gemini	♊	11 "	13 "	Scorpio	♏
12 Noon	2 "	Cancer	♋	12 Midnight	25 "	Scorpio	♏

MARCH —6—

A. M.					P. M.				
1 o'clock	11°	of	Sagittarius	♐	1 o'clock	18°	of	Cancer	♋
2 "	23	"	Sagittarius	♐	2 "	0	"	Leo	♌
3 "	7	"	Capricorn	♑	3 "	12	"	Leo	♌
4 "	22	"	Capricorn	♑	4 "	24	"	Leo	♌
5 "	11	"	Aquarius	♒	5 "	6	"	Virgo	♍
6 "	4	"	Pisces	♓	6 "	17	"	Virgo	♍
7 "	29	"	Pisces	♓	7 "	29	"	Virgo	♍
8 "	25	"	Aries	♈	8 "	11	"	Libra	♎
9 "	17	"	Taurus	♉	9 "	23	"	Libra	♎
10 "	6	"	Gemini	♊	10 "	5	"	Scorpio	♏
11 "	21	"	Gemini	♊	11 "	17	"	Scorpio	♏
12 Noon	5	"	Cancer	♋	12 Midnight	28	"	Scorpio	♏

MARCH —10—

A. M.					P. M.				
1 o'clock	14°	of	Sagittarius	♐	1 o'clock	21°	of	Cancer	♋
2 "	26	"	Sagittarius	♐	2 "	3	"	Leo	♌
3 "	11	"	Capricorn	♑	3 "	15	"	Leo	♌
4 "	27	"	Capricorn	♑	4 "	27	"	Leo	♌
5 "	16	"	Aquarius	♒	5 "	9	"	Virgo	♍
6 "	10	"	Pisces	♓	6 "	21	"	Virgo	♍
7 "	6	"	Aries	♈	7 "	2	"	Libra	♎
8 "	1	"	Taurus	♉	8 "	15	"	Libra	♎
9 "	23	"	Taurus	♉	9 "	27	"	Libra	♎
10 "	10	"	Gemini	♊	10 "	8	"	Scorpio	♏
11 "	26	"	Gemini	♊	11 "	20	"	Scorpio	♏
12 Noon	9	"	Cancer	♋	12 Midnight	2	"	Sagittarius	♐

MARCH —14—

A. M.					P. M.				
1 o'clock	17°	of	Sagittarius	♐	1 o'clock	25°	of	Cancer	♋
2 "	1	"	Capricorn	♑	2 "	7	"	Leo	♌
3 "	15	"	Capricorn	♑	3 "	18	"	Leo	♌
4 "	2	"	Aquarius	♒	4 "	0	"	Virgo	♍
5 "	22	"	Aquarius	♒	5 "	12	"	Virgo	♍

A. M.					P. M.				
6 o'clock	16°	of	Pisces	♓	6 o'clock	23°	of	Virgo	♍
7 "	13	"	Aries	♈	7 "	6	"	Libra	♎
8 "	7	"	Taurus	♉	8 "	18	"	Libra	♎
9 "	27	"	Taurus	♉	9 "	29	"	Libra	♎
10 "	14	"	Gemini	♊	10 "	11	"	Scorpio	♏
11 "	29	"	Gemini	♊	11 "	23	"	Scorpio	♏
12 Noon	12	"	Cancer	♋	12 Midnight	5	"	Sagittarius	♐

MARCH —18—

A. M.					P. M.				
1 o'clock	20°	of	Sagittarius	♐	1 o'clock	27°	of	Cancer	♋
2 "	4	"	Capricorn	♑	2 "	9	"	Leo	♌
3 "	19	"	Capricorn	♑	3 "	21	"	Leo	♌
4 "	7	"	Aquarius	♒	4 "	3	"	Virgo	♍
5 "	29	"	Aquarius	♒	5 "	15	"	Virgo	♍
6 "	24	"	Pisces	♓	6 "	27	"	Virgo	♍
7 "	19	"	Aries	♈	7 "	9	"	Libra	♎
8 "	13	"	Taurus	♉	8 "	21	"	Libra	♎
9 "	2	"	Gemini	♊	9 "	2	"	Scorpio	♏
10 "	18	"	Gemini	♊	10 "	14	"	Scorpio	♏
11 "	3	"	Cancer	♋	11 "	26	"	Scorpio	♏
12 Noon	15	"	Cancer	♋	12 Midnight	8	"	Sagittarius	♐

MARCH —22—

A. M.					P. M.				
1 o'clock	24°	of	Sagittarius	♐	1 o'clock	1°	of	Leo	♌
2 "	8	"	Capricorn	♑	2 "	13	"	Leo	♌
3 "	23	"	Capricorn	♑	3 "	24	"	Leo	♌
4 "	12	"	Aquarius	♒	4 "	6	"	Virgo	♍
5 "	5	"	Pisces	♓	5 "	18	"	Virgo	♍
6 "	0	"	Aries	♈	6 "	0	"	Libra	♎
7 "	26	"	Aries	♈	7 "	12	"	Libra	♎
8 "	18	"	Taurus	♉	8 "	23	"	Libra	♎
9 "	7	"	Gemini	♊	9 "	5	"	Scorpio	♏
10 "	22	"	Gemini	♊	10 "	17	"	Scorpio	♏
11 "	6	"	Cancer	♋	11 "	29	"	Scorpio	♏
12 Noon	19	"	Cancer	♋	12 Midnight	11	"	Sagittarius	♐

MARCH —26—

A. M.				P. M.				
1 o'clock	27° of	Sagittarius	♐	1 o'clock	4° of	Leo	♌
2 "	12 "	Capricorn	♑	2 "	16 "	Leo	♌
3 "	28 "	Capricorn	♑	3 "	28 "	Leo	♌
4 "	17 "	Aquarius	♒	4 "	9 "	Virgo	♍
5 "	11 "	Pisces	♓	5 "	21 "	Virgo	♍
6 "	7 "	Aries	♈	6 "	3 "	Libra	♎
7 "	2 "	Taurus	♉	7 "	15 "	Libra	♎
8 "	23 "	Taurus	♉	8 "	27 "	Libra	♎
9 "	11 "	Gemini	♊	9 "	9 "	Scorpio	♏
10 "	26 "	Gemini	♊	10 "	20 "	Scorpio	♏
11 "	10 "	Cancer	♋	11 "	2 "	Sagittarius	♐
12 Noon	22 "	Cancer	♋	12 Midnight	14 "	Sagittarius	♐

MARCH —30—

A. M.				P. M.				
1 o'clock	1° of	Capricorn	♑	1 o'clock	7° of	Leo	♌
2 "	16 "	Capricorn	♑	2 "	19 "	Leo	♌
3 "	3 "	Aquarius	♒	3 "	1 "	Virgo	♍
4 "	24 "	Aquarius	♒	4 "	12 "	Virgo	♍
5 "	18 "	Pisces	♓	5 "	24 "	Virgo	♍
6 "	15 "	Aries	♈	6 "	6 "	Libra	♎
7 "	9 "	Taurus	♉	7 "	18 "	Libra	♎
8 "	28 "	Taurus	♉	8 "	0 "	Scorpio	♏
9 "	15 "	Gemini	♊	9 "	12 "	Scorpio	♏
10 "	0 "	Cancer	♋	10 "	24 "	Scorpio	♏
11 "	13 "	Cancer	♋	11 "	5 "	Sagittarius	♐
12 Noon	25 "	Cancer	♋	12 Midnight	17 "	Sagittarius	♐

APRIL —3—

A. M.				P. M.				
1 o'clock	5° of	Capricorn	♑	1 o'clock	11° of	Leo	♌
2 "	20 "	Capricorn	♑	2 "	22 "	Leo	♌
3 "	8 "	Aquarius	♒	3 "	4 "	Virgo	♍
4 "	0 "	Pisces	♓	4 "	16 "	Virgo	♍
5 "	26 "	Pisces	♓	5 "	28 "	Virgo	♍

A. M.					P. M.				
6 o'clock	20°	of	Aries	♈	6 o'clock	10°	of	Libra	♎
7 "	13	"	Taurus	♉	7 "	21	"	Libra	♎
8 "	3	"	Gemini	♊	8 "	3	"	Scorpio	♏
9 "	19	"	Gemini	♊	9 "	15	"	Scorpio	♏
10 "	3	"	Cancer	♋	10 "	27	"	Scorpio	♏
11 "	16	"	Cancer	♋	11 "	8	"	Sagittarius	♐
12 Noon	29	"	Cancer	♋	12 Midnight	21	"	Sagittarius	♐

APRIL —7—

A. M.					P. M.				
1 o'clock	8°	of	Capricorn	♑	1 o'clock	13°	of	Leo	♌
2 "	24	"	Capricorn	♑	2 "	25	"	Leo	♌
3 "	13	"	Aquarius	♒	3 "	7	"	Virgo	♍
4 "	5	"	Pisces	♓	4 "	18	"	Virgo	♍
5 "	1	"	Aries	♈	5 "	0	"	Libra	♎
6 "	27	"	Aries	♈	6 "	12	"	Libra	♎
7 "	19	"	Taurus	♉	7 "	24	"	Libra	♎
8 "	8	"	Gemini	♊	8 "	6	"	Scorpio	♏
9 "	23	"	Gemini	♊	9 "	18	"	Scorpio	♏
10 "	7	"	Cancer	♋	10 "	29	"	Scorpio	♏
11 "	19	"	Cancer	♋	11 "	12	"	Sagittarius	♐
12 Noon	2	"	Leo	♌	12 Midnight	25	"	Sagittarius	♐

APRIL —10—

A. M.					P. M.				
1 o'clock	11°	of	Capricorn	♑	1 o'clock	16°	of	Leo	♌
2 "	28	"	Capricorn	♑	2 "	28	"	Leo	♌
3 "	17	"	Aquarius	♒	3 "	9	"	Virgo	♍
4 "	11	"	Pisces	♓	4 "	21	"	Virgo	♍
5 "	7	"	Aries	♈	5 "	3	"	Libra	♎
6 "	2	"	Taurus	♉	6 "	15	"	Libra	♎
7 "	23	"	Taurus	♉	7 "	27	"	Libra	♎
8 "	11	"	Gemini	♊	8 "	9	"	Scorpio	♏
9 "	26	"	Gemini	♊	9 "	20	"	Scorpio	♏
10 "	9	"	Cancer	♋	10 "	2	"	Sagittarius	♐
11 "	22	"	Cancer	♋	11 "	14	"	Sagittarius	♐
12 Noon	4	"	Leo	♌	12 Midnight	27	"	Sagittarius	♐

APRIL —14—

A. M.				P. M.			
1 o'clock	15° of	Capricorn	♑	1 o'clock	19° of	Leo	♌
2 "	3 "	Aquarius	♒	2 "	1 "	Virgo	♍
3 "	24 "	Aquarius	♒	3 "	12 "	Virgo	♍
4 "	18 "	Pisces	♓	4 "	24 "	Virgo	♍
5 "	14 "	Aries	♈	5 "	6 "	Libra	♎
6 "	8 "	Taurus	♉	6 "	18 "	Libra	♎
7 "	28 "	Taurus	♉	7 "	0 "	Scorpio	♏
8 "	15 "	Gemini	♊	8 "	12 "	Scorpio	♏
9 "	29 "	Gemini	♊	9 "	24 "	Scorpio	♏
10 "	13 "	Cancer	♋	10 "	5 "	Sagittarius	♐
11 "	25 "	Cancer	♋	11 "	17 "	Sagittarius	♐
12 Noon	7 "	Leo	♌	12 Midnight	1 "	Capricorn	♑

APRIL —18—

A. M.				P. M.			
1 o'clock	20° of	Capricorn	♑	1 o'clock	22° of	Leo	♌
2 "	7 "	Aquarius	♒	2 "	4 "	Virgo	♍
3 "	0 "	Pisces	♓	3 "	16 "	Virgo	♍
4 "	26 "	Pisces	♓	4 "	28 "	Virgo	♍
5 "	20 "	Aries	♈	5 "	9 "	Libra	♎
6 "	13 "	Taurus	♉	6 "	22 "	Libra	♎
7 "	3 "	Gemini	♊	7 "	3 "	Scorpio	♏
8 "	19 "	Gemini	♊	8 "	15 "	Scorpio	♏
9 "	3 "	Cancer	♋	9 "	27 "	Scorpio	♏
10 "	16 "	Cancer	♋	10 "	8 "	Sagittarius	♐
11 "	28 "	Cancer	♋	11 "	21 "	Sagittarius	♐
12 Noon	10 "	Leo	♌	12 Midnight	5 "	Capricorn	♑

APRIL —22—

A. M.				P. M.			
1 o'clock	23° of	Capricorn	♑	1 o'clock	25° of	Leo	♌
2 "	13 "	Aquarius	♒	2 "	7 "	Virgo	♍
3 "	5 "	Pisces	♓	3 "	18 "	Virgo	♍
4 "	1 "	Aries	♈	4 "	0 "	Libra	♎
5 "	27 "	Aries	♈	5 "	12 "	Libra	♎

A. M.					P. M.				
6 o'clock	19°	of	Taurus	♉	6 o'clock	24°	of	Libra	♎
7 "	3	"	Gemini	♊	7 "	5	"	Scorpio	♏
8 "	23	"	Gemini	♊	8 "	18	"	Scorpio	♏
9 "	7	"	Cancer	♋	9 "	29	"	Scorpio	♏
10 "	19	"	Cancer	♋	10 "	11	"	Sagittarius	♐
11 "	1	"	Leo	♌	11 "	24	"	Sagittarius	♐
12 Noon	13	"	Leo	♌	12 Midnight	8	"	Capricorn	♑

APRIL —26—

A. M.					P. M.				
1 o'clock	28°	of	Capricorn	♑	1 o'clock	28°	of	Leo	♌
2 "	19	"	Aquarius	♒	2 "	10	"	Virgo	♍
3 "	13	"	Pisces	♓	3 "	22	"	Virgo	♍
4 "	9	"	Aries	♈	4 "	4	"	Libra	♎
5 "	3	"	Taurus	♉	5 "	16	"	Libra	♎
6 "	24	"	Taurus	♉	6 "	27	"	Libra	♎
7 "	12	"	Gemini	♊	7 "	9	"	Scorpio	♏
8 "	27	"	Gemini	♊	8 "	21	"	Scorpio	♏
9 "	10	"	Cancer	♋	9 "	2	"	Sagittarius	♐
10 "	23	"	Cancer	♋	10 "	14	"	Sagittarius	♐
11 "	5	"	Leo	♌	11 "	28	"	Sagittarius	♐
12 Noon	16	"	Leo	♌	12 Midnight	12	"	Capricorn	♑

APRIL —30—

A. M.					P. M.				
1 o'clock	3°	of	Aquarius	♒	1 o'clock	1°	of	Virgo	♍
2 "	25	"	Aquarius	♒	2 "	13	"	Virgo	♍
3 "	18	"	Pisces	♓	3 "	24	"	Virgo	♍
4 "	15	"	Aries	♈	4 "	7	"	Libra	♎
5 "	9	"	Taurus	♉	5 "	19	"	Libra	♎
6 "	29	"	Taurus	♉	6 "	1	"	Scorpio	♏
7 "	16	"	Gemini	♊	7 "	12	"	Scorpio	♏
8 "	0	"	Cancer	♋	8 "	24	"	Scorpio	♏
9 "	14	"	Cancer	♋	9 "	6	"	Sagittarius	♐
10 "	26	"	Cancer	♋	10 "	18	"	Sagittarius	♐
11 "	8	"	Leo	♌	11 "	2	"	Capricorn	♑
12 Noon	19	"	Leo	♌	12 Midnight	16	"	Capricorn	♑

MAY —4—

A. M.				P. M.				
1 o'clock	9°	of	Aquarius ♒	1 o'clock	4°	of	Virgo	♍
2 "	0	"	Pisces ♓	2 "	16	"	Virgo	♍
3 "	26	"	Pisces ♓	3 "	28	"	Virgo	♍
4 "	22	"	Aries ♈	4 "	10	"	Libra	♎
5 "	15	"	Taurus ♉	5 "	22	"	Libra	♎
6 "	4	"	Gemini ♊	6 "	4	"	Scorpio	♏
7 "	20	"	Gemini ♊	7 "	15	"	Scorpio	♏
8 "	4	"	Cancer ♋	8 "	27	"	Scorpio	♏
9 "	17	"	Cancer ♋	9 "	9	"	Sagittarius	♐
10 "	29	"	Cancer ♋	10 "	21	"	Sagittarius	♐
11 "	11	"	Leo ♌	11 "	5	"	Capricorn	♑
12 Noon	22	"	Leo ♌	12 Midnight	20	"	Capricorn	♑

MAY —8—

A. M.				P. M.				
1 o'clock	14°	of	Aquarius ♒	1 o'clock	7°	of	Virgo	♍
2 "	7	"	Pisces ♓	2 "	19	"	Virgo	♍
3 "	3	"	Aries ♈	3 "	1	"	Libra	♎
4 "	29	"	Aries ♈	4 "	13	"	Libra	♎
5 "	20	"	Taurus ♉	5 "	25	"	Libra	♎
6 "	8	"	Gemini ♊	6 "	7	"	Scorpio	♏
7 "	24	"	Gemini ♊	7 "	18	"	Scorpio	♏
8 "	8	"	Cancer ♋	8 "	0	"	Sagittarius	♐
9 "	20	"	Cancer ♋	9 "	12	"	Sagittarius	♐
10 "	2	"	Leo ♌	10 "	25	"	Sagittarius	♐
11 "	14	"	Leo ♌	11 "	9	"	Capricorn	♑
12 Noon	25	"	Leo ♌	12 Midnight	25	"	Capricorn	♑

MAY —16—

A. M.				P. M.				
1 o'clock	25°	of	Aquarius ♒	1 o'clock	14°	of	Virgo	♍
2 "	20	"	Pisces ♓	2 "	25	"	Virgo	♍
3 "	16	"	Aries ♈	3 "	7	"	Libra	♎
4 "	10	"	Taurus ♉	4 "	19	"	Libra	♎
5 "	1	"	Gemini ♊	5 "	1	"	Scorpio	♏

A. M.					P. M.				
6 o'clock	16°	of	Gemini	♊	6 o'clock	13°	of	Scorpio	♏
7 "	1	"	Cancer	♋	7 "	24	"	Scorpio	♏
8 "	14	"	Cancer	♋	8 "	7	"	Sagittarius	♐
9 "	26	"	Cancer	♋	9 "	19	"	Sagittarius	♐
10 "	8	"	Leo	♌	10 "	2	"	Capricorn	♑
11 "	20	"	Leo	♌	11 "	17	"	Capricorn	♑
12 Noon	2	"	Virgo	♍	12 Midnight	5	"	Aquarius	♒

MAY —20—

A. M.					P. M.				
1 o'clock	2°	of	Pisces	♓	1 o'clock	17°	of	Virgo	♍
2 "	28	"	Pisces	♓	2 "	29	"	Virgo	♍
3 "	23	"	Aries	♈	3 "	11	"	Libra	♎
4 "	16	"	Taurus	♉	4 "	23	"	Libra	♎
5 "	6	"	Gemini	♊	5 "	4	"	Scorpio	♏
6 "	21	"	Gemini	♊	6 "	16	"	Scorpio	♏
7 "	5	"	Cancer	♋	7 "	27	"	Scorpio	♏
8 "	18	"	Cancer	♋	8 "	10	"	Sagittarius	♐
9 "	0	"	Leo	♌	9 "	22	"	Sagittarius	♐
10 "	11	"	Leo	♌	10 "	6	"	Capricorn	♑
11 "	23	"	Leo	♌	11 "	21	"	Capricorn	♑
12 Noon	5	"	Virgo	♍	12 Midnight	10	"	Aquarius	♒

MAY —24—

A. M.					P. M.				
1 o'clock	9°	of	Pisces	♓	1 o'clock	20°	of	Virgo	♍
2 "	4	"	Aries	♈	2 "	2	"	Libra	♎
3 "	29	"	Aries	♈	3 "	14	"	Libra	♎
4 "	22	"	Taurus	♉	4 "	26	"	Libra	♎
5 "	9	"	Gemini	♊	5 "	7	"	Scorpio	♏
6 "	25	"	Gemini	♊	6 "	19	"	Scorpio	♏
7 "	8	"	Cancer	♋	7 "	0	"	Sagittarius	♐
8 "	21	"	Cancer	♋	8 "	13	"	Sagittarius	♐
9 "	2	"	Leo	♌	9 "	26	"	Sagittarius	♐
10 "	14	"	Leo	♌	10 "	10	"	Capricorn	♑
11 "	26	"	Leo	♌	11 "	26	"	Capricorn	♑
12 Noon	8	"	Virgo	♍	12 Midnight	16	"	Aquarius	♒

MAY —28—

A. M.				P. M.			
1 o'clock	14° of	Pisces	♓	1 o'clock	23° of	Virgo	♍
2 "	11 "	Aries	♈	2 "	5 "	Libra	♎
3 "	5 "	Taurus	♉	3 "	17 "	Libra	♎
4 "	26 "	Taurus	♉	4 "	28 "	Libra	♎
5 "	13 "	Gemini	♊	5 "	10 "	Scorpio	♏
6 "	28 "	Gemini	♊	6 "	22 "	Scorpio	♏
7 "	12 "	Cancer	♋	7 "	3 "	Sagittarius	♐
8 "	24 "	Cancer	♋	8 "	16 "	Sagittarius	♐
9 "	5 "	Leo	♌	9 "	29 "	Sagittarius	♐
10 "	17 "	Leo	♌	10 "	14 "	Capricorn	♑
11 "	29 "	Leo	♌	11 "	1 "	Aquarius	♒
12 Noon	11 "	Virgo	♍	12 Midnight	20 "	Aquarius	♒

JUNE —1—

A. M.				P. M.			
1 o'clock	22° of	Pisces	♓	1 o'clock	26° of	Virgo	♍
2 "	18 "	Aries	♈	2 "	8 "	Libra	♎
3 "	12 "	Taurus	♉	3 "	20 "	Libra	♎
4 "	1 "	Gemini	♊	4 "	1 "	Scorpio	♏
5 "	17 "	Gemini	♊	5 "	13 "	Scorpio	♏
6 "	2 "	Cancer	♋	6 "	25 "	Scorpio	♏
7 "	15 "	Cancer	♋	7 "	7 "	Sagittarius	♐
8 "	27 "	Cancer	♋	8 "	19 "	Sagittarius	♐
9 "	9 "	Leo	♌	9 "	2 "	Capricorn	♑
10 "	21 "	Leo	♌	10 "	18 "	Capricorn	♑
11 "	2 "	Virgo	♍	11 "	6 "	Aquarius	♒
12 Noon	14 "	Virgo	♍	12 Midnight	27 "	Aquarius	♒

JUNE —5—

A. M.				P. M.			
1 o'clock	27° of	Pisces	♓	1 o'clock	29° of	Virgo	♍
2 "	22 "	Aries	♈	2 "	10 "	Libra	♎
3 "	15 "	Taurus	♉	3 "	22 "	Libra	♎
4 "	4 "	Gemini	♊	4 "	4 "	Scorpio	♏
5 "	20 "	Gemini	♊	5 "	15 "	Scorpio	♏

A. M.					P. M.				
6 "	4°	of	Cancer	♋	6 o'clock	27°	of	Scorpio	♏
7 "	17	"	Cancer	♋	7 "	9	"	Sagittarius	♐
8 "	0	"	Leo	♌	8 "	22	"	Sagittarius	♐
9 "	11	"	Leo	♌	9 "	6	"	Capricorn	♑
10 "	23	"	Leo	♌	10 "	21	"	Capricorn	♑
11 "	5	"	Virgo	♍	11 "	10	"	Aquarius	♒
12 Noon	17	"	Virgo	♍	12 Midnight	2	"	Pisces	♓

JUNE —9—

A. M.					P. M.				
1 o'clock	3°	of	Aries	♈	1 o'clock	2°	of	Libra	♎
2 "	29	"	Aries	♈	2 "	14	"	Libra	♎
3 "	20	"	Taurus	♉	3 "	25	"	Libra	♎
4 "	9	"	Gemini	♊	4 "	7	"	Scorpio	♏
5 "	24	"	Gemini	♊	5 "	19	"	Scorpio	♏
6 "	8	"	Cancer	♋	6 "	1	"	Sagittarius	♐
7 "	20	"	Cancer	♋	7 "	13	"	Sagittarius	♐
8 "	2	"	Leo	♌	8 "	26	"	Sagittarius	♐
9 "	14	"	Leo	♌	9 "	10	"	Capricorn	♑
10 "	26	"	Leo	♌	10 "	26	"	Capricorn	♑
11 "	8	"	Virgo	♍	11 "	16	"	Aquarius	♒
12 Noon	20	"	Virgo	♍	12 Midnight	9	"	Pisces	♓

JUNE —13—

A. M.					P. M.				
1 o'clock	11°	of	Aries	♈	1 o'clock	5°	of	Libra	♎
2 "	4	"	Taurus	♉	2 "	17	"	Libra	♎
3 "	26	"	Taurus	♉	3 "	28	"	Libra	♎
4 "	13	"	Gemini	♊	4 "	10	"	Scorpio	♏
5 "	28	"	Gemini	♊	5 "	21	"	Scorpio	♏
6 "	12	"	Cancer	♋	6 "	3	"	Sagittarius	♐
7 "	24	"	Cancer	♋	7 "	16	"	Sagittarius	♐
8 "	5	"	Leo	♌	8 "	29	"	Sagittarius	♐
9 "	23	"	Leo	♌	9 "	14	"	Capricorn	♑
10 "	29	"	Leo	♌	10 "	1	"	Aquarius	♒
11 "	11	"	Virgo	♍	11 "	20	"	Aquarius	♒
12 Noon	23	"	Virgo	♍	12 Midnight	14	"	Pisces	♓

JUNE —17—

A. M.				P. M.			
1 o'clock	16°	of Aries	♈	1 o'clock	7°	of Libra	♎
2 "	11 "	Taurus	♉	2 "	20 "	Libra	♎
3 "	1 "	Gemini	♊	3 "	1 "	Scorpio	♏
4 "	17 "	Gemini	♊	4 "	13 "	Scorpio	♏
5 "	2 "	Cancer	♋	5 "	25 "	Scorpio	♏
6 "	15 "	Cancer	♋	6 "	7 "	Sagittarius	♐
7 "	27 "	Cancer	♋	7 "	19 "	Sagittarius	♐
8 "	8 "	Leo	♌	8 "	3 "	Capricorn	♑
9 "	21 "	Leo	♌	9 "	18 "	Capricorn	♑
10 "	2 "	Virgo	♍	10 "	6 "	Aquarius	♒
11 "	14 "	Virgo	♍	11 "	27 "	Aquarius	♒
12 Noon	26 "	Virgo	♍	12 Midnight	22 "	Pisces	♓

JUNE —21—

A. M.				P. M.			
1 o'clock	24°	of Aries	♈	1 o'clock	11°	of Libra	♎
2 "	16 "	Taurus	♉	2 "	23 "	Libra	♎
3 "	6 "	Gemini	♊	3 "	5 "	Scorpio	♏
4 "	21 "	Gemini	♊	4 "	16 "	Scorpio	♏
5 "	5 "	Cancer	♋	5 "	28 "	Scorpio	♏
6 "	18 "	Cancer	♋	6 "	10 "	Sagittarius	♐
7 "	0 "	Leo	♌	7 "	23 "	Sagittarius	♐
8 "	11 "	Leo	♌	8 "	6 "	Capricorn	♑
9 "	23 "	Leo	♌	9 "	22 "	Capricorn	♑
10 "	5 "	Virgo	♍	10 "	11 "	Aquarius	♒
11 "	17 "	Virgo	♍	11 "	4 "	Pisces	♓
12 Noon	29 "	Virgo	♍	12 Midnight	28 "	Pisces	♓

JUNE —25—

A. M.				P. M.			
1 o'clock	0°	of Taurus	♉	1 o'clock	14°	of Libra	♎
2 "	22 "	Taurus	♉	2 "	26 "	Libra	♎
3 "	10 "	Gemini	♊	3 "	8 "	Scorpio	♏
4 "	25 "	Gemini	♊	4 "	19 "	Scorpio	♏
5 "	8 "	Cancer	♋	5 "	1 "	Sagittarius	♐

A. M.					P. M.				
6 o'clock	21°	of	Cancer	♋	6 o'clock	14°	of	Sagittarius	♐
7 "	3	"	Leo	♌	7 "	26	"	Sagittarius	♐
8 "	15	"	Leo	♌	8 "	11	"	Capricorn	♑
9 "	26	"	Leo	♌	9 "	27	"	Capricorn	♑
10 "	8	"	Virgo	♍	10 "	16	"	Aquarius	♒
11 "	20	"	Virgo	♍	11 "	9	"	Pisces	♓
12 Noon	2	"	Libra	♎	12 Midnight	5	"	Aries	♈

JUNE —29—

A. M.					P. M.				
1 o'clock	6°	of	Taurus	♉	1 o'clock	17°	of	Libra	♎
2 "	27	"	Taurus	♉	2 "	29	"	Libra	♎
3 "	14	"	Gemini	♊	3 "	11	"	Scorpio	♏
4 "	28	"	Gemini	♊	4 "	23	"	Scorpio	♏
5 "	12	"	Cancer	♋	5 "	5	"	Sagittarius	♐
6 "	24	"	Cancer	♋	6 "	17	"	Sagittarius	♐
7 "	6	"	Leo	♌	7 "	0	"	Capricorn	♑
8 "	18	"	Leo	♌	8 "	15	"	Capricorn	♑
9 "	0	"	Virgo	♍	9 "	2	"	Aquarius	♒
10 "	12	"	Virgo	♍	10 "	22	"	Aquarius	♒
11 "	23	"	Virgo	♍	11 "	16	"	Pisces	♓
12 Noon	5	"	Libra	♎	12 Midnight	13	"	Aries	♈

JULY —3—

A. M.					P. M.				
1 o'clock	12°	of	Taurus	♉	1 o'clock	20°	of	Libra	♎
2 "	2	"	Gemini	♊	2 "	2	"	Scorpio	♏
3 "	17	"	Gemini	♊	3 "	14	"	Scorpio	♏
4 "	2	"	Cancer	♋	4 "	25	"	Scorpio	♏
5 "	15	"	Cancer	♋	5 "	7	"	Sagittarius	♐
6 "	27	"	Cancer	♋	6 "	20	"	Sagittarius	♐
7 "	9	"	Leo	♌	7 "	3	"	Capricorn	♑
8 "	21	"	Leo	♌	8 "	18	"	Capricorn	♑
9 "	2	"	Virgo	♍	9 "	6	"	Aquarius	♒
10 "	14	"	Virgo	♍	10 "	27	"	Aquarius	♒
11 "	26	"	Virgo	♍	11 "	22	"	Pisces	♓
12 Noon	8	"	Libra	♎	12 Midnight	19	"	Aries	♈

JULY —7—

A. M.					P. M.				
1 o'clock	18°	of	Taurus	♉	1 o'clock	23°	of	Libra	♎
2 "	6	"	Gemini	♊	2 "	5	"	Scorpio	♏
3 "	22	"	Gemini	♊	3 "	17	"	Scorpio	♏
4 "	6	"	Cancer	♋	4 "	29	"	Scorpio	♏
5 "	18	"	Cancer	♋	5 "	11	"	Sagittarius	♐
6 "	0	"	Leo	♌	6 "	23	"	Sagittarius	♐
7 "	12	"	Leo	♌	7 "	7	"	Capricorn	♑
8 "	24	"	Leo	♌	8 "	23	"	Capricorn	♑
9 "	6	"	Virgo	♍	9 "	11	"	Aquarius	♒
10 "	17	"	Virgo	♍	10 "	4	"	Pisces	♓
11 "	29	"	Virgo	♍	11 "	0	"	Aries	♈
12 Noon	12	"	Libra	♎	12 Midnight	25	"	Aries	♈

JULY —11—

A. M.					P. M.				
1 o'clock	22°	of	Taurus	♉	1 o'clock	26°	of	Libra	♎
2 "	10	"	Gemini	♊	2 "	8	"	Scorpio	♏
3 "	26	"	Gemini	♊	3 "	20	"	Scorpio	♏
4 "	9	"	Cancer	♋	4 "	2	"	Sagittarius	♐
5 "	21	"	Cancer	♋	5 "	14	"	Sagittarius	♐
6 "	3	"	Leo	♌	6 "	27	"	Sagittarius	♐
7 "	15	"	Leo	♌	7 "	11	"	Capricorn	♑
8 "	27	"	Leo	♌	8 "	28	"	Capricorn	♑
9 "	9	"	Virgo	♍	9 "	17	"	Aquarius	♒
10 "	21	"	Virgo	♍	10 "	11	"	Pisces	♓
11 "	2	"	Libra	♎	11 "	7	"	Aries	♈
12 Noon	14	"	Libra	♎	12 Midnight	2	"	Taurus	♉

JULY —14—

A. M.					P. M.				
1 o'clock	26°	of	Taurus	♉	1 o'clock	29°	of	Libra	♎
2 "	14	"	Gemini	♊	2 "	11	"	Scorpio	♏
3 "	28	"	Gemini	♊	3 "	22	"	Scorpio	♏
4 "	12	"	Cancer	♋	4 "	5	"	Sagittarius	♐
5 "	24	"	Cancer	♋	5 "	17	"	Sagittarius	♐

A. M.					P. M.				
6 o'clock	6°	of	Leo	♌	6 o'clock	0°	of	Capricorn	♑
7 "	17	"	Leo	♌	7 "	15	"	Capricorn	♑
8 "	29	"	Leo	♌	8 "	2	"	Aquarius	♒
9 "	12	"	Virgo	♍	9 "	22	"	Aquarius	♒
10 "	23	"	Virgo	♍	10 "	6	"	Pisces	♓
11 "	5	"	Libra	♎	11 "	13	"	Aries	♈
12 Noon	17	"	Libro	♎	12 Midnight	6	"	Taurus	♉

JULY —18—

A. M.					P. M.				
1 o'clock	1°	of	Gemini	♊	1 o'clock	1°	of	Scorpio	♏
2 "	17	"	Gemini	♊	2 "	13	"	Scorpio	♏
3 "	2	"	Cancer	♋	3 "	25	"	Scorpio	♏
4 "	15	"	Cancer	♋	4 "	7	"	Sagittarius	♐
5 "	27	"	Cancer	♋	5 "	20	"	Sagittarius	♐
6 "	9	"	Leo	♌	6 "	3	"	Capricorn	♑
7 "	21	"	Leo	♌	7 "	19	"	Capricorn	♑
8 "	2	"	Virgo	♍	8 "	6	"	Aquarius	♒
9 "	14	"	Virgo	♍	9 "	28	"	Aquarius	♒
10 "	26	"	Virgo	♍	10 "	22	"	Pisces	♓
11 "	8	"	Libra	♎	11 "	18	"	Aries	♈
12 Noon	20	"	Libra	♎	12 Midnight	12	"	Taurus	♉

JULY —22—

A. M.					P. M.				
1 o'clock	6°	of	Gemini	♊	1 o'clock	5°	of	Scorpio	♏
2 "	22	"	Gemini	♊	2 "	16	"	Scorpio	♏
3 "	5	"	Cancer	♋	3 "	28	"	Scorpio	♏
4 "	18	"	Cancer	♋	4 "	11	"	Sagittarius	♐
5 "	0	"	Leo	♌	5 "	23	"	Sagittarius	♐
6 "	12	"	Leo	♌	6 "	7	"	Capricorn	♑
7 "	24	"	Leo	♌	7 "	22	"	Capricorn	♑
8 "	6	"	Virgo	♍	8 "	11	"	Aquarius	♒
9 "	17	"	Virgo	♍	9 "	4	"	Pisces	♓
10 "	29	"	Virgo	♍	10 "	29	"	Pisces	♓
11 "	12	"	Libra	♎	11 "	24	"	Aries	♈
12 Noon	23	"	Libra	♎	12 Midnight	17	"	Taurus	♉

JULY —26—

A. M.				P. M.				
1 o'clock	10°	of	Gemini ♊	1 o'clock	8°	of	Scorpio	♏
2 "	25	"	Gemini ♊	2 "	20	"	Scorpio	♏
3 "	9	"	Cancer ♋	3 "	2	"	Sagittarius	♐
4 "	21	"	Cancer ♋	4 "	14	"	Sagittarius	♐
5 "	3	"	Leo ♌	5 "	26	"	Sagittarius	♐
6 "	15	"	Leo ♌	6 "	11	"	Capricorn	♑
7 "	27	"	Leo ♌	7 "	27	"	Capricorn	♑
8 "	9	"	Virgo ♍	8 "	16	"	Aquarius	♒
9 "	20	"	Virgo ♍	9 "	10	"	Pisces	♓
10 "	2	"	Libra ♎	10 "	5	"	Aries	♈
11 "	14	"	Libra ♎	11 "	0	"	Taurus	♉
12 Noon	26	"	Libra ♎	12 Midnight	23	"	Taurus	♉

JULY —30—

A. M.				P. M.				
1 o'clock	14°	of	Gemini ♊	1 o'clock	11°	of	Scorpio	♏
2 "	29	"	Gemini ♊	2 "	23	"	Scorpio	♏
3 "	12	"	Cancer ♋	3 "	5	"	Sagittarius	♐
4 "	24	"	Cancer ♋	4 "	17	"	Sagittarius	♐
5 "	7	"	Leo ♌	5 "	0	"	Capricorn	♑
6 "	18	"	Leo ♌	6 "	15	"	Capricorn	♑
7 "	0	"	Virgo ♍	7 "	2	"	Aquarius	♒
8 "	12	"	Virgo ♍	8 "	22	"	Aquarius	♒
9 "	23	"	Virgo ♍	9 "	16	"	Pisces	♓
10 "	6	"	Libra ♎	10 "	13	"	Aries	♈
11 "	18	"	Libra ♎	11 "	7	"	Taurus	♉
12 Noon	29	"	Libra ♎	12 Midnight	27	"	Taurus	♉

AUGUST —3—

A. M.				P. M.				
1 o'clock	18°	of	Gemini ♊	1 o'clock	14°	of	Scorpio	♏
2 "	3	"	Cancer ♋	2 "	26	"	Scorpio	♏
3 "	15	"	Cancer ♋	3 "	8	"	Sagittarius	♐
4 "	28	"	Cancer ♋	4 "	21	"	Sagittarius	♐
5 "	10	"	Leo ♌	5 "	4	"	Capricorn	♑

A. M.					P. M.				
6 o'clock	21°	of	Leo	♌	6 o'clock	20°	of	Capricorn	♑
7 "	3	"	Virgo	♍	7 "	7	"	Aquarius	♒
8 "	15	"	Virgo	♍	8 "	29	"	Aquarius	♒
9 "	27	"	Virgo	♍	9 "	24	"	Pisces	♓
10 "	9	"	Libra	♎	10 "	20	"	Aries	♈
11 "	21	"	Libra	♎	11 "	13	"	Taurus	♉
12 Noon	2	"	Scorpio	♏	12 Midnight	3	"	Gemini	♊

AUGUST —7—

A. M.					P. M.				
1 o'clock	22°	of	Gemini	♊	1 o'clock	18°	of	Scorpio	♏
2 "	6	"	Cancer	♋	2 "	29	"	Scorpio	♏
3 "	19	"	Cancer	♋	3 "	11	"	Sagittarius	♐
4 "	1	"	Leo	♌	4 "	25	"	Sagittarius	♐
5 "	13	"	Leo	♌	5 "	8	"	Capricorn	♑
6 "	24	"	Leo	♌	6 "	24	"	Capricorn	♑
7 "	7	"	Virgo	♍	7 "	13	"	Aquarius	♒
8 "	8	"	Virgo	♍	8 "	5	"	Pisces	♓
9 "	0	"	Libra	♎	9 "	1	"	Aries	♈
10 "	12	"	Libra	♎	10 "	27	"	Aries	♈
11 "	24	"	Libra	♎	11 "	19	"	Taurus	♉
12 Noon	6	"	Scorpio	♏	12 Midnight	8	"	Gemini	♊

AUGUST —11—

A. M.					P. M.				
1 o'clock	26°	of	Gemini	♊	1 o'clock	21°	of	Scorpio	♏
2 "	9	"	Cancer	♋	2 "	2	"	Sagittarius	♐
3 "	22	"	Cancer	♋	3 "	14	"	Sagittarius	♐
4 "	4	"	Leo	♌	4 "	28	"	Sagittarius	♐
5 "	16	"	Leo	♌	5 "	12	"	Capricorn	♑
6 "	28	"	Leo	♌	6 "	28	"	Capricorn	♑
7 "	10	"	Virgo	♍	7 "	19	"	Aquarius	♒
8 "	21	"	Virgo	♍	8 "	13	"	Pisces	♓
9 "	3	"	Libra	♎	9 "	7	"	Aries	♈
10 "	15	"	Libra	♎	10 "	2	"	Taurus	♉
11 "	27	"	Libra	♎	11 "	24	"	Taurus	♉
12 Noon	9	"	Scorpio	♏	12 Midnight	12	"	Gemini	♊

AUGUST —15—

A. M.					P. M.				
1 o'clock	0°	of	Cancer	♋	1 o'clock	24°	of	Scorpio	♏
2 "	13	"	Cancer	♋	2 "	5	"	Sagittarius	♐
3 "	25	"	Cancer	♋	3 "	18	"	Sagittarius	♐
4 "	7	"	Leo	♌	4 "	2	"	Capricorn	♑
5 "	19	"	Leo	♌	5 "	16	"	Capricorn	♑
6 "	1	"	Virgo	♍	6 "	3	"	Aquarius	♒
7 "	12	"	Virgo	♍	7 "	24	"	Aquarius	♒
8 "	24	"	Virgo	♍	8 "	18	"	Pisces	♓
9 "	6	"	Libra	♎	9 "	15	"	Aries	♈
10 "	18	"	Libra	♎	10 "	9	"	Taurus	♉
11 "	0	"	Scorpio	♏	11 "	29	"	Taurus	♉
12 Noon	12	"	Scorpio	♏	12 Midnight	16	"	Gemini	♊

AUGUST —19—

A. M.					P. M.				
1 o'clock	3°	of	Cancer	♋	1 o'clock	27°	of	Scorpio	♏
2 "	16	"	Cancer	♋	2 "	9	"	Sagittarius	♐
3 "	28	"	Cancer	♋	3 "	21	"	Sagittarius	♐
4 "	10	"	Leo	♌	4 "	5	"	Capricorn	♑
5 "	22	"	Leo	♌	5 "	20	"	Capricorn	♑
6 "	4	"	Virgo	♍	6 "	9	"	Aquarius	♒
7 "	16	"	Virgo	♍	7 "	0	"	Pisces	♓
8 "	28	"	Virgo	♍	8 "	26	"	Pisces	♓
9 "	9	"	Libra	♎	9 "	22	"	Aries	♈
10 "	22	"	Libra	♎	10 "	15	"	Taurus	♉
11 "	3	"	Scorpio	♏	11 "	4	"	Gemini	♊
12 Noon	15	"	Scorpio	♏	12 Midnight	20	"	Gemini	♊

AUGUST —23—

A. M.					P. M.				
1 o'clock	7°	of	Cancer	♋	1 o'clock	0°	of	Sagittarius	♐
2 "	19	"	Cancer	♋	2 "	12	"	Sagittarius	♐
3 "	1	"	Leo	♌	3 "	25	"	Sagittarius	♐
4 "	13	"	Leo	♌	4 "	9	"	Capricorn	♑
5 "	24	"	Leo	♌	5 "	25	"	Capricorn	♑

A. M.					P. M.				
6 o'clock	7°	of	Virgo	♍	6 o'clock	14°	of	Aquarius	♒
7 "	18	"	Virgo	♍	7 "	7	"	Pisces	♓
8 "	0	"	Libra	♎	8 "	3	"	Aries	♈
9 "	12	"	Libra	♎	9 "	27	"	Aries	♈
10 "	24	"	Libra	♎	10 "	20	"	Taurus	♉
11 "	6	"	Scorpio	♏	11 "	8	"	Gemini	♊
12 Noon	18	"	Scorpio	♏	12 Midnight	24	"	Gemini	♊

AUGUST —27—

A. M.					P. M.				
1 o'clock	10°	of	Cancer	♋	1 o'clock	2°	of	Sagittarius	♐
2 "	22	"	Cancer	♋	2 "	15	"	Sagittarius	♐
3 "	5	"	Leo	♌	3 "	28	"	Sagittarius	♐
4 "	16	"	Leo	♌	4 "	13	"	Capricorn	♑
5 "	28	"	Leo	♌	5 "	29	"	Capricorn	♑
6 "	10	"	Virgo	♍	6 "	20	"	Aquarius	♒
7 "	22	"	Virgo	♍	7 "	13	"	Pisces	♓
8 "	4	"	Libra	♎	8 "	9	"	Aries	♈
9 "	16	"	Libra	♎	9 "	4	"	Taurus	♉
10 "	27	"	Libra	♎	10 "	24	"	Taurus	♉
11 "	9	"	Scorpio	♏	11 "	12	"	Gemini	♊
12 Noon	21	"	Scorpio	♏	12 Midnight	28	"	Gemini	♊

AUGUST —31—

A. M.					P. M.				
1 o'clock	14°	of	Cancer	♋	1 o'clock	6°	of	Sagittarius	♐
2 "	26	"	Cancer	♋	2 "	19	"	Sagittarius	♐
3 "	8	"	Leo	♌	3 "	2	"	Capricorn	♑
4 "	19	"	Leo	♌	4 "	17	"	Capricorn	♑
5 "	1	"	Virgo	♍	5 "	5	"	Aquarius	♒
6 "	13	"	Virgo	♍	6 "	25	"	Aquarius	♒
7 "	25	"	Virgo	♍	7 "	20	"	Pisces	♓
8 "	7	"	Libra	♎	8 "	16	"	Aries	♈
9 "	19	"	Libra	♎	9 "	10	"	Taurus	♉
10 "	1	"	Scorpio	♏	10 "	0	"	Gemini	♊
11 "	12	"	Scorpio	♏	11 "	17	"	Gemini	♊
12 Noon	24	"	Scorpio	♏	12 Midnight	1	"	Cancer	♋

SEPTEMBER —4—

A. M.				P. M.			
1 o'clock	17° of	Cancer	♋	1 o'clock	9° of	Sagittarius	♐
2 "	29 "	Cancer	♋	2 "	22 "	Sagittarius	♐
3 "	11 "	Leo	♌	3 "	6 "	Capricorn	♑
4 "	23 "	Leo	♌	4 "	21 "	Capricorn	♑
5 "	4 "	Virgo	♍	5 "	10 "	Aquarius	♒
6 "	17 "	Virgo	♍	6 "	2 "	Pisces	♓
7 "	28 "	Virgo	♍	7 "	28 "	Pisces	♓
8 "	10 "	Libra	♎	8 "	24 "	Aries	♈
9 "	22 "	Libra	♎	9 "	16 "	Taurus	♉
10 "	4 "	Scorpio	♏	10 "	4 "	Gemini	♊
11 "	15 "	Scorpio	♏	11 "	20 "	Gemini	♊
12 Noon	27 "	Scorpio	♏	12 Midnight	5 "	Cancer	♋

SEPTEMBER —8—

A. M.				P. M.			
1 o'clock	20° of	Cancer	♋	1 o'clock	12° of	Sagittarius	♐
2 "	2 "	Leo	♌	2 "	25 "	Sagittarius	♐
3 "	14 "	Leo	♌	3 "	9 "	Capricorn	♑
4 "	25 "	Leo	♌	4 "	25 "	Capricorn	♑
5 "	7 "	Virgo	♍	5 "	15 "	Aquarius	♒
6 "	19 "	Virgo	♍	6 "	7 "	Pisces	♓
7 "	1 "	Libra	♎	7 "	3 "	Aries	♈
8 "	13 "	Libra	♎	8 "	29 "	Aries	♈
9 "	25 "	Libra	♎	9 "	21 "	Taurus	♉
10 "	7 "	Scorpio	♏	10 "	9 "	Gemini	♊
11 "	18 "	Scorpio	♏	11 "	24 "	Gemini	♊
12 Noon	0 "	Sagittarius	♐	12 Midnight	8 "	Cancer	♋

SEPTEMBER —12—

A. M.				P. M.			
1 o'clock	23° of	Cancer	♋	1 o'clock	15° of	Sagittarius	♐
2 "	5 "	Leo	♌	2 "	29 "	Sagittarius	♐
3 "	17 "	Leo	♌	3 "	14 "	Capricorn	♑
4 "	28 "	Leo	♌	4 "	1 "	Aquarius	♒
5 "	11 "	Virgo	♍	5 "	20 "	Aquarius	♒

A. M.					P. M.				
6 o'clock	22°	of	Virgo	♍	6 o'clock	15°	of	Pisces.	♓
7 "	4	"	Libra	♎	7 "	11	"	Aries	♈
8 "	16	"	Libra	♎	8 "	5	"	Taurus	♉
9 "	27	"	Libra	♎	9 "	26	"	Taurus	♉
10 "	10	"	Scorpio	♏	10 "	13	"	Gemini	♊
11 "	21	"	Scorpio	♏	11 "	28	"	Gemini	♊
12 Noon	3	"	Sagittarius	♐	12 Midnight	12	"	Cancer	♋

SEPTEMBER —16—

A. M.					P. M.				
1 o'clock	27°	of	Cancer	♋	1 o'clock	19°	of	Sagittarius	♐
2 "	8	"	Leo	♌	2 "	2	"	Capricorn	♑
3 "	20	"	Leo	♌	3 "	18	"	Capricorn	♑
4 "	2	"	Virgo	♍	4 "	6	"	Aquarius	♒
5 "	13	"	Virgo	♍	5 "	27	"	Aquarius	♒
6 "	25	"	Virgo	♍	6 "	22	"	Pisces	♓
7 "	7	"	Libra	♎	7 "	17	"	Aries	♈
8 "	19	"	Libra	♎	8 "	12	"	Taurus	♉
9 "	1	"	Scorpio	♏	9 "	1	"	Gemini	♊
10 "	13	"	Scorpio	♏	10 "	17	"	Gemini	♊
11 "	24	"	Scorpio	♏	11 "	2	"	Cancer	♋
12 Noon	7	"	Sagittarius	♐	12 Midnight	15	"	Cancer	♋

SEPTEMBER —20—

A. M.					P. M.				
1 o'clock	29°	of	Cancer	♋	1 o'clock	22°	of	Sagittarius	♐
2 "	11	"	Leo	♌	2 "	5	"	Capricorn	♑
3 "	22	"	Leo	♌	3 "	21	"	Capricorn	♑
4 "	4	"	Virgo	♍	4 "	9	"	Aquarius	♒
5 "	16	"	Virgo	♍	5 "	1	"	Pisces	♓
6 "	28	"	Virgo	♍	6 "	26	"	Pisces	♓
7 "	10	"	Libra	♎	7 "	22	"	Aries	♈
8 "	22	"	Libra	♎	8 "	15	"	Taurus	♉
9 "	3	"	Scorpio	♏	9 "	5	"	Gemini	♊
10 "	15	"	Scorpio	♏	10 "	21	"	Gemini	♊
11 "	27	"	Scorpio	♏	11 "	5	"	Cancer	♋
12 Noon	9	"	Sagittarius	♐	12 Midnight	18	"	Cancer	♋

SEPTEMBER —24—

A. M.				P. M.			
1 o'clock	2° of	Leo	♌	1 o'clock	26° of	Sagittarius	♐
2 "	14 "	Leo	♌	2 "	11 "	Capricorn	♑
3 "	26 "	Leo	♌	3 "	27 "	Capricorn	♑
4 "	8 "	Virgo	♍	4 "	16 "	Aquarius	♒
5 "	20 "	Virgo	♍	5 "	9 "	Pisces	♓
6 "	2 "	Libra	♎	6 "	5 "	Aries	♈
7 "	14 "	Libra	♎	7 "	0 "	Taurus	♉
8 "	26 "	Libra	♎	8 "	22 "	Taurus	♉
9 "	8 "	Scorpio	♏	9 "	10 "	Gemini	♊
10 "	19 "	Scorpio	♏	10 "	25 "	Gemini	♊
11 "	1 "	Sagittarius	♐	11 "	9 "	Cancer	♋
12 Noon	13 "	Sagittarius	♐	12 Midnight	21 "	Cancer	♋

SEPTEMBER —28—

A. M.				P. M.			
1 o'clock	6° of	Leo	♌	1 o'clock	0° of	Capricorn	♑
2 "	17 "	Leo	♌	2 "	14 "	Capricorn	♑
3 "	29 "	Leo	♌	3 "	2 "	Aquarius	♒
4 "	11 "	Virgo	♍	4 "	22 "	Aquarius	♒
5 "	23 "	Virgo	♍	5 "	16 "	Pisces	♓
6 "	5 "	Libra	♎	6 "	12 "	Aries	♈
7 "	17 "	Libra	♎	7 "	7 "	Taurus	♉
8 "	29 "	Libra	♎	8 "	27 "	Taurus	♉
9 "	11 "	Scorpio	♏	9 "	14 "	Gemini	♊
10 "	22 "	Scorpio	♏	10 "	29 "	Gemini	♊
11 "	4 "	Sagittarius	♐	11 "	12 "	Cancer	♋
12 Noon	16 "	Sagittarius	♐	12 Midnight	24 "	Cancer	♋

OCTOBER —2—

A. M.				P. M.			
1 o'clock	9° of	Leo	♌	1 o'clock	3° of	Capricorn	♑
2 "	21 "	Leo	♌	2 "	18 "	Capricorn	♑
3 "	2 "	Virgo	♍	3 "	16 "	Aquarius	♒
4 "	14 "	Virgo	♍	4 "	27 "	Aquarius	♒
5 "	26 "	Virgo	♍	5 "	22 "	Pisces	♓

A. M.					P. M.				
6 o'clock	8°	of	Libra	♎	6 o'clock	18°	of	Aries	♈
7 "	20	"	Libra	♎	7 "	12	"	Taurus	♉
8 "	2	"	Scorpio	♏	8 "	2	"	Gemini	♊
9 "	13	"	Scorpio	♏	9 "	18	"	Gemini	♊
10 "	25	"	Scorpio	♏	10 "	2	"	Cancer	♋
11 "	7	"	Sagittarius	♐	11 "	15	"	Cancer	♋
12 Noon	19	"	Sagittarius	♐	12 Midnight	27	"	Cancer	♋

OCTOBER —6—

A. M.					P. M.				
1 o'clock	11°	of	Leo	♌	1 o'clock	6°	of	Capricorn	♑
2 "	23	"	Leo	♌	2 "	22	"	Capricorn	♑
3 "	5	"	Virgo	♍	3 "	10	"	Aquarius	♒
4 "	17	"	Virgo	♍	4 "	3	"	Pisces	♓
5 "	28	"	Virgo	♍	5 "	28	"	Pisces	♓
6 "	10	"	Libra	♎	6 "	24	"	Aries	♈
7 "	22	"	Libra	♎	7 "	17	"	Taurus	♉
8 "	4	"	Scorpio	♏	8 "	5	"	Gemini	♊
9 "	16	"	Scorpio	♏	9 "	21	"	Gemini	♊
10 "	28	"	Scorpio	♏	10 "	5	"	Cancer	♋
11 "	10	"	Sagittarius	♐	11 "	18	"	Cancer	♋
12 Noon	22	"	Sagittarius	♐	12 Midnight	0	"	Leo	♌

OCTOBER —10—

A. M.					P. M.				
1 o'clock	15°	of	Leo	♌	1 o'clock	11°	of	Capricorn	♑
2 "	27	"	Leo	♌	2 "	27	"	Capricorn	♑
3 "	8	"	Virgo	♍	3 "	17	"	Aquarius	♒
4 "	20	"	Virgo	♍	4 "	11	"	Pisces	♓
5 "	2	"	Libra	♎	5 "	7	"	Aries	♈
6 "	14	"	Libra	♎	6 "	2	"	Taurus	♉
7 "	27	"	Libra	♎	7 "	23	"	Taurus	♉
8 "	9	"	Scorpio	♏	8 "	11	"	Gemini	♊
9 "	19	"	Scorpio	♏	9 "	26	"	Gemini	♊
10 "	˙2	"	Sagittarius	♐	10 "	9	"	Cancer	♋
11 "	14	"	Sagittarius	♐	11 "	22	"	Cancer	♋
12 Noon	26	"	Sagittarius	♐	12 Midnight	4	"	Leo	♌

OCTOBER —14—

A. M.				P. M.			
1 o'clock	18°	of Leo	♌	1 o'clock	15°	of Capricorn	♑
2 "	0	" Virgo	♍	2 "	2	" Aquarius	♒
3 "	12	" Virgo	♍	3 "	22	" Aquarius	♒
4 "	23	" Virgo	♍	4 "	16	" Pisces	♓
5 "	6	" Libra	♎	5 "	13	" Aries	♈
6 "	18	" Libra	♎	6 "	7	" Taurus	♉
7 "	29	" Libra	♎	7 "	27	" Taurus	♉
8 "	11	" Scorpio	♏	8 "	15	" Gemini	♊
9 "	22	" Scorpio	♏	9 "	29	" Gemini	♊
10 "	5	" Sagittarius	♐	10 "	12	" Cancer	♋
11 "	17	" Sagittarius	♐	11 "	25	" Cancer	♋
12 Noon	0	" Capricorn	♑	12 Midnight	7	" Leo	♌

OCTOBER —18—

A. M.				P. M.			
1 o'clock	21°	of Leo	♌	1 o'clock	19°	of Capricorn	♑
2 "	3	" Virgo	♍	2 "	7	" Aquarius	♒
3 "	15	" Virgo	♍	3 "	29	" Aquarius	♒
4 "	27	" Virgo	♍	4 "	24	" Pisces	♓
5 "	9	" Libra	♎	5 "	20	" Aries	♈
6 "	20	" Libra	♎	6 "	13	" Taurus	♉
7 "	2	" Scorpio	♏	7 "	3	" Gemini	♊
8 "	14	" Scorpio	♏	8 "	19	" Gemini	♊
9 "	26	" Scorpio	♏	9 "	3	" Cancer	♋
10 "	8	" Sagittarius	♐	10 "	16	" Cancer	♋
11 "	21	" Sagittarius	♐	11 "	28	" Cancer	♋
12 Noon	4	" Capricorn	♑	12 Midnight	10	" Leo	♌

OCTOBER —22—

A. M.				P. M.			
1 o'clock	24°	of Leo	♌	1 o'clock	24°	of Capricorn	♑
2 "	6	" Virgo	♍	2 "	13	" Aquarius	♒
3 "	18	" Virgo	♍	3 "	5	" Pisces	♓
4 "	0	" Libra	♎	4 "	1	" Aries	♈
5 "	12	" Libra	♎	5 "	27	" Aries	♈

A. M.				P. M.			
6 o'clock	24° of	Libra	♎	6 o'clock	19° of	Taurus	♉
7 "	5 "	Scorpio	♏	7 "	7 "	Gemini	♊
8 "	17 "	Scorpio	♏	8 "	23 "	Gemini	♊
9 "	29 "	Scorpio	♏	9 "	7 "	Cancer	♋
10 "	11 "	Sagittarius	♐	10 "	19 "	Cancer	♋
11 "	24 "	Sagittarius	♐	11 "	1 "	Leo	♌
12 Noon	7 "	Capricorn	♑	12 Midnight	13 "	Leo	♌

OCTOBER —26—

A. M.				P. M.			
1 o'clock	28° of	Leo	♌	1 o'clock	28° of	Capricorn	♑
2 "	9 "	Virgo	♍	2 "	19 "	Aquarius	♒
3 "	21 "	Virgo	♍	3 "	13 "	Pisces	♓
4 "	3 "	Libra	♎	4 "	8 "	Aries	♈
5 "	15 "	Libra	♎	5 "	2 "	Taurus	♉
6 "	27 "	Libra	♎	6 "	24 "	Taurus	♉
7 "	9 "	Scorpio	♏	7 "	11 "	Gemini	♊
8 "	20 "	Scorpio	♏	8 "	27 "	Gemini	♊
9 "	2 "	Sagittarius	♐	9 "	10 "	Cancer	♋
10 "	14 "	Sagittarius	♐	10 "	22 "	Cancer	♋
11 "	27 "	Sagittarius	♐	11 "	5 "	Leo	♌
12 Noon	12 "	Capricorn	♑	12 Midnight	16 "	Leo	♌

OCTOBER —30—

A. M.				P. M.			
1 o'clock	1° of	Virgo	♍	1 o'clock	3° of	Aquarius	♒
2 "	12 "	Virgo	♍	2 "	24 "	Aquarius	♒
3 "	24 "	Virgo	♍	3 "	19 "	Pisces	♓
4 "	6 "	Libra	♎	4 "	15 "	Aries	♈
5 "	18 "	Libra	♎	5 "	9 "	Taurus	♉
6 "	0 "	Scorpio	♏	6 "	29 "	Taurus	♉
7 "	12 "	Scorpio	♏	7 "	16 "	Gemini	♊
8 "	23 "	Scorpio	♏	8 "	0 "	Cancer	♋
9 "	5 "	Sagittarius	♐	9 "	13 "	Cancer	♋
10 "	17 "	Sagittarius	♐	10 "	26 "	Cancer	♋
11 "	1 "	Capricorn	♑	11 "	8 "	Leo	♌
12 Noon	16 "	Capricorn	♑	12 Midnight	19 "	Leo	♌

NOVEMBER —3—

A. M.				P. M.				
1 o'clock	3°	of	Virgo ♍	1 o'clock	9°	of	Aquarius	♒
2 "	15	"	Virgo ♍	2 "	0	"	Pisces	♓
3 "	27	"	Virgo ♍	3 "	26	"	Pisces	♓
4 "	9	"	Libra ♎	4 "	22	"	Aries	♈
5 "	21	"	Libra ♎	5 "	14	"	Taurus	♉
6 "	3	"	Scorpio ♏	6 "	3	"	Gemini	♊
7 "	15	"	Scorpio ♏	7 "	19	"	Gemini	♊
8 "	27	"	Scorpio ♏	8 "	3	"	Cancer	♋
9 "	8	"	Sagittarius ♐	9 "	16	"	Cancer	♋
10 "	21	"	Sagittarius ♐	10 "	29	"	Cancer	♋
11 "	4	"	Capricorn ♑	11 "	11	"	Leo	♌
12 Noon	20	"	Capricorn ♑	12 Midnight	22	"	Leo	♌

NOVEMBER —7—

A. M.				P. M.				
1 o'clock	7°	of	Virgo ♍	1 o'clock	13°	of	Aquarius	♒
2 "	18	"	Virgo ♍	2 "	7	"	Pisces	♓
3 "	0	"	Libra ♎	3 "	2	"	Aries	♈
4 "	12	"	Libra ♎	4 "	27	"	Aries	♈
5 "	24	"	Libra ♎	5 "	20	"	Taurus	♉
6 "	6	"	Scorpio ♏	6 "	8	"	Gemini	♊
7 "	18	"	Scorpio ♏	7 "	23	"	Gemini	♊
8 "	29	"	Scorpio ♏	8 "	7	"	Cancer	♋
9 "	12	"	Sagittarius ♐	9 "	20	"	Cancer	♋
10 "	25	"	Sagittarius ♐	10 "	2	"	Leo	♌
11 "	8	"	Capricorn ♑	11 "	14	"	Leo	♌
12 Noon	25	"	Capricorn ♑	12 Midnight	25	"	Leo	♌

NOVEMBER —11—

A. M.				P. M.				
1 o'clock	10°	of	Virgo ♍	1 o'clock	20°	of	Aquarius	♒
2 "	22	"	Virgo ♍	2 "	13	"	Pisces	♓
3 "	4	"	Libra ♎	3 "	9	"	Aries	♈
4 "	16	"	Libra ♎	4 "	4	"	Taurus	♉
5 "	27	"	Libra ♎	5 "	25	"	Taurus	♉

A. M.				P. M.				
6 o'clock	9°	of	Scorpio ♏	6 o'clock	12°	of	Gemini	♊
7 "	21	"	Scorpio ♏	7 "	28	"	Gemini	♊
8 "	2	"	Sagittarius ♐	8 "	11	"	Cancer	♋
9 "	15	"	Sagittarius ♐	9 "	23	"	Cancer	♋
10 "	28	"	Sagittarius ♐	10 "	5	"	Leo	♌
11 "	12	"	Capricorn ♑	11 "	17	"	Leo	♌
12 Noon	29	"	Capricorn ♑	12 Midnight	28	"	Leo	♌

NOVEMBER —15—

A. M.				P. M.				
1 o'clock	13°	of	Virgo ♍	1 o'clock	25°	of	Aquarius	♒
2 "	25	"	Virgo ♍	2 "	20	"	Pisces	♓
3 "	6	"	Libra ♎	3 "	16	"	Aries	♈
4 "	19	"	Libra ♎	4 "	10	"	Taurus	♉
5 "	1	"	Scorpio ♏	5 "	0	"	Gemini	♊
6 "	12	"	Scorpio ♏	6 "	16	"	Gemini	♊
7 "	24	"	Scorpio ♏	7 "	1	"	Cancer	♋
8 "	6	"	Sagittarius ♐	8 "	14	"	Cancer	♋
9 "	18	"	Sagittarius ♐	9 "	26	"	Cancer	♋
10 "	2	"	Capricorn ♑	10 "	8	"	Leo	♌
11 "	17	"	Capricorn ♑	11 "	20	"	Leo	♌
12 Noon	5	"	Aquarius ♒	12 Midnight	2	"	Virgo	♍

NOVEMBER —19—

A. M.				P. M.				
1 o'clock	16°	of	Virgo ♍	1 o'clock	2°	of	Pisces	♓
2 "	28	"	Virgo ♍	2 "	27	"	Pisces	♓
3 "	10	"	Libra ♎	3 "	23	"	Aries	♈
4 "	22	"	Libra ♎	4 "	15	"	Taurus	♉
5 "	4	"	Scorpio ♏	5 "	4	"	Gemini	♊
6 "	15	"	Scorpio ♏	6 "	20	"	Gemini	♊
7 "	27	"	Scorpio ♏	7 "	4	"	Cancer	♋
8 "	9	"	Sagittarius ♐	8 "	17	"	Cancer	♋
9 "	21	"	Sagittarius ♐	9 "	29	"	Cancer	♋
10 "	5	"	Capricorn ♑	10 "	11	"	Leo	♌
11 "	20	"	Capricorn ♑	11 "	23	"	Leo	♌
12 Noon	9	"	Aquarius ♒	12 Midnight	5	"	Virgo	♍

NOVEMBER —23—

A. M.				P. M.				
1 o'clock	19°	of	Virgo ♍	1 o'clock	8°	of	Pisces	♓
2 "	1	"	Libra ♎	2 "	3	"	Aries	♈
3 "	13	"	Libra ♎	3 "	29	"	Aries	♈
4 "	25	"	Libra ♎	4 "	20	"	Taurus	♉
5 "	7	"	Scorpio ♏	5 "	9	"	Gemini	♊
6 "	18	"	Scorpio ♏	6 "	24	"	Gemini	♊
7 "	0	"	Sagittarius ♐	7 "	8	"	Cancer	♋
8 "	12	"	Sagittarius ♐	8 "	20	"	Cancer	♋
9 "	25	"	Sagittarius ♐	9 "	2	"	Leo	♌
10 "	9	"	Capricorn ♑	10 "	14	"	Leo	♌
11 "	25	"	Capricorn ♑	11 "	26	"	Leo	♌
12 Noon	14	"	Aquarius ♒	12 Midnight	7	"	Virgo	♍

NOVEMBER —27—

A. M.				P. M.				
1 o'clock	22°	of	Virgo ♍	1 o'clock	14°	of	Pisces	♓
2 "	4	"	Libra ♎	2 "	10	"	Aries	♈
3 "	16	"	Libra ♎	3 "	8	"	Taurus	♉
4 "	28	"	Libra ♎	4 "	26	"	Taurus	♉
5 "	10	"	Scorpio ♏	5 "	13	"	Gemini	♊
6 "	21	"	Scorpio ♏	6 "	28	"	Gemini	♊
7 "	3	"	Sagittarius ♐	7 "	13	"	Cancer	♋
8 "	15	"	Sagittarius ♐	8 "	24	"	Cancer	♋
9 "	29	"	Sagittarius ♐	9 "	5	"	Leo	♌
10 "	14	"	Capricorn ♑	10 "	17	"	Leo	♌
11 "	0	"	Aquarius ♒	11 "	29	"	Leo	♌
12 Noon	20	"	Aquarius ♒	12 Midnight	11	"	Virgo	♍

DECEMBER —1—

A. M.				P. M.				
1 o'clock	25°	of	Virgo ♍	1 o'clock	21°	of	Pisces	♓
2 "	7	"	Libra ♎	2 "	16	"	Aries	♈
3 "	19	"	Libra ♎	3 "	10	"	Taurus	♉
4 "	1	"	Scorpio ♏	4 "	1	"	Gemini	♊
5 "	13	"	Scorpio ♏	5 "	17	"	Gemini	♊

A. M.				P. M.				
6 o'clock	25°	of	Scorpio ♏	6 o'clock	2°	of	Cancer	♋
7 "	7	"	Sagittarius ♐	7 "	15	"	Cancer	♋
8 "	19	"	Sagittarius ♐	8 "	27	"	Cancer	♋
9 "	2	"	Capricorn ♑	9 "	9	"	Leo	♌
10 "	17	"	Capricorn ♑	10 "	21	"	Leo	♌
11 "	5	"	Aquarius ♒	11 "	2	"	Virgo	♍
12 Noon	27	"	Aquarius ♒	12 Midnight	14	"	Virgo	♍

DECEMBER —5—

A. M.				P. M.				
1 o'clock	28°	of	Virgo ♍	1 o'clock	26°	of	Pisces	♓
2 "	10	"	Libra ♎	2 "	22	"	Aries	♈
3 "	21	"	Libra ♎	3 "	15	"	Taurus	♉
4 "	3	"	Scorpio ♏	4 "	4	"	Gemini	♊
5 "	15	"	Scorpio ♏	5 "	20	"	Gemini	♊
6 "	27	"	Scorpio ♏	6 "	4	"	Cancer	♋
7 "	9	"	Sagittarius ♐	7 "	17	"	Cancer	♋
8 "	21	"	Sagittarius ♐	8 "	29	"	Cancer	♋
9 "	5	"	Capricorn ♑	9 "	11	"	Leo	♌
10 "	20	"	Capricorn ♑	10 "	22	"	Leo	♌
11 "	9	"	Aquarius ♒	11 "	4	"	Virgo	♍
12 Noon	0	"	Pisces ♓	12 Midnight	16	"	Virgo	♍

DECEMBER —9—

A. M.				P. M.				
1 o'clock	2°	of	Libra ♎	1 o'clock	5°	of	Aries	♈
2 "	14	"	Libra ♎	2 "	0	"	Taurus	♉
3 "	25	"	Libra ♎	3 "	22	"	Taurus	♉
4 "	8	"	Scorpio ♏	4 "	10	"	Gemini	♊
5 "	19	"	Scorpio ♏	5 "	25	"	Gemini	♊
6 "	1	"	Sagittarius ♐	6 "	9	"	Cancer	♋
7 "	13	"	Sagittarius ♐	7 "	21	"	Cancer	♋
8 "	26	"	Sagittarius ♐	8 "	3	"	Leo	♌
9 "	10	"	Capricorn ♑	9 "	15	"	Leo	♌
10 "	26	"	Capricorn ♑	10 "	27	"	Leo	♌
11 "	16	"	Aquarius ♒	11 "	8	"	Virgo	♍
12 Noon	9	"	Pisces ♓	12 Midnight	20	"	Virgo	♍

DECEMBER —13—

A. M.				P. M.				
1 o'clock	5°	of	Libra	♎	1 o'clock	12°	of Aries	♈
2 "	17	"	Libra	♎	2 "	6	" Taurus	♉
3 "	28	"	Libra	♎	3 "	27	" Taurus	♉
4 "	10	"	Scorpio	♏	4 "	14	" Gemini	♊
5 "	22	"	Scorpio	♏	5 "	29	" Gemini	♊
6 "	4	"	Sagittarius	♐	6 "	12	" Cancer	♋
7 "	16	"	Sagittarius	♐	7 "	24	" Cancer	♋
8 "	29	"	Sagittarius	♐	8 "	6	" Leo	♌
9 "	14	"	Capricorn	♑	9 "	18	" Leo	♌
10 "	1	"	Aquarius	♒	10 "	0	" Virgo	♍
11 "	21	"	Aquarius	♒	11 "	12	" Virgo	♍
12 Noon	15	"	Pisces	♓	12 Midnight	23	" Virgo	♍

DECEMBER —18—

A. M.				P. M.				
1 o'clock	9°	of	Libra	♎	1 o'clock	20°	of Aries	♈
2 "	21	"	Libra	♎	2 "	13	" Taurus	♉
3 "	2	"	Scorpio	♏	3 "	3	" Gemini	♊
4 "	14	"	Scorpio	♏	4 "	19	" Gemini	♊
5 "	26	"	Scorpio	♏	5 "	3	" Cancer	♋
6 "	8	"	Sagittarius	♐	6 "	16	" Cancer	♋
7 "	21	"	Sagittarius	♐	7 "	28	" Cancer	♋
8 "	4	"	Capricorn	♑	8 "	10	" Leo	♌
9 "	19	"	Capricorn	♑	9 "	22	" Leo	♌
10 "	7	"	Aquarius	♒	10 "	4	" Virgo	♍
11 "	29	"	Aquarius	♒	11 "	16	" Virgo	♍
12 Noon	24	"	Pisces	♓	12 Midnight	27	" Virgo	♍

DECEMBER —23—

A. M.				P. M.				
1 o'clock	12°	of	Libra	♎	1 o'clock	28°	of Aries	♈
2 "	24	"	Libra	♎	2 "	20	" Taurus	♉
3 "	6	"	Scorpio	♏	3 "	9	" Gemini	♊
4 "	18	"	Scorpio	♏	4 "	24	" Gemini	♊
5 "	0	"	Sagittarius	♐	5 "	8	" Cancer	♋

A. M.				P. M.			
6 o'clock	12° of	Sagittarius	♐	6 o'clock	20° of	Cancer	♋
7 "	25 "	Sagittarius	♐	7 "	2 "	Leo	♌
8 "	9 "	Capricorn	♑	8 "	14 "	Leo	♌
9 "	25 "	Capricorn	♑	9 "	26 "	Leo	♌
10 "	14 "	Aquarius	♒	10 "	7 "	Virgo	♍
11 "	7 "	Pisces	♓	11 "	19 "	Virgo	♍
12 Noon	2 "	Aries	♈	12 Midnight	1 "	Libra	♎

DECEMBER —28—

A. M.				P. M.			
1 o'clock	16° of	Libra	♎	1 o'clock	5° of	Taurus	♉
2 "	28 "	Libra	♎	2 "	26 "	Taurus	♉
3 "	10 "	Scorpio	♏	3 "	13 "	Gemini	♊
4 "	22 "	Scorpio	♏	4 "	28 "	Gemini	♊
5 "	4 "	Sagittarius	♐	5 "	12 "	Cancer	♋
6 "	16 "	Sagittarius	♐	6 "	24 "	Cancer	♋
7 "	29 "	Sagittarius	♐	7 "	6 "	Leo	♌
8 "	14 "	Capricorn	♑	8 "	17 "	Leo	♌
9 "	1 "	Aquarius	♒	9 "	0 "	Virgo	♍
10 "	21 "	Aquarius	♒	10 "	12 "	Virgo	♍
11 "	14 "	Pisces	♓	11 "	23 "	Virgo	♍
12 Noon	11 "	Aries	♈	12 Midnight	6 "	Libra	♎

PART IV

HOW TO CAST A HOROSCOPE

HOW TO CAST A HOROSCOPE

The instructions given in this chapter are for beginners in the science. The author has been told frequently by those who have read extensively on the subject of Astrology that they find it difficult to follow any of the rules given in the various works on the subject, as they are generally too technical and complicated. For this reason these directions have been abbreviated; but they are sufficiently accurate to prove of value to the layman. Non-technical terms are employed wherever possible, and minute calculations, such as corrections from Standard to Local Mean Time, or from Local Mean Time to Sidereal Time, have been omitted.

A horoscope is a map or chart indicating the positions of the Sun, the Moon and seven planets in relation to the earth and to the zodiac for any given moment of time. While it is possible to calculate the horoscope with great precision for any instant of time, so few know exactly the moment of their birth, unfortunately, that for ordinary judgment the rules given herein will suffice.

In Diagram 1 the center represents the earth and the outer circle the space of the heavens which is divided into twelve equal sections called "houses." The term "cusp" is used to indicate the line that divides one house from another. The first house begins with the horizontal line on the left side of the circle and the cusp of the first house is called the Ascendant, as the Sun, the Moon and the planets from this point on ascend, or arise, and are visible in our horizon.

The sign of the zodiac rising at a person's birth, termed the Ascendant, signifies man's outward appearance and everything which has to do with the personality, and is

MIDHEAVEN OR ZENITH

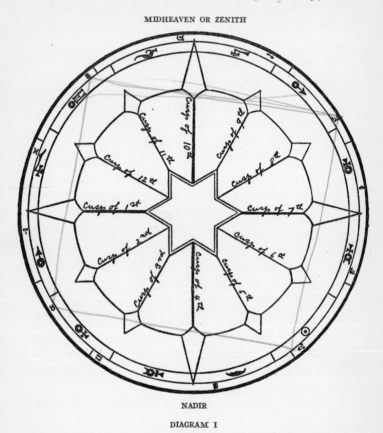

NADIR

DIAGRAM I

therefore considered one of the most important factors in diagnosing the horoscope. In order to verify the calculations, after having placed the signs on each of the twelve divisions, it is recommended that the student refer to the Table of Ascendants (Part III), which will show at a glance whether his figures are correct, for if the Ascendant has been calculated accurately, the signs on the cusps of the other houses will generally be found to be in their right places.

FINDING THE CUSPS OF THE HOUSES

In order to erect a horoscope for any given time, it will be necessary to refer to Raphael's Ephemeris (for the year of birth desired), which contains the zodiacal positions of the Sun, Moon and planets.

Sidereal Time of Birth.—Turning to the required month and day in the Ephemeris, a column will be found on the left, headed "Sidereal Time." If the birth be before noon, deduct from the Sidereal Time the difference between the time of birth and noon of the same day; if the birth happened after noon, then add to the Sidereal Time the time between noon and the time of birth. In the case of a morning birth, if the Sidereal Time will not permit the deduction, then add 24 hours to it, and make your subtraction; in like manner, if, when adding the time of birth to the Sidereal Time, the total exceeds 24 hours, then subtract this (24) from the result, which gives the correct Sidereal Time of birth. Again, it must be taken into account whether Daylight Saving Time was in operation at the time the person was born; if so, subtract one hour from the clock time, and then proceed as above.

Cusps of the Houses.—Having ascertained the correct Sidereal Time of birth, turn to the Table of Houses at the end of Raphael's Ephemeris, and in the column marked Sidereal Time, find this figure or the nearest thereto as computed above. It will be noted in this table that the figures 10, 11, 12, Ascendant 2 and 3 occupy the top line. These represent the cusps of six of the houses, or from the Midheaven to the 4th. The remaining six houses occupy the other half of the circle, and we insert on their cusps the same degrees of the opposite signs, thus completing the twelve houses. (The signs and those opposite each one, are shown at the beginning of Part I.)

The signs and degrees for the cusps of the 10th, 11th, 2nd, Ascendant and 3rd houses of the horoscope are on the same horizonal line with Sidereal Time.

As an example, we will proceed to erect a figure for the moment of the New Year, which is 0 A. M. January 1, 1928. If we turn to the Ephemeris for 1928, we find Sidereal Time to be 18 hours, 39 minutes and 37 seconds (or for practical purposes 18 hours, 49 minutes). Since the Ephemeris is calculated for Greenwich or London at noon of each day, and since 0 A. M., or the beginning of the New Year, is twelve hours previous to noon (from which all calculations are made as stated before) we subtract 12 hours from 18 hours and 40 minutes, giving the result of 6 hours and 40 minutes.

We now turn to the Table of Houses and find the nearest Sidereal Time to be 6 hours, 39 minutes and 11 seconds, which gives us 9 degrees of Cancer on the cusp of the 10th house; 12 degrees of Leo on the eleventh house; 13 degrees of Virgo on the twelfth; 7 degrees, 47 minutes of Libra on the first or Ascendant; 4 of Scorpio on the cusp of the second; and 5 of Sagittarius on the third. We fill in the remaining six cusps with the same number of degrees, but with the opposite signs. Our cusps are now complete.

How to Place the Planets in the Houses.—In order to insert the planets in their proper places in the map, we refer to January 1 in the 1928 Ephemeris. In the column headed "Long." (abbreviation of longitude signifying the planets' positions in the zodiac), and under the planetary symbols, we find the planets' positions expressed in degrees and minutes, and seconds in the case of the Sun and Moon. The student realizes, of course, that each sign of the zodiac contains 30 degrees, each degree 60 minutes, and each minute 60 seconds. When the seconds exceed 30, one minute may be added, and if under thirty, they can be omitted.

Birth Time Changed to Greenwich Time.—The planets' places given in the Ephemeris are calculated for noon at Greenwich or London, as already stated, and therefore we must change New York time to Greenwich time. This is done by adding the difference in time between New York and Greenwich to the time of birth of the New Year (or with an individual their hour of birth). As the earth turns around on its axis once in twenty-four hours (the circumference containing 360 degrees), it is obvious that every degree must represent four minutes of time. As the longitude for New York is approximately 75 degrees west of Greenwich, and each degree of longitude is equal to four minutes of time, we consequently find that the difference in time between New York and Greenwich is five hours; we now add this five hours to 0 A. M. of January 1, 1928, which gives us 5 A. M. This, subtracted from noon, upon which all calculations in the Ephemeris are based, gives a 7-hour correction for the Sun, Moon and planets.

The Sun's Position.—The Sun moves approximately 1

degree, or 60 minutes, in 24 hours, and, if we divide 24 hours by 60 minutes, we will find that the Sun moves 2½ minutes per hour. Multiplying 2½ by 7, gives 17 minutes and 30 seconds. As the corrected time was previous to noon (5 A. M.), this amount must be subtracted from the position of the Sun in the "Ephemeris" for January 1, 1928, which is 9 degrees, 50 minutes of Capricorn, making the Sun for January 1 at New York City, in 9 degrees, 32 minutes of Capricorn.

The Moon's Position.—The movement of the Moon is more erratic, varying from 12 to 15 degrees in 24 hours. One degree for each two hours, or 30 minutes per hour, is sufficiently accurate in correcting the Moon for the use of the beginner. We now multiply the 7 hours by 30 minutes, or one-half a degree, which will give 3 degrees, 30 minutes correction, which must be subtracted from the Moon's position at noon, 23 degrees, 19 minutes of Aries, leaving 19 degrees, 49 minutes of Aries for the Moon's position at New York City for January 1, 1928, at 0 A. M.

This is not quite exact, as the Moon on December 31, 1927, was in 9 degrees 10 minutes of Aries, and on January 1, 1928, it was in 23 degrees 19 minutes, or a difference of 14 degrees and 9 minutes for the twenty-four hours; in this case it would make a difference in the position of the Moon of 35 minutes, but, unless one were using secondary directions or arcs, it would have no material effect in determining the Moon's influence.

A remark made by the author's preceptor, Dr. J. Heber Smith, when teaching her how to erect a figure, made a deep impression. This was to the effect that the type of mind that "fussed" over the minutes and seconds in drawing up a chart never made a good astrological diagnostician, such minds being too literal and their spiritual perception too limited. As an example, he stated that the charts drawn by Professor Lester (his contemporary, and whom he considered the wisest Astrologer of his period), "looked as if a hen had walked over the paper." Dr. Smith's opinion has been borne out by the author in her own experience with pupils. Raphael, under whose supervision the ephemerides upon which all Astrologers are dependent are prepared, in drawing his charts in his daily work, does not consider it necessary to put in anything but the degrees of the planets; which still further goes to prove that the more one knows of the truths of the science, the more one realizes that he is dealing with the Cosmos and that unless the Astrologer has background, years of experience and much worldly wisdom, he is in danger of depending too much on mathematics and too little on the things that count.

Sometimes the author is asked how long it would be necessary to study Astrology in order to master the science, and she is always reminded at such times of a remark made by Regulus in 1889, to the effect that he had been studying Astrology thirty-five years and he realized that he had only scratched the surface of its vast possibilities.

The Planets' Positions.—For all practical purposes the other planets may be inserted in the map as found in the Ephemeris. Should it be desired to calculate the exact positions of the planets (including the Sun and Moon), the student will find on the last sheet of Raphael's Ephemeris, a table of Proportional Logarithms, with a rule and example at the end of the page; but as many students will find themselves puzzled by the propor-

tional logarithms, a more simple method is given below. In cases where a planet is close to the end or beginning of a sign it is more necessary to ascertain its
exact position, and it should be accurately calculated.
The planets are moving, not only at various rates, but
because of the relative motion of the earth in the ecliptic
at certain periods in any year they appear to be moving
backwards. At such times, they are said to be retrograde;
this is signified by the symbol ℞, or the symbol which is
used on all apothecary's prescriptions. When a planet
turns direct, the letter D is inserted in the column. The
Sun and Moon, of course, are never retrograde.

Placing the Planets in the Houses.—Now that the
Sun and Moon have been rectified, we will proceed to
place them and the planets in their proper houses on
the chart. To assist the beginner, let him think of the
first house or Ascendant as being 9 o'clock on the face
of a watch or clock, and remember that, in order that
the planets may rise, the signs on the cusps of the
houses must move backwards. This again comes from the
fact that it is the earth that moves on its axis, causing the
Sun to appear to rise, as in reality, the heavenly bodies
remain practically stationary for the twenty-four hours.
Therefore it is necessary to remember that the planets go
with the clock, and the signs rise in the opposite direction.

Referring to Diagram 2, which shows the positions of
the heavens or the twelve houses at the beginning of the
New Year, and the degrees of the zodiac on the cusp of
each house, we will proceed to place the planets in this
diagram.

We found that the Moon, after being corrected, was in
19 degrees Aries 49 minutes, and as 7 Aries, 47 minutes is

on the cusp of the seventh house, we must place the Moon in the seventh house. We found that the Sun, after being corrected, was in 9 degrees Capricorn 32 minutes, and as 9 degrees Capricorn was on the cusp of the fourth house,

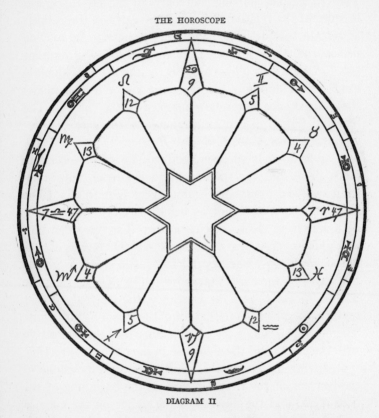

THE HOROSCOPE

DIAGRAM II

we must place the Sun just over the line in the fourth house, because it is more than 9 degrees. As already stated for easy reckoning, we have not corrected the planets, and will therefore proceed to place them in their right positions. Neptune, being in 28 degrees Leo, 56 minutes, will occupy the eleventh house, as 12 of Leo is on the cusp. Uranus, being in 29 degrees Pisces, 43 minutes, will be

THE HOROSCOPE

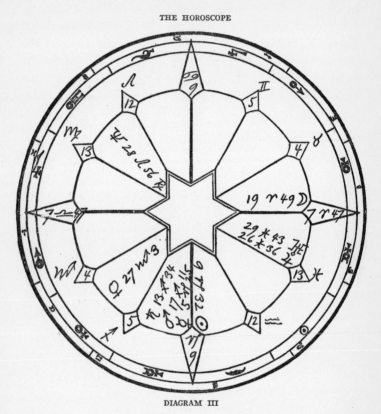

DIAGRAM III

placed in the sixth house, as 13 degrees of Pisces is on the cusp of the sixth house. Jupiter being in 26 Pisces, 36 minutes, will also be placed in the sixth house, preceding Uranus. Saturn being in 13 degrees Sagittarius, 34 minutes, will be in the third house, as 5 degrees of Sagittarius is on the cusp. Mars being in 17 degrees Sagittarius 11 minutes, will follow Saturn in the same house. Venus, being in 27 Scorpio 3 minutes, will be in the second house, as 4 degrees of Scorpio is on the cusp. Mercury, being in 5 degrees Capricorn 25, will also be placed in the third house, as 9 degrees of Capricorn is on the cusp of the fourth house; 5 degrees being less than 9 degrees, it must be placed in the preceding house. Diagram 3 illustrates the complete figure or horoscope for the year 1928, January 1, 0 A. M.

PART V

HORARY ASTROLOGY

HORARY ASTROLOGY

As stated in "The Bowl of Heaven," the Ancients, in their Horary Astrology, considered only the mundane position of the heavens at the time the individual sought an answer to his query. It can at once be seen that if two or more persons present their queries at exactly the same time, they would with this method get exactly the same diagnosis, irrespective of what their immediate need might be. Horary Astrology, as practiced by the author, considers also the position of the heavens in relation to the radical chart of the individual. With this method, which is explained below, each person would receive the information bearing on the particular problem involving his life at the moment.

For instance, and for the benefit of the beginner, take the exact time the question is asked and work out for this time the Ascendant, or first house, as well as the cusps of the other eleven houses; just as you would if drawing a natal chart. Instead, however, of placing in this chart the planets as they appear in the heavens at the moment the question is asked, the querent's radical planets should be placed in this chart. The Astrologer should now proceed to read the chart in the same manner as if it were the radix, for the chart as it now stands might be considered the horoscope for the birth of the idea, just as the natal chart is the horoscope for the birth of the individual. The description given for the twelve houses can be utilized either in ascertaining the effects of the planets in the life of the individual or its effects on the horary question.

Just as the position of Saturn in any of the twelve houses in the natal chart indicates the source from which we must expect discipline, restricted conditions and the most serious disappointments that the native will find it necessary to meet during his lifetime, so the position of Saturn in the horary figure shows the source of his present worry. For instance, if Saturn is found in the first house, or Ascendant, of the horary figure, the Astrologer must instruct his querent that he is facing depressed health conditions, that he is about to pass through a temporary cloud, and that he may meet with a disappointment of some kind.

If Saturn is in the second house, or house of money, it is safe to assume that the querent has come for enlightenment on some business involving finance, and he should be cautioned against taking any undue risks where money is involved.

Just as Saturn stands for limitation, sorrow, obstacles and delays, and even death of a project or person, Uranus indicates the unexpected, and the querent should be informed that he must not take too seriously any good or ill fortune which may be promised or threatened in any department of life designated by the position of Uranus in one of the twelve houses in which it may happen to fall.

Where Neptune, which stands for the psychic forces, is placed in the horary figure, it always indicates some form of intrigue or camouflage, as this planet is nearly always unfortunate in its influence on the material or mundane plane.

Where Jupiter, which is the "Greater Fortune" and

stands for harmony and prosperity, is placed in the horary figure, it always indicates from what source the querent is enjoying happiness or prosperity and from what source he can look for favorable conditions concerning the matters connected with the particular house in which Jupiter is found at the moment.

This is a sufficient key to make it possible for the student or Astrologer to determine from what angle or department of life the influence of any planet will be felt. There is not adequate space here to give details regarding the nine planets and the twelve houses; the author plans to do this in another volume.

As an example of the manner in which the author utilizes this branch of Astrology, not only in her professional life but also at any and all times, the following may be noted: During her recent visit to London, when she and Alec Stewart, co-editor of Raphael's Astronomical Ephemeris and Editor of the monthly magazine "Star Lore," were guests at dinner of a well-known British financier, who is a client of Mr. Stewart's, the butler announced an urgent call on the telephone. Our host was informed that his brother was dangerously ill, and when he returned to the drawing-room and informed his guests of the purport of the message, the author turned to Mr. Stewart and said "You will find, if you draw a horary figure for this moment, that our host's Saturn will be in the third house" (brothers and sisters). This was done almost immediately, and true to form, Saturn *was* in the third house!

A much more significant example is that of the late Philip Payne, of the New York *Mirror,* who lost his life with the ill-fated, *Old Glory,* in her attempt to fly to Rome. He was for some years a client of the author, and, at the time his chart was consulted as to whether this feat would meet with success, his Saturn, Uranus, and Mars were all about to rise, clearly indicating the long delays before starting off, the unexpected happenings, and the ultimate disaster which overtook him and his companions. It is further interesting to note that, on September 6, 1927, at 12.23 P. M., when *Old Glory* hopped off from Old Orchard, Saturn in the heavens was exactly on the Ascendant.

In strong contrast to this figure, at the time Colonel Charles A. Lindbergh hopped off from Mineola, L. I., on May 20, 1927, 6.51 A. M., true time, the Sun and Mercury had just risen, Venus was close to the Ascendant, and the "Greater Fortune," Jupiter and Uranus, the planet of the unexpected, were in the Midheaven. The charts drawn for the time of the flights of these men are not, however, horary figures. They are, rather, the natal charts of the ventures.

Horary Astrology practically proves that there are no accidents in the Universe, and that everything happens according to law and order. In substantiating this belief, the author has found that when, because of the unavoidable delay, either on her part or that of the client, the appointment has been held over, it invariably develops that the horary figure, as drawn from the exact moment when consultation takes place, indicates the problem about which he is desirous of obtaining information; and, had there been no delay, the horary figure would not have indicated his problem or offered any assistance in its solution.

This branch of the science must not be used for asking questions out of mere curiosity or in a spirit of levity.

Whenever a horary figure seems meaningless, it is either because the question is not worth while or it was erected at a time when nothing very vital was pending, and in such cases the natal chart should be relied upon.

The question often arises as to whether the time when the querent first conceives an idea or the time when the question is put to the Astrologer is the correct time for erecting the horary figure. The author has found that where it is possible for the querent to place definitely the moment of the birth of the *idea*, or the time when the proposition was presented to him, this would be the radical figure, which should be considered in combination with that drawn for the time when the question was propounded to the Astrologer.

PART VI

DESCRIPTION OF THE TWELVE HOUSES

THE TWELVE HOUSES

In order that the student may understand and make use of the New Horary Astrology, it is necessary to have a knowledge of the twelve houses, which might be considered the "mansions in the sky." The circumference of the zodiacal belt contains 360 degrees; consequently, each house or sign contains thirty degrees.

In Part I, we have considered the twelve signs of the zodiac, showing in what way they affect the body, the character, the disposition and the mental and moral attributes, as well as the possibilities for success or failure. The twelve houses describe the environment and circumstances, the possibilities and limitations of every phase of destiny with which each individual is confronted in his journey through life.

In order to determine the strength or importance of any particular house, it is necessary to examine, first, the lord of that house and his aspects, and, second, any planets that may be present in that house, and their aspects. There is also a third consideration, and one of great importance; i. e., whether the nature of the sign is itself sympathetic to that of the house. For example, when fifteen degrees of Aries are rising at New York, the signs lie in regular order without any duplication or cutting out; Taurus is on the cusp of the second, Gemini the third, and so on; this is an ideal arrangement, for there is then a natural correspondence between the meaning of the signs and that of the houses. Thus, the mercurial sign Gemini is obviously a good sign to rule the house that describes the mind; Libra, ruled by Venus, is sympathetic for marriage, and its judicial character makes it sympathetic to partnerships of all kinds. Leo, the heart sign, naturally occupies the cusp of the house of pleasure (the fifth); Aquarius, the human sign, corresponds naturally to the house of friends (the eleventh). This arrangement, however, is very rare. Because of the difference in latitude in places either very far north or very far south, we never find these twelve signs on these twelve houses exactly; and, again, it is only in one horoscope out of twelve, or even less, since Aries is the sign of short Ascension, that we find Aries rising. We consequently very often find rather unsympathetic conditions confronting the average mortal. If we find a Saturnian sign (Capricorn) on the cusp of the house of pleasure, or a martial sign (Aries and Scorpio) on the cusp of that of friends, we must conclude that the native is to meet many disappointments in his search for pleasure, and encounter many clashes with his friends. The slow and obstinate Taurus on the cusp of the third house, which has to do with the mind, or the elusive Gemini on the cusp of the fourth house, which has to do with the early environment as well as with the end of life, would be undesirable both for the mentality and for the blessing of repose in the home. In some future volume, therefore, it will be necessary to discuss in turn the influence of every sign upon every house in the heavens.

Unfortunately, unless the exact hour of birth is known, it is impossible to draw a sufficiently accurate figure of the heavens to enable the Astrologer to use the cusps to any advantage; this lack of accuracy on the part of the average person in regard to their time of birth is respon-

sible for many of the errors of judgment in diagnosing
a horoscope. The layman does not understand that a
slight absence of harmony may interfere with the perfect
operation of a powerful configuration. To borrow an
analogy from a science of a different order, consider the
automobile. The machine may be in absolute order, the
engine going, the wheels ready to turn, but the machine
does not move, because the clutch has not been let in.
As an example, the great Napoleon had Sagittarius on the
cusp of the third house; the lord, Jupiter, is in Scorpio,
which gives great sense of reality and thoroughness to the
mind, but the quickness of the mind is determined by the
fact that it is Sagittarius and not Scorpio or Pisces which
occupies the cusp of the third house. Had either of these
signs been there, we should have had a mind much slower,
more receptive, with probably some mystical turn to it.
In other words, we might have had a great man of science
rather than a great man of action.

In the case of Cléo de Mérode, we find the Moon on
the cusp of the seventh house, the Sun, Jupiter, Mercury
and Venus within it. One could not imagine a stronger
indication that the native would marry early and often.
Jupiter is in opposition to Neptune, but otherwise there
are no bad aspects. The only reason for her failing to undertake the great gamble is the presence of Virgo on the
cusp of the seventh house. This, of course, is equivalent
to saying that people with Pisces rising often remain un-
married, and this is usually the case, unless Mercury be
aspected in such a way as to transform the ordinary indication, or unless Libra occupies a very large portion of
the seventh house, so that by the time the native arrives
at a marriageable age, that sign, by the operation of

directions, has come to occupy the cusp of the seventh house, when other combinations must be taken into consideration.

We must therefore always be on the lookout for some lack of sympathy between the meaning of the sign and that of the house, so that we may see whether or no the ordinary influences of the planets will be inhibited from operating.

DESCRIPTION OF THE TWELVE HOUSES [1]

Ascendant.—The first house, which mundanely is Aries, and ruled over by Mars, signifies man's outward appearance and everything which has to do with the personality. It rules the head and determines the degree of activity or repression of the individual. In questions pertaining to the affairs of nations, and universal conditions generally, the first house signifies the masses, or general state of that locality or kingdom where the figure is erected.

The House of Money.—The second house, which mundanely is Taurus and ruled over by Venus, signifies the financial circumstances or fortune, profit or gain, loss or damage, and all movable goods of the individual. It rules the throat and determines the degree of prosperity which the native will enjoy. In questions pertaining to the affairs of nations or conditions generally, the second house signifies national wealth, banking activities and matters which concern revenue in general.

House of Relatives.—The third house, which mundanely is Gemini and ruled over by Mercury, signifies brothers, sisters, neighbors, environment of the family,

[1] Tables of the Houses are given at the end of Raphael's Ephemeris.

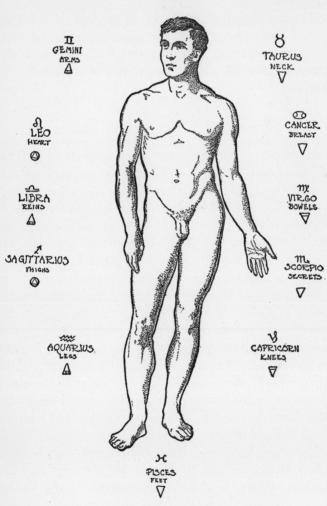

ARIES
HEAD & FACE
♈

GEMINI Ⅱ
ARMS
♊

TAURUS ♉
NECK
♉

LEO ♌
HEART
♌

CANCER ♋
BREAST
♋

LIBRA ♎
REINS
♎

VIRGO ♍
BOWELS
♍

SAGITTARIUS ♐
THIGHS
♐

SCORPIO ♏
SECRETS
♏

AQUARIUS ♒
LEGS
♒

CAPRICORN ♑
KNEES
♑

PISCES ♓
FEET
♓

THE TWELVE HOUSES

short journeys, correspondence and messages of all kinds, the degree of mentality, perception and adaptability of the individual, and determines the native's relations with all these departments. It rules the shoulders, arms, hands and fingers. In questions pertaining to national affairs, it rules over transportation, whether it be by railways, common carriers, post office, telegraph, telephone or radio. It also stands for libraries and public education generally.

The House of the Home.—The fourth house, which mundanely is Cancer, and ruled over by the Moon, signifies the father or mother, inherited tendencies, the environment during the early childhood and old age, fixed possessions such as real estate, of the individual. It rules the stomach and breast, and determines the native's relations with his father and mother, environment, and the state of his property holdings. In questions pertaining to national affairs, it rules over mines, agriculture, gardens, crops, public buildings, and determines the termination or end of anything.

The House of Pleasure.—The fifth house, which mundanely is Leo, and ruled over by the Sun, signifies love affairs, entertainment, speculation, and children, of the individual. It rules the heart and back, and determines the degree of success or failure in the native's love affairs and pleasures, his speculative operations, and matters concerning offspring. In questions pertaining to national affairs, it rules over ambassadors, banquets, theaters, and education generally.

The House of Health and Service.—The sixth house, which mundanely is Virgo, and ruled over by Mercury, signifies the needs, afflictions, and care of the body, servants, inferiors, dress and hygiene, grandparents, uncles and aunts, and domestic animals, of the individual. It rules the intestines and solar plexus, and determines the state of the native's health, his ability to get on with servants and inferiors, and his relations with grandparents, uncles and aunts, and small animals. In questions pertaining to national affairs, it rules over the working classes generally; over industries, public health and sanitation.

The House of Marriage and Partnerships.—The seventh house, which mundanely is Libra, and ruled over by Venus, signifies marriage, business partnerships, and public enemies, of the individual. It rules the veins, the kidneys (and in the case of a woman, the ovaries), and determines the degree of happiness and success derived through marriage and partnerships, and the type of public enemies the native may have. In questions pertaining to national affairs, it rules over foreign relations, peace, war and international relationships.

The House of Death.—The eighth house, which mundanely is Scorpio, and ruled over by Mars, signifies the inheritance, legacies, wills and the goods of the dead, of the individual. It rules the organs of generation, and determines all questions regarding inheritance, and the type of death of the native. In questions pertaining to national affairs, it signifies the death of national rulers, and matters that may be involved because of such deaths.

The House of Religion and Philosophy.—The ninth house, which mundanely is Sagittarius, and ruled over by Jupiter, signifies religion, philosophy, long journeys, particularly by water, and the relations with foreigners, of the individual. It has rule over abstract thought, dreams and visions, as distinguished from the concrete concerns of the third house. It rules the hips and thighs, and determines the religious and philosophical beliefs of the native, and the amount of travel and success he will enjoy in distant countries. In questions pertaining to national affairs, it rules over churches, law-courts, shipping, cables, and the findings of science.

The House of Business and Honor.—The tenth house, which mundanely is Capricorn, and ruled over by Saturn, signifies ambition, fame, worldly position, power, promotion, elevation, the calling or authority, of the individual. It also signifies either the father or mother, as in the fourth house. (Some authorities claim that the fourth house rules the father, and the tenth the mother, but the author has not been able to prove that this is correct.) It rules the skeleton, and particularly the knees, and determines the degree of success in business and the honor of the native. In questions pertaining to national affairs, it rules over the upper classes, or those in power and authority (as did the sixth house the masses and those who serve), rulers, such as presidents, kings and dictators.

The House of Friends.—The eleventh house, which mundanely is Aquarius and ruled over by Uranus, signifies the friendships and the aspirations of the individual. It rules the legs, particularly the ankles, and determines the native's relations with friends, his position towards humanity, and the degree of harmony or inharmony of life in relation to his fellowman. In questions pertaining to national affairs it rules over the counselors, associates or allies of the nation.

The House of Secret Enemies.—The twelfth house, which mundanely is Pisces, and ruled over by Neptune,

signifies unseen difficulties, impairment of the senses, se-
clusion, forced or otherwise, and secret enemies of the
individual. It rules the extremities, and determines the
amount of freedom enjoyed by the native, and the degree to which he will be forced to submerge his own personality, in his subservience to others. In questions pertaining to national affairs, it rules prisons, hospitals and
asylums, and all matters pertaining to such institutions.

PART VII

FREE WILL VERSUS DESTINY

FREE WILL VERSUS DESTINY

The questions asked the author most frequently are these—"Does Astrology teach fatality?" "Do the stars indicate circumstances or conditions over which the individual can have no control?" "Does Astrology help us find our true niche in the Universe?"

These queries have suggested this chapter. It should be clearly understood that the stars only indicate what will come to pass if intelligence and Free Will are not used to change the natural course of events. The wise man coöperates with the stars, the fool thinks he rules them. As William Henley says:

> "It matters not how strait the gate,
> How charged with punishment the scroll,
> I am the Master of my Fate,
> I am the Captain of my Soul."

The horoscope indicates the pattern on which the life is built, and if we are not familiar with this pattern, we are in danger of blurring it. Through Astrology we are not only made familiar with the details of it, but are helped to coöperate with its plan, and so we make our lives faithful to that plan, and by so doing, add to our own happiness, efficiency and usefulness in the world.

While Astrology points out the potentialities, capabilities and limitations of the individual, how far we shall develop the desirable traits and overcome those which are undesirable, depends upon the exercise of

Free Will. In other words, Astrology points the way and helps us to maintain a balance between the mental and the physical.

Astrology points out the weak spots in our character, and gives the reason why we are not successful in reaching our goal. It also points out when we are in danger of suffering through our weakness and when misfortune is likely to overtake us. Character is Destiny, and "to be forewarned is to be forearmed."

It is further possible through Astrology to ascertain for what work we are best fitted, and the times and seasons when opportunity will be presented for establishing ourselves in that work.

> "There is a tide in the affairs of men,
>   Which, taken at the flood, leads on to fortune;
>   Omitted, all the voyage of their life
>   Is bound in shallows and in miseries."
>
> (JULIUS CÆSAR.)

Had Napoleon exercised intelligence and taken the warning of his professional astrologer that he would suffer defeat if he met Wellington at Waterloo, his whole destiny and that of France might have been changed. Had Abraham Lincoln been informed through Astrology that he was under accidental and treacherous vibrations (which was the case at the time), he might have exercised his Free Will and avoided making himself a target by appearing in so public a place as a theater the night he was assassinated.

In attempting to arrive at a solution of our problem, it is necessary to study man in his relation to the Universe. Grounded in the structure of the Cosmos is the law of fatality. Life is a chain of successive causes and effects, link upon link. But whereas fatality is the process of Nature, freedom is the essence of *human nature*. Free Will is our highest possession. Free Will makes man a moral being; indeed morality is always a choice among alternatives. Otherwise, there would be Kismet, fatalism, helplessness, irresponsibility, leaving no justification for the punishment of crime or for paying the penalty of ignorance or wrong-doing, and, on the other hand, for awarding merit to intelligence and virtue.

Charles Fleischer, in his Essay on Human Nature, asserts this equation: "Animal nature plus Vision, plus Will, equals Human Nature."

Perhaps the secret of the common readiness to accept fatality as a finality is, in what modern psychology calls "defense mechanism"—a willingness to blame the stars and circumstances and whatever appears to be outside of ourselves, as the ultimate determining forces and factors in our lives. Herein is the point of the suggestion of Cassius—"It is not in our stars, but in ourselves, dear Brutus, that we are underlings."

In this connection I wish to remind the reader of Voltaire's subtle suggestion that if there were no God, mankind would invent one. So also it should be said to those who insist upon fatality that if there were no Free Will, we should have to invent it. Man is not really man, a child of the divine, unless he is a free moral agent, using intelligence and will to determine his own life.

The old hymn reads: "My mind to me a kingdom is." It might be added, my soul gives me dominion over life. To speak further in traditional terms, the real "sin against the Holy Ghost" is the refusal to recognize this supreme truth—*that the soul's dominion and authority is the very essence and the meaning of human life.* In other words, each individual is finally responsible for his own choice of conduct.

Fatalism only exists on the material plane. The soul is not shackled by Fate. Through Astrology we can ascertain what is likely to happen, but it is not the mission of the astrologer to determine how the events which are preordained shall influence each individual. This depends upon one's own Free Will and the degree of development one has attained and which will determine one's mental attitude toward anything which may happen. One will receive results through one's opportunities in proportion to the use one makes of them.

Knowledge is power, and Astrology is the Master Key to the lock of Truth. By knowing what our destiny indicates, and when we are headed straight for the rocks unless we use our intelligence and our Free Will to study the causes which threaten disaster, it behooves us first, to ascertain what pitfalls lie ahead, and then to exercise our choice to determine the best course to avert the catastrophe. If, for instance, we are told there has been a washout on the road and then we proceed heedlessly, we are exercising neither our Free Will nor our good judgment. It was inevitable that the washout occurred, but it depends upon us alone whether we shall succumb to the menace threatened.

On the other hand, Astrology points out the best and shortest and safest route to a given goal. Also, it offers solutions to our problems and it is the part of self-interested wisdom and enlightened Free Will to use gratefully this beneficent guidance of the stars. Astrology reveals us to ourselves—our physical and psychical make-up, our tendencies and our possibilities. Astrology makes it possible for us to analyze and diagnose ourselves, and so to play the part of self-healing physicians, thus curing the causes of illness and fertilizing the roots of our well-being. Astrology might also be likened to the search-light that brings to vision the iceberg, but in no way forces the captain to go around it.

With the help that Astrology brings, we may use our intelligence and Free Will both to avert dangers and to convert opportunity to our advantage. It opens wide fields of important knowledge regarding human life, and enlarges our sphere of consciousness, thus enabling one to be Master, rather than servant—dictator to, rather than victim of, circumstances.

Destiny brings us experience, but Free Will determines what use we shall make of the experience in shaping our lives. Fate knocks at the door, but it is up to us to bid her enter or keep her out. Dryden says:

"Fortune at some hour to all is kind;
The lucky have whole days which still they choose;
The unlucky have but hours,
And those they lose."

The "unlucky" can well be termed those unfortunate human beings who drift with the tide or oppose it, instead of adjusting their course to its ebb and flow by exercising intelligent Free Will.

"One ship drives east and another drives west
With the self-same winds that blow;
'Tis the set of the sails

And not the gales
Which tell us the way to go.

Like the winds of the sea are the ways of fate,
As we voyage along through life,
'Tis the set of the soul
That decides its goal,
And not the calm or the strife."

Life is evolution, fostered by vision and will. Consider the seaman, equipped with chart, compass and rudder. He has marked advantage over one who tries to navigate without these helps, and who, therefore, drifts blindly at the mercy of wind and wave. So Astrology renders incalculable service to even self-directing human beings by furnishing them the informative equivalents of the mariner's chart, compass and rudder. Again, our career is like a voyage. It is as though we were embarking, let us say, for Cherbourg. Fate determines our destination, but with our Free Will we decide whether we shall spend the period on shipboard in indulging our appetites —perhaps to the point of debauch—or in using the time for valuable work, in making friends, or in rest and thought.

Astrology being the emancipator from ignorance, helps the individual to understand himself, and also, through understanding his fellowman better, to be more sympathetic and more tolerant. In a large sense, Astrology teaches the true meaning of the Brotherhood of Man— by knowing and respecting one's self and one's fellows.

The assistance that Astrology gives in diagnosing disease is of invaluable assistance to medicine. Those physicians and surgeons who have put aside their prejudice and have taken advantage of the findings of Astrology (as did the physicians of old), have an added power in helping mankind, and in understanding their own science.

In the last analysis, the balance between fatalism and Free Will is suggested by Democracy, the idealistic expression of our American civilization and of the whole modern human trend. True Democracy means self-government, self-direction, self-control.

So this interpretation of the uses of Astrology makes Man, the Individual, the free arbiter of his fate through the use of vision, intelligence and will.

Character is Destiny. It is the resultant of the life-long, conscious use of the Cosmic Forces that vibrate through our human stuff. This dowers you with that dynamic vitality, which is your normal heritage as a creative human being, and entitles you to YOUR PLACE IN THE SUN.